The Essential Dalai Lama

The Essential Dalai Lama

His Important Teachings

Edited by
Rajiv Mehrotra

**HODDER
MOBIUS**

First published in Great Britain in 2005 by Hodder & Stoughton
A division of Hodder Headline

This paperback edition published in 2006

A Mobius paperback

4

A CIP catalogue record for this title is
available from the British Library

ISBN 978 0 340 83495 4

Printed and bound by Clays Ltd, St Ives plc

Hodder Headline's policy is to use papers that are natural, renewable
and recyclable products and made from wood grown in sustainable forests.
The logging and manufacturing processes are expected to conform to the
environmental regulations of the country of origin.

Hodder & Stoughton Ltd
A division of Hodder Headline
338 Euston Road
London NW1 3BH

The merit gained
from the compilation
of this book
and from reading it
is dedicated to
the long life and good health
of my guru
Gyalwa Rinpoche,
His Holiness the Dalai Lama
and
to lifting the veils of our collective ignorance
that it might lead to the end of suffering
for all sentient beings.

Acknowledgements

The Foundation for Universal Responsibilty and I owe our deep gratitude to His Holiness the Dalai Lama and his office for their encouragement of my efforts to put together this collection. Special thanks are due to Mr Tenzin Geyche, Ven Lhakdor, Mr Tenzin Takhla and my Tibetan family of Tendzin Choegyal and Rinchen Khando la. Many of His Holiness's publishers have been most generous and spontaneous in responding to our request for permission to print these extracts. It is a truly collective offering.

Penguin India under the stewardship of David Davidar has been truly wonderful and, more recently, V.K. Karthika has been a constant source of encouragement and patient support. My enduring appreciation to Krishan Chopra, my first commissioning editor at Penguin, who gave me the courage to attempt being an author. Paromita Mohanchandra has been a most reassuring, patient and calm presence during the final difficult stages of publishing the book.

A word of appreciation to Shalini Srinivas for her invaluable comments and suggestions on the manuscript. My gratitude to Simmi Bali Mahajan, R.Lalitha, Divya Sharma and Tulika Srivastava for their help in putting the manuscript together. At the Foundation Mrs Raji Ramanan and Kunjo Tashi are an enduring source of support.

My life and work are deeply touched by the memory of my late mother Shanti Mehrotra and my family—my father Har Narain Mehrotra, Kalpana, Iqbal, Preeti, Satish, Nishat, Ambika, Priyal, Mallika, Anuja, Sarada Gopinath and above all my wife, Meenakshi Gopinath, who remains my best friend, ever. I celebrate our continuing journey together.

CONTENTS

~

PREFACE

The Foundation for Universal Responsibility is honoured, blessed and privileged to offer this introductory collection of writings by one of the great spiritual teachers and philosophers of our time Tenzin Gyatso, His Holiness the XIV Dalai Lama.

While drawing upon his training and primary commitment to the Tibetan Buddhist Mahayana Gelupa tradition this collection essentially offers the Dalai Lama's teachings and perspectives on Buddhism, its interface with other traditions, the cultivation of universal ethical values and the pursuit of happiness.

The Dalai Lama reaches out to a global following with a vision that is transforming, secular and accessible to all. The essence of his teachings lies in powerful methods of training the mind and a wisdom that juxtaposes a profound expression of compassion bred from insights into patterns of inter-connectedness that lead inevitably to an activist sense of universal responsibility. His vision touches potent personal chords and invigorates our common humanity.

Buddhahood is not the exclusive preserve of the historical Buddha, but a state of insight and being, accessible to all humans. Though the Dalai Lama himself is at pains not to stake such a claim, describing himself as merely a 'simple Buddhist monk', millions of his followers, both Tibetans and others, regard him as a 'Living Buddha'. He is revered as a reincarnation of the compassionate Buddha, Avalokteshwara, the fourteenth incarnation in the line of Dalai Lamas—bodhisattvas, who choose to reincarnate to provide spiritual and temporal leadership to Tibetans and to teach and serve all humanity.

Being ascribed the qualities of a Buddha has not obliged the Dalai Lama to play out that role to nurture an image he must serve. People identify with him because he is intensely human and quick to acknowledge that he is fallible and that his own quest is a long journey only just begun. He has not hesitated, for the sake of appearances, to acknowledge that he experiences emotions such as anger every day, or that,on occasion, on seeing a beautiful woman, he has to remind himself that he is a monk.

The methods and the wisdom that His Holiness the Dalai Lama teaches draw upon not just scriptural authority but the passion, the clarity and the power that can only come when accumulated wisdom carries with it the eloquent authority and conviction of lived experience, belief and logic. To this day the Dalai Lama, even as the pre-eminent Buddhist teacher, continues a rigorous, daily personal practice of receiving new teachings on traditions and techniques, from other lamas and teachers, that can and must be handed down only through personal oral transmission. It is a powerful and real humility that drives his continuing quest for perfection and insight into the true nature of a reality that penetrates all delusion. He himself continually engages in and evolves the very practices that he teaches. Because he himself is open about acknowledging his own mundane emotions and experiences he is able to empathize and relate to us the better, we who are deep in the illusions of samsara.

He combines rationality, humanism and religious tradition as the foundations for the moral responses to the great challenges of our century. He has sought to learn, and wants Buddhism also to learn, from the modern discoveries of science and through closer contact with other faith traditions of how, together, a deeper understanding of the ultimate nature of reality and ultimate truth (if there is one) might emerge.

The Dalai Lama has argued that religion must be willing to modify its understanding and assumptions, if the empiricism and instruments of science prove some of its myths and assumptions are wrong. If the latest techniques of photography prove that Mt. Meru does not exist here on earth we must accept that. It does not mean, however, that just because science cannot validate the principle of reincarnation, for instance, that it is false. If the Bible evokes a more proactive idea of service than the Buddhist concept of the Bodhisattva, indeed Buddhism can learn from it and celebrate it as he does. The Dalai Lama engages in a week-long dialogue each year with eminent scientists from around the world. It is an opportunity to learn from them, and for them to learn from him. He has introduced the study of science in the monks' curriculum. For him and his flock of monks there are frequent in-depth exchanges with practitioners of other faiths that include visits to their places of pilgrimage and experiments with some of their practices.

As a teacher his word is not absolute, his path not the only one. In the tradition of the Buddha himself he discourages formal conversion to Buddhism unless it follows careful consideration deeply driven by an inner compulsion and imperative, and only when there is no felt alternative. He encourages us to learn from Buddhism and practise those principles that appeal to us without necessarily becoming a Buddhist.

The Dalai Lama urges that surrender to any teacher, including himself, must follow intense scrutiny of the master and careful consideration by the student. The aspirant cannot and must not abdicate responsibility. The teacher does not necessarily embody perfection. He is in human form. The teaching must meet the dictates of logic, reason and common sense before it is accepted and practised. It is only in the highest stages of practice, initiation and transmission, after the teacher and the aspirant have truly tested and evaluated each other, often over lifetimes, that real surrender and a deep bonding between the two takes place. The karma of the teacher and student, more aptly described as guru and chela, are then intertwined and becomes a sacred relationship.

Buddhism is often perceived as a sombre, austere philosophy of negation. The Dalai Lama, embodying its highest aspirations, is a living testament to its philosophy of a full, joyous life of action. His ever-smiling face and deep infectious laughter are his most persuasive teachings.

His Holiness rarely formally sits down to write. His 'writings' are invariably edited transcriptions of oral teachings. They are usually simultaneously translated into several languages and later transcribed and edited for publications, and this compilation draws upon these sources. His Holiness usually speaks of and teaches more complex ideas in Tibetan, frequently breaking out into what he describes as 'my broken English' when he feels the need to establish a more direct rapport with his audiences or, occasionally, when he feels his translator has missed a significant nuance. Over the decades, certainly in the early years of his public life, this role was performed by a number of different editors and translators and often, the language and the rhythm of his writings seem at variance. Ultimately there is no substitute for being in the physical presence of a great master. His Holiness communicates with, and has an impact on, those privileged to be in his physical presence at numerous levels, and in ways no printed word can capture.

We present this compilation that it might point the reader in a direction that will whet an appetite for the real impact of listening to a living master.

This book celebrates and commemorates one of the great embodiments of humanity and the human potential to be truly human, as we celebrate his seventieth year in this life on earth on 6 July, 2005.

Rajiv Mehrotra
Trustee—Secretary
Foundation for Universal Responsibility
of His Holiness the Dalai Lama
New Delhi
July 2005

I

THE VISION

WORDS OF TRUTH

A PRAYER

Honouring and Invoking the Great Compassion
of the Three Jewels; the Buddha, the Teachings,
and the Spiritual Community

O Buddhas, Bodhisattvas, and disciples
  of the past, present, and future
Having remarkable qualities
Immeasurably vast as the ocean,
Who regard all helpless sentient beings
 as your only child;
Please consider the truth of my anguished pleas.
Buddha's full teachings dispel the pain of worldly
  existence and self-oriented peace;
May they flourish, spreading prosperity and happiness
  throughout this spacious world.
O holders of the Dharma: scholars
  and realized practitioners;
May your tenfold virtuous practice prevail.
Humble sentient beings, tormented
  by sufferings without cease,
Completely suppressed by seemingly endless
  and terribly intense negative deeds,
May all their fears from unbearable war, famine,
  and disease be pacified,
To freely breathe an ocean of happiness and well-being.
And particularly the pious people
  of the Land of Snows who, through various means,
  are mercilessly destroyed by barbaric hordes
  on the side of darkness,

Kindly let the power of your compassion arise,
To quickly stem the flow of blood and tears.
Those unrelentingly cruel ones, objects of compassion,
Maddened by delusion's evils,
    wantonly destroy themselves and others;
May they achieve the eye of wisdom,
    knowing what must be done and undone,
And abide in the glory of friendship and love.
May this heartfelt wish of total freedom for all Tibet,
Which has been awaited for a long time,
    be spontaneously fulfilled;
Please grant soon the good fortune to enjoy
The happy celebration of spiritual with temporal rule.
O protector Chenrezig, compassionately care for
    those who have undergone myriad hardships,
Completely sacrificing their most cherished lives,
    bodies, and wealth,
For the sake of the teachings, practitioners,
    people, and nation.
Thus, the protector Chenrezig made vast prayers
Before the Buddhas and Bodhisativas
To fully embrace the Land of Snows;
May the good results of these prayers now quickly appear.
By the profound interdependence of emptiness
    and relative forms,
Together with the force of great compassion
    in the Three Jewels and their Words of Truth,
And through the power
    of the infallible law of actions and their fruits,
May this truthful prayer be unhindered
    and quickly fulfilled.

ONE

THE QUEST FOR HUMAN HAPPINESS[*]

I am a comparative newcomer to the modern world. Although I fled my homeland as long ago as 1959, and although my life since then as a refugee in India has brought me into much closer contact with contemporary society, my formative years were spent largely cut off from the realities of the twentieth century. This was partly due to my appointment as Dalai Lama. I became a monk at a very early age. It also reflects the fact that we Tibetans had chosen—mistakenly, in my view—to remain isolated behind the high mountain ranges which separate our country from the rest of the world. Today, however, I travel a great deal, and it is my good fortune continuously to be meeting new people.

Moreover, individuals from all walks of life come to see me. Many—especially those who make the effort to travel to the Indian hill-station at Dharamsala where I live in exile—arrive seeking something. Among these are people who have cancer and with AIDS-related illnesses. Then, of course, there are fellow Tibetans with their own tales of hardship and suffering. Unfortunately, many have unrealistic expectations, believing that I have healing powers or that I can give some sort of blessing. But I am only an ordinary human being. The best I can do is try to help them by sharing in their suffering.

For my part, meeting innumerable others from all over the world and from every walk of life reminds me of our basic sameness as human beings. Indeed, the more I see of the world, the clearer it becomes that no matter what our situation, whether we are rich or poor, educated or

---

[*] From *Ethics for the New Millennium*, Riverhead Books, Penguin Putman Inc., 1999.

not, of one race, gender, religion or another, we all desire to be happy and to avoid suffering. Our every intended action, in a sense our whole life, how we choose to live it within the context of the limitations imposed by our circumstances—can be seen as our answer to the great question which confronts us all: 'How am I to be happy?'

We are sustained in this great quest for happiness, it seems to me, by hope. We know, even if we do not admit it, that there can be no guarantee of a better, happier life than the one we are leading today. As an old Tibetan proverb puts it, 'The next life or tomorrow—we can never be certain which will come first'. But we hope to go on living. We hope that through this or that action we can bring about happiness. Everything we do, not only as individuals but also at the level of society, can be seen in terms of this fundamental aspiration. Indeed, it is one shared by all sentient beings. The desire or inclination to be happy and to avoid suffering knows no boundaries. It is in our nature. As such, it needs no justification and is validated by the simple fact that we naturally and correctly want this.

And this is precisely what we see in countries both rich and poor. Everywhere, by all means imaginable, people are striving to improve their lives. Yet strangely, my impression is that those living in the materially developed countries, for all their industry, are in some ways less satisfied, are less happy, and to some extent suffer more than those living in the least developed countries. Indeed, if we compare the rich with the poor, it often seems that those with nothing are, in fact, the least anxious, though they are plagued with physical pains and suffering. As for the rich, while a few know how to use their wealth intelligently— that is to say, not in luxurious living but by sharing it with the needy— many do not. They are so caught up with the idea of acquiring still more that they make no room for anything else in their lives. In their absorption, they actually lose the dream of happiness, which riches were to have provided. As a result, they are constantly tormented, torn between doubt about what might happen and the hope of gaining more, and plagued with mental and emotional suffering—even though outwardly they may appear to be leading entirely successful and comfortable lives. This is suggested both by the high degree and by the disturbing prevalence among the populations of the materially developed countries of anxiety, discontent, frustration, uncertainty, and depression. Moreover, this inner suffering is clearly connected with growing confusion as to what constitutes morality and what its foundations are.

I am often reminded of this paradox when I go abroad. It frequently happens that when I arrive in a new country, at first everything seems very pleasant, very beautiful. Everybody I meet is very friendly. There is nothing to complain about. But then, day by day as I listen, I hear people's problems, their concerns and worries. Below the surface, so many feel uneasy and dissatisfied with their lives. They experience feelings of isolation; then follows depression. The result is the troubled atmosphere which is such a feature of the developed world.

This paradox whereby inner—or we could say psychological and emotional—suffering is so often found amid material wealth is readily apparent throughout much of the West. Indeed, it is so pervasive that we might wonder whether there is something in Western culture which predisposes people living there to such kinds of suffering. This I doubt. So many factors are involved. Clearly, material development itself has a role to play. But we can also cite the increasing urbanization of modern society, where high concentrations of people live in close proximity to one another. In this context, consider that in place of our dependence on one another for support, today, wherever possible, we tend to rely on machines and services. Whereas formerly, farmers would call in all their family members to help with the harvest, today they simply telephone a contractor. We find modern living organized so that it demands the least possible direct dependence on others. The more or less universal ambition seems to be for everyone to own their own house, their own car, their own computer, and so on in order to be as independent as possible. This is natural and understandable. We can also point to the increasing autonomy that people enjoy as a result of advances in science and technology. In fact, it is possible today to be far more independent of others than ever before. But with these developments, there has arisen a sense that my future is not dependent on my neighbour but rather on my job or, at most, my employer. This in turn encourages us to suppose that because others are not important for my happiness, their happiness is not important to me.

We have, in my view, created a society in which people find it harder and harder to show one another basic affection. In place of the sense of community and belonging, which we find such a reassuring feature of less wealthy (and generally rural) societies, we find a high degree of loneliness and alienation. Despite the fact that millions live in close proximity to one another, it seems that many people, especially among the old, have no one to talk to but their pets. Modern industrial society often strikes me as being like a huge self-propelled machine. Instead of human beings in charge, each individual is a tiny, insignificant component with no choice but to move when the machine moves.

Clearly, a major reason for modern society's devotion to material progress is the very success of science and technology. Now the wonderful thing about these forms of human endeavor is that they bring immediate satisfaction. They're unlike prayer, the results of which are, for the most part, invisible—if indeed prayer works at all. And we are impressed by results. What could be more normal? Unfortunately, this devotion encourages us to suppose that the keys to happiness are material well-being on the one hand and the power conferred by knowledge on the other. And while it is obvious to anyone who gives this mature thought that the former cannot bring us happiness by itself, it is perhaps less apparent that the latter cannot. But the fact is knowledge alone cannot provide the happiness that springs from inner development that is not reliant on external factors. Indeed, though our very detailed and specific knowledge of external phenomena is an immense achievement, the urge to reduce, to narrow down in pursuit of it, far from bringing us happiness can actually be dangerous. It can cause us to lose touch with the wider reality of human experience and, in particular, our dependence on others.

We need also to recognize what happens when we rely too much on the external achievements of science. For example, as the influence of religion declines, there is mounting confusion with respect to the problem of how best we are to conduct ourselves in life. In the past, religion and ethics were closely intertwined. Now, many people, believing that science has 'disproved' religion, make the further assumption that because there appears to be no final evidence for any spiritual authority, morality itself must be a matter of individual preference. And whereas in the past, scientists and philosophers felt a pressing need to find solid foundations on which to establish immutable laws and absolute truths, nowadays this kind of research is held to be futile. As a result, we see a complete reversal, heading toward the opposite extreme, where ultimately nothing exists any longer, where reality itself is called into question. This can only lead to chaos.

In saying this, I do not mean to criticize scientific endeavor. I have learned a great deal from my encounters with scientists, and I see no obstacle to engaging in dialogue with them even when their perspective is one of radical materialism. Indeed, for as long as I can remember, I have been fascinated by the insights of science. As a boy, there was a time when I was rather more interested in learning about the mechanics of an old film projector I found in the storerooms of the summer residence of the Dalai Lama than in my religious and scholastic studies. My concern is rather that we are apt to overlook the limitations of science. In replacing religion as the final source of knowledge in popular estimation, science begins to look a bit like another religion itself. With this comes a similar danger on the part of some of its adherents of blind faith in its principles and, correspondingly, to intolerance of alternative views. That this supplanting of religion has taken place is not surprising, however, given science's extraordinary achievements. Who could fail to be impressed at our ability to land people on the moon? Yet the fact remains that if, for example, we were to go to a nuclear physicist and say, 'I am facing a moral dilemma, what should I do? he or she could only shake their head and suggest we look elsewhere for an answer. Generally speaking, a scientist is in no better position than a lawyer in this respect. For while both science and the law can help us forecast the likely consequence of our actions, neither can tell us how we ought to act in a moral sense. Moreover, we need to recognize the limits of scientific inquiry itself. For example, though we have been aware of human consciousness for millennia, and though it has been the subject of investigation throughout history, despite scientists' best efforts they still do not understand what it actually is, or why it exists, how it functions, or what is its essential nature. Neither can science tell us what the substantial cause of consciousness is, nor what its effects are. Of course, consciousness belongs to that category of phenomena without form, substance, or colour. It is not susceptible to investigation by external means. But this does not mean such things do not exist, merely that science cannot find them.

Should we, therefore, abandon scientific inquiry on the grounds that it has failed us? Certainly not. Nor do I mean to suggest that the goal of prosperity for all is invalid. Because of our nature, bodily and physical experiences play a dominant role in our lives. The achievements of science and technology clearly reflect our desire to attain a better, more comfortable existence. This is very good. Who could fail to applaud many of the advances of modern medicine?

At the same time, I think it is genuinely true that members of certain traditional, rural communities do enjoy greater harmony and tranquility than those settled in our modern cities. For example, in the Spiti area of northern India, it remains the custom for locals not to lock their houses when they go out. It is expected that a visitor who finds the house empty would go in and help themselves to a meal while waiting for the family to return. The same obtained in Tibet in former times. This is not to say that there is no crime in such places. As in the case of pre-occupation Tibet, such things did of course happen occasionally. But when they did, people would raise their eyebrows in surprise. It was a rare and unusual event. By contrast, in some modern cities, if a day goes by without a murder, it is a remarkable event. With urbanization has come disharmony.

We must be careful not to idealize old ways of life, however. The high level of cooperation we find in undeveloped rural communities may be based more on necessity than on goodwill. People recognize it as an alternative to greater hardship. And the contentment we perceive may actually have more to do with ignorance. These people may not realize or imagine that any other way of life is possible. If they did, very likely they would embrace it eagerly. The challenge we face is therefore to find some means of enjoying the same degree of harmony and tranquility as those more traditional communities while benefiting fully from the material developments of the world as we find it at the dawn of a new millennium. To say otherwise is to imply that these communities should not even try to improve their standard of living. Yet, I am quite certain that, for example, the majority of Tibet's nomads would be very glad to have the latest thermal clothing for winter, smokeless fuel to cook with, the benefits of modern medicine, and a portable television in their tents. And I, for one, would not wish to deny them these. Modern society, with all its benefits and defects, has emerged within the context of innumerable causes and conditions. To suppose that merely by abandoning material progress we could overcome all our problems would be shortsighted. That would be to ignore their underlying causes. Besides, there is still much in the modern world to be optimistic about.

There are countless people in the most developed countries who are active in their concern for others. Nearer home, I think of the enormous kindness we Tibetan refugees have been shown by those whose personal resources were also quite limited. For example, our children have benefited immeasurably from the selfless contribution of their Indian teachers, many of whom have been compelled to live under difficult conditions far away from their homes. On a wider scale, we might also consider the growing appreciation of fundamental human rights all over the world. This represents a very positive development in my view. The way in which the international community generally responds to natural disasters with immediate aid is also a wonderful feature of the modern world. Increasing recognition that we cannot forever continue to mistreat our natural environment without facing serious consequences is likewise a cause for hope. Moreover, I believe that, thanks largely to modern communications, people are probably more accepting of diversity now. And standards of literacy and education throughout the world are in general higher than ever before. Such positive developments I take to be an indication of what we humans are capable of.

Recently, I had the opportunity to meet the Queen Mother in England. She has been a familiar figure to me throughout my life, so this gave me great pleasure. But what was particularly encouraging was to hear her opinion, as a woman as old as the twentieth century itself, that people have become much more aware of others than when she was young. In those days, she said, people were interested mainly in their own countries whereas today there is much more concern for the inhabitants of other countries. When I asked her whether she was optimistic about the future, she replied in the affirmative without hesitation.

Yet, unlike the sufferings of sickness, old age, and death, none of these problems is by nature inevitable. Nor are they due to any lack of knowledge. When we think carefully, we see that they are all ethical problems. They each reflect our understanding of what is right and wrong, of what is positive and what is negative, of what is appropriate and what is inappropriate. But beyond this we can point to something more fundamental: a neglect of what I call our inner dimension.

What do I mean by this? According to my understanding, our overemphasis on material gain reflects an underlying assumption that what it can buy can, by itself alone, provide us with all the satisfaction we require. Yet by nature, the satisfaction material gain can provide us with will be limited to the level of the senses. If it were true that we human beings were no different from animals, this would be fine. However, given the complexity of our species—in particular, the fact of our having thoughts and emotions as well as imaginative and critical faculties—it is obvious that our needs transcend the merely sensual. The prevalence of anxiety, stress, confusion, uncertainty, and depression among those whose basic needs have been met is a clear indication of this. Our problems, both those we experience externally—such as wars, crime, and violence—and those we experience internally—our emotional and psychological sufferings—cannot be solved until we address this underlying neglect. That is why the great movements of the last hundred years and more—democracy, liberalism, socialism—have all failed to deliver the universal benefits they were supposed to provide, despite many wonderful ideas. A revolution is called for, certainly. But not a political, an economic, or even a technical revolution. We have had enough experience of these during the past century to know that a purely external approach will not suffice. What I propose is a spiritual revolution.

TWO

~

OUR GLOBAL FAMILY*

When I meet people in different parts of the world, I am always reminded that we are all basically alike: We are all human beings. Maybe we have different clothes, our skin is of a different colour, or we speak different languages. That is on the surface. But basically, we are the same human beings. That is what binds us to each other. That is what makes it possible for us to understand each other and to develop friendship and closeness.

Because we all share this small planet Earth, we have to learn to live in harmony and peace with each other and with nature. That is not just a dream, but a necessity. We are dependent on each other in so many ways that we can no longer live in isolated Communities and ignore what is happening outside those communities. We need to help each other when we have difficulties, and we must share the good fortune that we enjoy. I speak to you as just another human being; as a simple monk. If you find what I say useful, then I hope you will try to practice it.

The realization that we are all basically the same human beings, who seek happiness and try to avoid suffering, is very helpful in developing a sense of brotherhood and sisterhood; a warm feeling of love and compassion for others. This, in turn, is essential if we are to survive in this ever shrinking world we live in. For if we each selfishly pursue only what we believe to be in our own interest, without caring about the needs of others, we not only may end up harming others but also ourselves. This fact has become very clear during the course of this century. We know that to wage a nuclear war today for example, would

---

* Excerpt from the Nobel Peace Prize Speech from *The Spirit of Tibet: Universal Heritage*, published by Allied Publishers Ltd.

be a form of suicide; or that by polluting the air or the oceans, in order to achieve some short-term benefit, we are destroying the very basis for our survival. As individuals and nations are becoming increasingly interdependent, therefore, we have no other choice than to develop what I call a sense of universal responsibility.

Today, we are truly a global family. What happens in one part of the world may affect us all. This, of course, is not only true of the negative things that happen, but is equally valid for the positive developments. We not only know what happens elsewhere, thanks to the extraordinary modern communications technology, we are also directly affected by events that occur far away. We feel a sense of sadness when children are starving in eastern Africa. Similarly, we feel a sense of joy when a family is reunited after decades of separation by the Berlin Wall. Our crops and livestock are contaminated and our health and livelihood threatened when a nuclear accident happens miles away in another country. Our own security is enhanced when peace breaks out between warring parties in other continents.

But war or peace; the destruction or the protection of nature; the violation or promotion of human rights and democratic freedoms; poverty or material well being; the lack of moral and spiritual values or their existence and development; and the breakdown or development of human understanding, are not isolated phenomena that can be analyzed and tackled independently of one another. In fact, they are very much interrelated at all levels and need to be approached with that understanding.

Peace, in the sense of the absence of war, is of little value to someone who is dying of hunger or cold. It will not remove the pain of torture inflicted on a prisoner of conscience. It does not comfort those who have lost their loved ones in floods caused by senseless deforestation in a neighbouring country. Peace can only last where human rights are respected, where the people are fed, and where individuals and nations are free. True peace with one self and with the world around us can only be achieved through the development of mental peace. The other phenomena mentioned above are similarly interrelated. Thus, for example, we see that a clean environment, wealth or democracy mean little in the face of war, especially nuclear war, and that material development is not sufficient to ensure human happiness.

Material progress is of course important for human advancement. In Tibet, we paid too little attention to technological and economic development, and today we realize that this was a mistake. At the same time, material development without spiritual development can also cause serious problems. In some countries too much attention is paid to external things and very little importance is given to inner development. I believe both are important and must be developed side by side so as to achieve a good balance between them. Tibetans are always described by foreign visitors as being a happy, jovial people. This is part of our national character, formed by cultural and religious values that stress the importance of mental peace through the generation of love and kindness to all other living sentient beings, both human and animal. Inner peace is the key: If you have inner peace, the external problems do not affect your deep sense of peace and tranquility. In that state of mind you can deal with situations with calmness and reason, while keeping your inner happiness. That is very important. Without this inner peace, no matter how comfortable your life is materially, you may still be worried, disturbed or unhappy because of circumstances.

Clearly, it is of great importance, therefore, to understand the interrelationship among these and other phenomena, and to approach and attempt to solve problems in a balanced way that takes these different aspects into consideration. Of course it is not easy. But it is of little benefit to try to solve one problem if doing so creates an equally serious new one. So really we have no alternative: we must develop a sense of universal responsibility not only in the geographic sense, but also in respect to the different issues that confront our planet.

Responsibility does not only lie with the leaders of our countries or with those who have been appointed or elected to do a particular job. It lies with each of us individually. Peace, for example, starts within each one of us. When we have inner peace, we can be at peace with those around us. When our Community is in a state of peace, it can share that peace with neighbouring communities, and so on. When we feel love and kindness towards others, it not only makes others feel loved and cared for, but it helps us also to develop inner happiness and peace. And there are ways in which we can consciously work to develop feelings

15

of love and kindness. For some of us, the most effective way to do so is through religious practice. For others it may be non-religious practices. What is important is that we each make a sincere effort to take our responsibility for each other and for the natural environment we live in seriously.

Reason, courage, determination, and the inextinguishable desire for freedom can ultimately win. In the struggle between forces of war, violence and oppression on the one hand, and peace, reason and freedom on the other, the latter are gaining the upper hand. This realization fills us Tibetans with hope that some day we too will once again be free.

THREE

~

COMPASSION*

I think that every human being has an innate sense of I. We cannot explain why that feeling is there, but it is. Along with it comes a desire for happiness and a wish to overcome suffering. This is quite justified, we have a natural right to achieve as much happiness as possible, and we also have the right to overcome suffering.

The whole of human history has developed on the basis of this feeling. In fact it is not limited to human beings; from the Buddhist point of view, even the tiniest insect has this feeling and, according to its capacity, is trying to gain some happiness and avoid unhappy situations.

However, there are some major differences between human beings and other animal species. They stem from human intelligence. On account of our intelligence, we are much more advanced and have a greater capacity. We are able to think much further into the future, and our memory is powerful enough to take us back many years. Furthermore, we have oral and written traditions which remind us of events many centuries ago. Now, thanks to scientific methods, we can even examine events which occurred millions of years ago.

So our intelligence makes us very smart, but at the same time, precisely because of that fact, we also have more doubts and suspicions, and hence more fears. I think the imagination of fear is much more developed in humans than in other animals. In addition, the many conflicts within the human family and within one's own family, not to mention the conflicts within the community and between nations, as well as the internal conflicts within the individual—all conflicts and

* From *The Heart of the Buddha's Path*, Thorsons, an Imprint of HarperCollins*Publishers*, 1999.

contradictions arise from the different ideas and views our intelligence brings. So unfortunately, intelligence can sometimes create a quite unhappy state of mind. In this sense, it becomes another source of human misery. Yet, at the same time, I think that ultimately intelligence is the tool with which we can overcome all these conflicts and differences.

From this point of view, of all the various species of animal on the planet, human beings are the biggest troublemakers. That is clear. I imagine that if there were no longer any humans on the planet, the planet itself would be safer! Certainly millions of fish, chicken and other small animals might enjoy some sort of genuine liberation!

It is therefore important that human intelligence be utilized in a constructive way. That is the key. If we utilize its capacity properly, then not only human beings would become less harmful to each other, and to the planet, but also individual human beings would be happier in themselves. It is in our hands. Whether we utilize our intelligence in the right way or the wrong way is up to us. Nobody can impose their values on us. How can we learn to use our capacity constructively? First, we need to recognize our nature and then, if we have the determination, there is a real possibility of transforming the human heart.

On this basis, I will speak today on how a human being can find happiness as an individual, because I believe the individual is the key to all the rest. For change to happen in any community, the initiative must come from the individual. If the individual can become a good, calm, peaceful person, this automatically brings a positive atmosphere to the family around him or her. When parents are warm-hearted, peaceful and calm people, generally speaking their children will also develop that attitude and behaviour.

The way our attitude works is such that it is often troubled by outside factors, so one side of the issue is to eliminate the existence of trouble around you. The environment, meaning the surrounding situation, is a very important factor for establishing a happy frame of mind. However, even more important is the other side of the issue, which is one's own mental attitude.

The surrounding situation may not be so friendly, it may even be hostile, but if your inner mental attitude is right, then the situation will not disturb your inner peace. On the other hand, if your attitude is not right, then even if you are surrounded by good friends and the best facilities, you cannot be happy. This is why mental attitude is more important than external conditions. Despite this, it seems to me that many people are more concerned about their external conditions, and neglect the inner attitude of mind. I suggest that we should pay more attention to our inner qualities.

There are a number of qualities which are important for mental peace, but from the little experience I have, I believe that one of the most important factors is human compassion and affection, a sense of caring.

Let me explain what we mean by compassion. Usually, our concept of compassion or love refers to the feeling of closeness we have with our friends and loved ones. Sometimes compassion also carries a sense of pity. This is wrong—any love or compassion which entails looking down on the other is not genuine compassion. To be genuine, compassion must be based on respect for the other, and on the realization that others have the right to be happy and overcome suffering just as much as you. On this basis, since you can see that others are suffering, you develop a genuine sense of concern for them.

As for the closeness we feel towards our friends, this is usually more like attachment than compassion. Genuine compassion should be unbiased. If we only feel close to our friends, and not to our enemies, or to the countless people who are unknown to us personally and towards whom we are indifferent, then our compassion is only partial or biased.

Compassion also brings us a certain inner strength. Once it is developed, it naturally opens an inner door, through which we can communicate with other fellow human beings, and even other sentient beings, with ease, and heart to heart. On the other hand, if you feel hatred and ill-feeling towards others, they may feel similarly towards you, and as a result suspicion and fear will automatically create a distance between you and make communication difficult. You will then feel lonely and isolated.

Compassion naturally creates a positive atmosphere, and as a result you feel peaceful and content. Wherever there lives a compassionate person, there is always a pleasant atmosphere. Even dogs and birds approach the person easily. Almost fifty years ago, I used to keep some birds in the Norbulingka Summer Palace, in Lhasa. Among them was a small parrot. At that time I had an elderly attendant whose appearance was somewhat unfriendly—he had very round, stern eyes—but he was always feeding this parrot with nuts and so on. So whenever the attendant would appear, just the sound of his footsteps or his coughing would mean the parrot would show some excitement. The attendant had an extraordinarily friendly manner with that small bird, and the parrot also had an amazing response to him. On a few occasions I fed him some nuts but he never showed such friendliness to me, so I started to poke him with a stick, hoping he might react differently; the result was totally negative. I was using more force than the bird had, so it reacted accordingly.

Therefore, if you want a genuine friend, first you must create a positive atmosphere around you. We are social animals, after all, and friends are very important. How can you bring a smile to people's faces? If you remain stony and suspicious, it is very difficult. Perhaps if you have power or money, some people may offer you an artificial smile, but a genuine smile will only come from compassion.

The question is how to develop compassion. In fact, can we really develop this unbiased compassion at all? My answer is that we definitely can. I believe that human nature is gentle and compassionate, although many people, both in the past and now, think that human nature is basically aggressive. Let us examine this point.

At the time of conception, and while we are in our mothers womb, our mother's compassionate and peaceful mental state is a very positive factor for our development. If the mother's mind is very agitated, it is harmful for us. And that is just the beginning of life! Even the parents' state of mind at conception itself is important. If a child is conceived through rape, for example, then the child will be unwanted, which is a terrible thing. For conception to take place properly, it should come from genuine love and mutual respect, not just mad passion. It is not enough to have some casual love affair, the two partners should know each other well and respect each other as people, and this is the basis for a happy marriage. Furthermore, marriage itself should be for life, or at least should be long lasting. Life should properly start from such a situation.

Then, according to medical science, in the few weeks after birth, the child's brain is still growing. During that period, the experts claim that physical touch is a crucial factor for the proper development of the brain. This alone shows that the mere growth of our body requires another's affection.

After birth, one of the first acts on the mother's side is to give milk, and from the child's side it is to suckle. Milk is often considered a symbol of compassion. Without it, traditionally the child cannot survive. Through the process of suckling there comes a closeness between mother and child. If that closeness is not there, then the child will not seek its mother's breast, and if the mother is feeling dislike towards the child her milk may not come freely. So milk comes with affection. This means that the first act of our life, that of taking milk, is a symbol of affection. I am always reminded of this when I visit a church and see Mary carrying Jesus as a small baby; that, to me, is a symbol of love and affection.

It has been found that those children who grow up in homes where there is love and affection have a healthier physical development and study better at school. Conversely, those who lack human affection have more difficulty in developing physically and mentally. These children also find it difficult to show affection when they grow up, which is such a great tragedy.

Now let us look at the last moment of our lives—death. Even at the time of death, although the dying person can no longer benefit much from his friends, if he is surrounded by friends his mind may be more calm. Therefore throughout our lives, from the very beginning right up to our death, human affection plays a very important role.

An affectionate disposition not only makes the mind more peaceful and calm, but it affects our body in a positive way too. On the other hand, hatred, jealousy and fear upset our peace of mind, make us agitated and affect our body adversely. Even our body needs peace of mind, and is not suited to agitation. This shows that an appreciation of peace of mind is in our blood.

Therefore, although some may disagree, I feel that although the aggressive side of our nature is part of life, the dominant force of life is human affection. This is why it is possible to strengthen that basic goodness which is our human nature.

We can also approach the importance of compassion through intelligent reasoning. If I help another person, and show concern for him or her, then I myself will benefit from that. However, if I harm others, eventually I will be in trouble. I often joke, half sincerely and half seriously, saying that if we wish to be truly selfish then we should be wisely selfish rather than foolishly selfish. Our intelligence can help to adjust our attitude in this respect. If we use it well, we can gain insight as to how we can fulfill our own self-interest by leading a compassionate way of life. It would even be possible to argue that being compassionate is ultimately selfish.

In this context, I do not think that selfishness is wrong. Loving oneself is crucial. If we do not love ourselves, how can we love others? It seems that when some people talk of compassion, they have the notion that it entails a total disregard for one's own interests—a sacrificing of one's interests. This is not the case. In fact genuine love should first be directed at oneself.

There are two different senses of self. One has no hesitation in harming other people, and that is negative and leads to trouble. The other is based on determination, will-power and self-confidence, and that sense of I is very necessary. Without it, how can we develop the confidence we need to carry out any task in life? Similarly, there are two types of desire also. However, hatred is invariably negative and destructive of harmony.

How can we reduce hatred? Hatred is usually preceded by anger. Anger rises as a reactive emotion, and gradually develops into a feeling of hatred. The skilful approach here is first to know that anger is negative. Often people think that as anger is part of us, it is better to express it, but I think this is misguided. You may have grievances or resentment due to your past and by expressing your anger you might be able to finish with them. That is very possible. Usually, however, it is better to check your anger, and then gradually, year by year, it diminishes. In my experience, this works best when you adopt the position that anger is negative and it is better not to feel it. That position itself will make a difference.

Whenever anger is about to come, you can train yourself to see the object of your anger in a different light. Any person or circumstance which causes anger is basically relative; seen from one angle it makes you angry, but seen from another perspective you may discover some good things in it. We lost our country, for example, and became refugees. If we look at our situation from that angle, we might feel frustration and sadness, yet the same event has created new opportunities—meeting with other people from different religious traditions, and so on. Developing a more flexible way of seeing things helps us cultivate a more balanced mental attitude. This is one method.

There are other situations where you might fall sick, for example, and the more you think about your sickness the worse your frustration becomes. In such a case, it is very helpful to compare your situation with the worst case scenario related to your illness, or with what would have happened if you had caught an even more serious illness, and so on. In this way, you can console yourself by realizing that it could have been much worse. Here again, you train yourself to see the relativity of your situation. If you compare it with something that is much worse, this will immediately reduce your frustration.

Similarly, if difficulties come they may appear enormous when you look at them closely, but if you approach the same problem from a wider perspective, it appears smaller. With these methods, and by developing a larger outlook, you can reduce your frustration whenever you face problems. You can see that constant effort is needed, but if you apply it in this way, then the angry side of you will diminish. Meanwhile, you strengthen your compassionate side and increase your good potential. By combining these two approaches, a negative person can be transformed into a kind one. This is the method we use to effect that transformation.

In addition, if you have religious faith, it can be useful in extending these qualities. For example, the Gospels teach us to turn the other cheek, which clearly shows the practice of tolerance. For me, the main message of the Gospels is love for our fellow human beings, and the reason we should develop this is because we love God. I understand this in the sense of having infinite love. Such religious teachings are very powerful to increase and extend our good qualities. The Buddhist approach presents a very clear method. First, we try to consider all sentient beings as equal. Then we consider that the lives of all beings are just as precious as our own, and through this we develop a sense of concern for others.

What of the case of someone who has no religious faith? Whether we follow a religion or not is a matter of individual right. It is possible to manage without religion, and in some cases it may make life simpler! But when you no longer have any interest in religion, you should not neglect the value of good human qualities. As long as we are human beings, and members of human society, we need human compassion. Without that, you cannot be happy. Since we all want to be happy, and to have a happy family and friends, we have to develop compassion and affection. It is important to recognize that there are two levels of spirituality, one with religious faith, and one without. With the latter, we simply try to be a warm-hearted person.

We should also remember that once we cultivate a compassionate attitude, non-violence comes automatically. Non-violence is not a diplomatic word, it is compassion in action. If you have hatred in your heart, then very often your actions will be violent, whereas if you have compassion in your heart, your actions will be non-violent.

As I said earlier, as long as human beings remain on this earth there will always be disagreements and conflicting views. We can take that as given. If we use violence in order to reduce disagreements and conflict, then we must expect violence every day and I think the result of this is terrible. Furthermore, it is actually impossible to eliminate disagreements through violence. Violence only brings even more resentment and dissatisfaction.

Non-violence, on the other hand, means dialogue, it means using language to communicate. And dialogue means compromise, listening to others' views, and respecting others' rights, in a spirit of reconciliation. Nobody will be 100 per cent winner, and nobody will be 100 per cent loser. That is the practical way. In fact, that is the only way. Today, as the world becomes smaller and smaller, the concept of 'us' and 'them' is almost out-dated. If our interests existed independently of those of others, then it would be possible to have a complete winner and a complete loser, but since in reality we all depend on one another, our interests and those of others are very interconnected. So how can you gain 100 per cent victory? It is impossible. You have to share, half-half, or if at all possible 60 per cent this side and 40 per cent the other side! Without this approach, reconciliation is impossible.

The reality of the world today means that we need to learn to think in this way. This is the basis of my own approach—the 'middle way' approach. Tibetans will not be able to gain 100 per cent victory for, whether we like it or not, the future of Tibet very much depends on China. Therefore, in the spirit of reconciliation, I advocate a sharing of interests so that genuine progress is possible. Compromise is the only way. Through non-violent means we can share views, feelings and rights, and in this way we can solve the problem.

I sometimes call the twentieth century a century of bloodshed, a century of war. In this century there have been more conflicts, more bloodshed and more weapons than ever before. Now, on the basis of the experience we have all had in this century, and of what we have learned from it, I think we should look to the next century to be one of dialogue. The principle of non-violence should be practised everywhere. This cannot be achieved simply by sitting here and praying. It means work and effort, and yet more effort.

~

FOUR

UNIVERSAL RESPONSIBILITY*

I always believe that we human beings are all essentially the same—mentally, emotionally and physically.

I want to make clear, however—perhaps even warn you—that you should not expect too much. There are no miracles. I am very sceptical of such things. It is very dangerous if people come to my talks believing that the Dalai Lama has some kind of healing power, for example. I myself doubt those who claim to have the power to heal. Some time ago, at a large gathering in England, I said the same thing. At that time I told the audience that if there is a real healer out there, I want to show that person my skin problems. Sometimes it can be quite pleasant to scratch the itch, but as the Indian Buddhist master Nagarjuna said, 'It's better not to have the itching than to have the pleasure of scratching.' Anyway, so far, I have never met such a person. However, if you are here simply out of curiosity, that's perfectly fine. I'm very happy to have this opportunity to talk to you and would also like to express my deep appreciation to those who have organized this event.

The fundamental thing is that everyone wants a happy, successful life. This is not only our goal but our legitimate right as well. The question then arises, how do we achieve this happy life? When material and spiritual development are combined, however, we can achieve our goal of a happy life. Therefore, while focusing on material development, it is essential that we pay attention to inner values as well.

When I use the word 'spiritual,' I don't necessarily mean religious faith. It is quite obvious that there are two levels of spirituality—spirituality with religious faith and that without. Obviously, an

---

* From *Illuminating the Path to Enlightenment*, Thubten Dhargye Ling, 2002.

individual can manage to lead a meaningful life without religious faith, but you can't be a happy person without the spirituality of basic human values. As long as we remain human, there is no way that we can neglect this.

What are these basic human values? There are two levels. On one level, there is the sense of caring for one another, sharing with one another—the sense of oneness that comes from seeing all people as brothers and sisters in a single human family, bringing respect, tolerance and self-discipline. We even find some of these qualities in the animal kingdom. However, on another level, because of our human intelligence and understanding of far-reaching consequences, we can deliberately increase certain qualities and try to restrain others. In this way, humans are much more sophisticated than animals.

Human beings and animals both have the same basic desire for happiness or satisfaction. This is common to all sentient beings. The unique thing about us, however, is our intelligence. The desire to attain happiness, pleasure and satisfaction mainly through the five senses is not a uniquely human thing; there is not much to distinguish us from animals in this regard. What does distinguish us from animals, however, is our ability to use our faculty of intelligence in our quest to fulfill our natural desire to be happy and overcome suffering. It is this ability to judge between the long-term and short-term consequences of our behaviour and actions that really distinguishes us from animals; utilizing our unique human qualities in the right way is what proves us to be true human beings.

Another important factor is that there are two kinds of pain and pleasure—pain and pleasure on the physical, or sensory, level and those on the mental level. If we examine our daily lives, it will become clear that we can subdue physical pain mentally. When we are happy and calm, we can easily ignore physical discomfort, such as pain and unpleasant sensations. When, however, we are unhappy or disturbed, then even the best of external factors, such as good companions, money and fame, cannot make us happy. This suggests that no matter how powerful our sensory experiences might be, they cannot overwhelm our state of mind; mental experience is superior to physical. It is in this mental realm of happiness and suffering or pain and pleasure that

27

the application of human intelligence plays a tremendously influential role.

Human intelligence itself is neutral; it is just an instrument that can be utilized in either destructive or constructive ways. For example, many of our sufferings come about as the result of the power of our imagination and ability to think about the future, which can create doubt, expectation, disappointment and fear. Animals don't have these problems. If an animal finds good food and shelter and there are no immediate disturbances, it can exist quite peacefully, but even when we human beings are well fed and surrounded by good companions, nice music and so forth, our sophistication and expectations don't allow us to relax. Human intelligence, in other words, is a source of worry and problems. The unhappiness that arises from an overactive imagination cannot be resolved by material means.

Human intelligence, therefore, can be very influential either negatively or positively. The key factor in directing it more positively is having the right mental attitude. To have a happy life—happy days and happy nights—it is extremely important to combine our human intelligence with basic human values. If our minds are peaceful, open and calm during the day, our dreams will reflect these experiences and be happy. If during the day we experience fear, agitation and doubt, we will continue to encounter troubles in our dreams. Therefore, to have happiness twenty-four hours a day, we must have the right mental attitude.

Instead of thinking about money and material things every minute of the day, we should pay more attention to our inner world. It is interesting to ask ourselves such questions as, 'Who am I?' and 'Where is my I?' Usually, we take our 'I' for granted. We feel that within us, there is something solid and independent that is the owner of our mind, body and possessions; if we reflect on and examine where this so-called powerful and precious self actually resides, it will prove to be quite useful. We should also ask, 'What is the mind? Where is it?' because the greatest of all disturbing forces are the negative emotions. When these destructive emotions are fully developed, we become their slave; as if mad. Therefore, when negative emotions arise, it is useful to inquire, 'Where does all this come from?'

The key factor in developing and increasing basic human values—the sense of caring for and sharing with one another—is human affection, a feeling of closeness with one another. Medical science also teaches us that emotions play a very important role in health. Fear and hatred, for example, are very bad for us. Also, when negative emotions arise strongly, certain parts of our brain become blocked and our intelligence cannot function properly. We can see from our daily experience as well that strong negative emotions can make us uncomfortable and tense, leading to problems with digestion and sleep and causing some of us to resort to tranquilizers, sleeping pills, alcohol or other drugs.

Furthermore, when certain negative emotions develop they can disturb our body's natural balance, resulting in high blood pressure and other kinds of disease. One medical researcher presented data at a conference showing that people who frequently use words such as 'I,' 'me' and 'mine' have a greater risk of heart attack. Thus, it seems that if you want to have a heart attack, you should repeat these words like a mantra and all the time say, 'I, I, I, I, I, I.'

If we think of ourselves as very precious and absolute, our whole mental focus becomes very narrow and limited and even minor problems can seem unbearable. The actual beneficiary of the practice of compassion and caring for others is oneself. We may have the impression that the main beneficiaries of the practice of compassion are those on the receiving end; that the practice of compassion is relevant only for those concerned about others and irrelevant for those who are not, because its main benefit goes to others. This is a mistake. The immediate benefit of practising compassion is actually experienced by the practitioner.

Because our mind broadens and we feel more comfortable when we think about humanity and the welfare of others, if we can generate this kind of mental attitude, whenever we meet someone, we will feel that here is another human brother or sister and will immediately be able to communicate with ease. When we think only about ourselves, our inner door remains closed and we find it very difficult to communicate with our fellow human beings.

I am a seventy-year-old Buddhist monk and in a few months I will be seventy-one. The greater part of my life has not been happy. Most people already know about my difficult experiences. When I was fifteen I lost my freedom; at the age of twenty-four I lost my country. Now, forty-one years have passed since I became a refugee and news from my homeland is always very saddening. Yet inside, my mental state seems quite peaceful. Bad news tends to go in one ear and out the other; not much remains stuck within my mind. The result is that my peace of mind is not too disturbed.

This is not because I'm some kind of special person. I joke with my Chinese friends about the Chinese term *huo-fo*, which means 'living Buddha.' The very term itself is dangerous; it's completely wrong. The Tibetan word is 'lama'; in Sanskrit, it's 'guru.' There's no hint of 'living Buddha' in these words, so I have no idea how the Chinese got 'living Buddha' out of them. Anyway, whether people call me a living Buddha, a god-king or, in some cases, a devil or counter-revolutionary, it doesn't matter. The reality is that I'm just a human being; a simple Buddhist monk. There are no differences between us, and according to my own experience, if we pay more attention to our inner world then our lives can be happier. You can achieve many things as a result of living in a materially developed society, but if, in addition, you pay more attention to your inner world, your life will become much richer and more complete.

Through training our minds we can become more peaceful. This will give us greater opportunities for creating the peaceful families and human communities that are the foundation of world peace. With inner strength, we can face problems on the familial, societal and even global levels in a more realistic way. Non-violence does not mean passivity. We need to solve problems through dialogue in a spirit of reconciliation. This is the real meaning of non-violence and the source of world peace.

This approach can also be very useful in ecology. We always hear about a better environment, world peace, non-violence and so forth, but such goals are not achieved through the application of regulations or United Nations resolutions; it takes individual transformation. Once we have developed a peaceful society in which problems are negotiated through dialogue, we can seriously think about demilitarization—

first on the national level; then on the regional level; and finally, on the global level. However, it will be very difficult to achieve these things unless individuals themselves undergo a change within their own minds.

II

BUDDHIST PERSPECTIVES

FIVE

~

INTRODUCTION*

Studying Buddhist teachings is a bit like doing construction work upon our minds. This kind of work is not always easy, but some of its aspects make it less difficult. For example, we don't need money, labourers, technicians or technology. Everything we require is already there, within our mind. Therefore, with the right kind of effort and awareness, mental development can be easy.

I sometimes feel a little hesitant about giving Buddhist teachings in the West, because I think that it is better and safer for people to stay within their own religious tradition. But out of the millions of people who live in the West, naturally there will be some who find the Buddhist approach more effective or suitable. Even among Tibetans, there are those who practice Islam instead of Buddhism. If you do adopt Buddhism as your religion, however, you must still maintain an appreciation for the other major religious traditions. Even if they no longer work for you, millions of other people have received immense benefit from them in the past and continue to do so. Therefore, it is important for you to respect them.

The teachings we are studying here are based on two texts: *A Lamp for the Path to Enlightenment* (Tib: *Jang-chub lam-gyi dron-ma*) by the Indian master Atisha Dipamkara Shrijnana, and *Lines of Experience* (Tib: *Lam-rim nyam-gur or Lam-rim nyam-len dor-du*), by Lama Tsong Khapa.

The skillful and compassionate Shakyamuni Buddha taught diverse types of Buddhadhara within a collection of 84,000 scriptures for the diverse mental dispositions and spiritual inclinations of his listeners.

---

* From *Illuminating the Path to Enlightenment*, Thubten Dhargye Ling, 2002.

The essence of all these teachings is presented in such excellent treatises as Atisha's *Lamp for the Path*, which presents the systematic approach of an individual on the path to enlightenment.

With this as a basis, Lama Tsong Khapa composed three versions of lam-rim texts: an extensive version known as the *Great Exposition of the Path to Enlightenment*, a medium-length version known as the *Middling Exposition of the Stages of the Path*; and the text we are studying here, the *Short Exposition of the Stages of the Path*, which is also called *Lines of Experience or Songs of Spiritual Experience*.

Although I am the one explaining the texts we'll be studying here, you don't necessarily have to see me as your spiritual teacher. Instead, you can take my explanations to heart by relating to me more as a spiritual friend or colleague. Furthermore, don't simply believe what I say without question, but use it as a basis for personal reflection and, in that way, develop your understanding of the Dharma.

Whenever we engage in teaching, studying or listening to the Buddhadharma, it is very important to ensure that we adopt the correct motivation and attitude within our hearts and minds. We do this by taking refuge in the Three Jewels (Buddha, Dharma and Sangha) and reaffirming our generation of the mind of enlightenment (the altruistic intention) through reciting the following verse three times:

> I take refuge until I am enlightened
> In the Buddha, the Dharma and the Sangha.
> By the positive potential I generate
> Through studying these teachings,
> May I attain buddhahood for the benefit of all.

It is also traditional at the beginning of a teaching to recite verses making salutations to the Buddha, such as those that appear in Nagarjuna's text, *Fundamentals of the Middle Way*. At the conclusion of this text, there is a verse that states, 'I salute the Buddha who revealed the path that pacifies all suffering.' The Buddha presented the path that pacifies all suffering in the following way.

Since the sufferings we all wish to avoid result from fundamentally mistaken ways of viewing the world, the way we eliminate them is by cultivating a correct understanding of the nature of reality. Therefore, in this verse, Nagarjuna salutes the Buddha for revealing the path that shows us how to cultivate a correct understanding of the nature of reality.

The Purpose of Dharama Practice

What is the purpose of the Dharma? Just like other spiritual traditions, Buddhadharma is an instrument for training the mind—something we use to try to work out the problems that we all experience; problems that originate mainly at the mental level. Negative emotional forces create mental unrest, such as unhappiness, fear, doubt, frustration and so forth; these negative mental states then cause us to engage in negative activities, which in turn bring us more problems and more suffering. Practising Dharma is a way of working out these problems, be they long-term or immediate. In other words, Dharma protects us from unwanted suffering.

Buddhadharma means bringing discipline and inner tranquility into our mind. Therefore, when we talk about transforming our mind and developing inner qualities, the only way we can do this is to utilize the mind itself. There is nothing else we can use to bring about such change. Thus, we should realize that much of what we do not desire— unwanted events, unhappiness and suffering—actually comes about as a result of our mistaken way of viewing the world and our destructive thoughts and emotions. These negative minds create both immediate unhappiness and future suffering as well.

Underlying all of this is a fundamental ignorance, a fundamentally flawed way of perceiving reality. In Buddhism, this is called 'self-grasping,' or 'grasping at self-existence.' Since this is the case, the way to eliminate negative aspects of mind and the suffering they create is to see through the delusion of these mental processes and cultivate their opponent— the wisdom that is correct insight into the ultimate nature of reality. Through cultivating this insight and applying it as an antidote, we will be able to dispel the suffering and undesirable events in our lives.

To succeed in this, we must first recognize what the negative and positive aspects of mind are and be able to distinguish between them.

Once we develop a clear understanding of the negative aspects of mind and their destructive potential, the wish to distance ourselves from them will arise naturally within us. Similarly, when we recognize the positive aspects of mind and their potential benefit, we will naturally aspire to gain and enhance these mental qualities. Such transformation of mind cannot be imposed on us from the outside but happens only on the basis of voluntary acceptance and great enthusiasm inspired by a clear awareness of the benefits to be gained.

Time is always moving, minute-by-minute and second-by-second. As time moves on, so do our lives. Nobody can stop this movement. However, one thing is in our own hands, and that is whether or not we waste the time that we have; whether we use it in a negative way or a constructive way. The passage of time through which we live our lives is the same for all of us and there is also a basic equality between those of us who are a part of this time. The difference lies in our state of mind and motivation.

Proper motivation does not come about simply by our being aware that one kind of motivation is right and another wrong. Awareness alone does not change motivation. It takes effort. If we make this effort wisely, we will attain a positive, desirable result, but unwise effort is akin to self-torture. Therefore, we need to know how to act.

This issue of making a wise use of effort is very important. For example, even external development, such as the construction of a building, requires a tremendous amount of diligence and care. You need to take into account its exact location, the suitability of the environment, the climate and so forth. Having taken all those factors into account, you can then build a reliable and appropriate structure.

Similarly, when you make an effort in the realm of mental experience, it is important to first have a basic understanding of the nature of mind, thoughts and emotions, and also to take into account the complexity of the human physiological condition and how it interfaces with the surrounding environment.

Therefore, it is important for you to have a wide, comprehensive knowledge of things so that you don't exert all your effort blindly pursuing your goal on the basis of a single point. That's not the way of the intelligent, the way of the wise. The way of the wise is to exert effort on the basis of much wider knowledge.

In the Tibetan Buddhist tradition, there are more than one hundred volumes of *Kangyur*—sutras attributed to the Buddha himself—and more than two hundred volumes of *Tengyur*—the collection of authoritative commentaries written by such Indian masters as Nagarjuna and Asanga. If you were to distill the meaning of all of these sutras and their commentaries and incorporate them into your practice, you would make tremendous strides in terms of realization and spiritual progress, but if you treat all this great literature simply as an object of veneration and seek instead some smaller text on which to base your practice, then although you will receive some benefit, your spiritual progress will not be that great.

Intellectual and Experiential Understanding

It is important to be able to differentiate between two levels of understanding. One is the superficial, intellectual level, where on the basis of reading, studying or listening to teachings, we distinguish between negative and positive qualities of mind and recognize their nature and origin. The other is the deeper, experiential level, where we actually cultivate and generate positive qualities within ourselves.

Although it can be challenging to develop an intellectual understanding of certain topics, it is generally easier because it can be cultivated merely by reading texts or listening to teachings. Experiential understanding is far more difficult to develop, since it comes about only as a result of sustained practice. At the experiential level, your understanding is also accompanied by a strong component of feeling; your understanding is essentially a felt experience.

Because experiential understanding is thus accompanied by powerful emotions, you can see that although many emotions are destructive, there are positive emotional states as well. Actually, human beings could not survive without emotion. Emotion is an integral part of being human; without it, there would be no basis for life. However, we also know that many of our problems and conflicts are entangled with strong emotions. When certain emotions arise within our hearts and minds, they create an immediate disturbance, which isn't only temporary but can lead to negative long-term consequences, especially when we interact with other people.

When other types of emotion arise, however, they immediately induce a sense of strength and courage, creating a more positive atmosphere in general and leading to positive long-term consequences, including our health. Putting aside the question of spiritual practice for the moment, we can see that even from the perspective of mundane day-to-day life, there are destructive emotions and those that are constructive.

The Tibetan term for Dharma is *cho*, which has the literal connotation of 'changing,' or 'bringing about transformation.' When we talk about transforming the mind, we are referring to the task of diminishing the force of destructive thoughts and emotions while developing the force of those that are constructive and beneficial. In this way, through the practice of Dharma, we transform our undisciplined mind into one that is disciplined.

The Basis for Transformation

How do we know that it is possible to transform our mind? There are two bases for this. One is the fundamental law of impermanence; that all things and events are subject to transformation and change. If we examine this more deeply, we will realize that at every instant, everything that exists is going through a process of change. Even though, for example, we speak of yesterday's person as existing unchanged today, we are all aware at a gross, experiential level of the laws of impermanence; that, for instance, even the earth on which we live will one day come to an end.

If things and events did not have the nature of changing from moment to moment, we would be unable to explain how transformation takes place over time. When we reduce vast passages of time down to very brief ones, we can realize that things are actually changing from moment to moment. Modern technology helps us see some of these changes; the development of a biological organism, for example, can be observed through a microscope. Also, at a subtle theoretical level, certain observations indicate the extremely dynamic nature of physical reality.

This transient and impermanent nature of reality is not to be understood in terms of something coming into being, remaining for a while and then ceasing to exist. That is not the meaning of impermanence at the subtle level. Subtle impermanence refers to the fact that the moment things and events come into existence, they are already impermanent in nature; the moment they arise, the process of their disintegration has already begun. When something comes into being from its causes and conditions, the seed of its cessation is born along with it. It is not that something comes into being and then a third factor or condition causes its disintegration. That is not how to understand impermanence. Impermanence means that as soon as something comes into being, it has already started to decay.

If you limit your understanding of impermanence to something's continuum, you will comprehend only gross impermanence. You will feel that when certain causes and conditions give rise to something, it remains unchanged as long as the factors that sustain its existence remain unchanged, and begins to disintegrate only when it encounters adverse circumstances. This is gross impermanence.

If, however, you deepen your understanding of impermanence by approaching it at the subtle level—the moment-to-moment change undergone by all phenomena—you will realize how as soon as something comes into being, its cessation has also begun.

At first you might feel that coming into being and coming to cessation are contradictory processes, but when you deepen your understanding of impermanence, you will realize that coming into being (birth) and cessation (death) are, in a sense, simultaneous. Thus, the fundamental law of impermanence (the transitory nature of all phenomena) gives us one basis for the possibility of transforming our minds.

The second premise for the possibility of transforming our minds is again one that we can perceive in the reality of the external physical world, where we see that certain things are in conflict with others. We can call this the law of contradiction. For example, heat and cold, darkness and light and so forth are opposing forces—enhancing one automatically diminishes the other. In some cases this is a gradual process, in others, instantaneous. For instance, when you switch on a light, darkness in a room is immediately dispelled.

If you look at the mental world of thoughts and emotions in the same way, you will again find many opposing forces, such that when you encourage and develop certain types of emotions, those that contradict them automatically diminish in intensity. This natural fact of our consciousness, where opposite forces contradict one another, provides another premise for the possibility of change and transformation.

When we take two types of thought or emotion that directly oppose one another, the question arises, which reflects the true state of affairs and which is a false way of relating to the world? The answer is that those thoughts and emotions that are strongly grounded in experience and reason are the ones with truth on their side, whereas those that are contrary to the way things exist, no matter how powerful they may be at any given time, are actually unstable. Since they lack valid grounding in experience and reason, they do not have a firm foundation.

Also, if we take two kinds of emotion that directly oppose one other and examine them to see what distinguishes one from the other; another feature we notice is that they differ in their long-term effects.

There are certain types of emotion that give us temporary relief or satisfaction, but when we examine them with our faculty of intelligence— the insight that enables us to judge between long- and short-term benefits and shortcomings—we find that in the long run they are destructive and harmful; they cannot be supported by reason or insight. The moment the light of intelligence shines on destructive emotions, they no longer have any support.

There are other types of emotion, however, that may seem a bit disturbing at the time but actually have long-term benefits, and are, therefore, reinforced by reason and insight, supported by intelligence. Therefore, positive emotions are ultimately more powerful than negative ones because their potential for development is greater.

These two premises—the laws of impermanence and contradiction—allow us to see the possibility of bringing about transformation within ourselves.

Investigating the Nature of Reality

All this suggests the importance of having a deeper knowledge of the nature of the mind and its various aspects and functions in general, and the nature and complexity of emotion in particular. Also, since we realize that many of our problems arise from a fundamentally flawed way of perceiving and relating to the world, it becomes important for us to be able to examine whether or not our perception accords with the true nature of reality. Understanding the true nature of reality is crucial, as it is our perception of reality that lies at the heart of how we relate to the world. However, reality here means not just the immediate facts of our experience and environment but the entire expanse of reality, because many of our thoughts and emotions arise not only as a result of the immediate physical environment but also out of abstract ideas.

Therefore, in the Buddha's teaching, we find a great deal of discussion on the nature of reality in terms of the eighteen constituents, the twelve sources, the five aggregates and so forth and how it relates to the practitioner's quest for enlightenment. If the Buddhist path were simply a matter of faith and cultivating deep devotion to the Buddha, there would have been no need for him to explain the nature of reality in such technical and complex terms. From this perspective, then, the Buddha's teaching can be described as an exploration of the nature of reality.

Just as scientific disciplines place tremendous emphasis on the need for objectivity on the part of the scientist, Buddhism also emphasizes the importance of examining the nature of reality from an objective stance. You cannot maintain a point of view simply because you like it or because it accords with your preset metaphysical or emotional prejudices. If your view of reality is based simply on fantasy or conjecture, there will be no possibility of your being able to cultivate that view to an infinite level.

When you are engaged in the Buddhist path of the exploration of the nature of reality, there are principally two faculties at work in your mind. One is the faculty of investigation, which subjects reality to analysis. In Buddhist language this is described as 'wisdom,' or 'insight.' Then there is the faculty of 'method,' or 'skilful means,' which is the faculty that allows you to deepen your courage and tolerance and generates the powerful motivational force that sustains you in your spiritual quest.

Question. Your Holiness, you said that all phenomena are subject to impermanence. Is the pure, unobstructed nature of mind also subject to impermanence? Does this nature of mind have a birth and a death?

His Holiness. When we speak about the nature of mind in a Buddhist context, we have to understand that it can be understood on two different levels—the ultimate level of reality, where the nature of mind is understood in terms of its emptiness of inherent existence, and the relative, or conventional, level, which refers to the mere quality of luminosity, knowing and experience.

If your question relates to the mind's conventional nature, then just as the mind itself goes through a process of change and flux, so does the nature of mind. This already indicates that the nature of mind is an impermanent phenomenon. However, if you are asking about the mind's emptiness, then we need to consider that even though the mind's emptiness is not a transient phenomenon—that is, not subject to causes and conditions—it cannot be posited independent of a given object.

In other words, the emptiness of mind cannot exist independently of mind itself. The emptiness of mind is nothing other than its utter lack of intrinsic, or inherent, existence. Therefore, as different states of mind come and go, new instances of the emptiness of mind also occur.

SIX

LAYING THE GROUNDWORK*

The Need to Reform Our Mind

Why are we gathered here today? Not for business, and not to attend a spectacle or show. The essential thing for today is to listen to a Buddhist address. To what end? To reform our mind. What must be reformed in our mind?

Generally speaking, among all animals that experience themselves as an 'I,' the avoidance of suffering and the desire to be joyful are altogether natural. All animals, each as it can, bend every effort to avoid suffering and to attain well-being. All animal species, down to the most minuscule, seek to avoid suffering and to find well-being, and it is in this manner that each one goes forward in its struggle for survival.

When the Buddhist teachings mention 'all animate beings,' clearly they mean all beings that reject suffering and desire pleasure. Meanwhile, the ability to discern good and evil is far greater in human beings than in other animals. I think this is why, in human society, where spiritual discernment has the most power, religious faith has come to light. Visions, philosophies, and spiritual theories are all born in human society.

The human being's power of discernment is aided by our many technologies and sciences, but it is because of our wish to be happy and not to suffer that our discernment is actually used. However, each time this discernment is employed, its very use creates a multitude of problems and sufferings.

I speak here only of what everyone can see on this planet. I say

* From *Buddha Heart, Buddha Mind*, The Crossroad Publishing Company, 2000.

nothing of the gods, the dragons, and the perfume eaters. With the three worlds, the six classes of beings, or the four births of which the Buddhist texts speak, things expand even more. There are many other beings, all endowed with the ability to discern. In brief, human discernment is a good thing and very powerful, but always ready to secure us a little more suffering.

When animals have a full belly and a temperature that suits them, they relax and become tranquil. We human beings have all external circumstances favorable to us, but by the very fact of our hopes and our apprehensions, we often find ourselves in the greatest displeasure. Each time human discernment ought to intervene, albeit differently for each of us, we see again that our malaise is most intense, and hopes and apprehensions are most abundant. But this is not all. On this planet the most destructive being, all things considered, is the human being. One could almost say that if the human being did not exist, there would be much more peace and the environment would be better-off.

If the human being did not exist, the fish and the innumerable other animals sensible to pleasure and pain would not suffer being exploited by humans. For those who exploit animals, animal life does not have the same value as human life. If the human being did not exist, some claim, there would be far fewer animals—without the human being, animals would only eat each other up! But would this not be a sort of natural equilibrium? If we think about it, would it not be better to desire the disappearance of the human being?

And yet all living beings, of whatever kind, love one another. So human beings love one another and can have concern for others. Our concern comes from our power of discerning, which is how we can develop our sense of compassion. But is it only the human being who has this capability? Among all animals, unselfishness, limited as it may be, brings benefits. Among the social animals, however, infinite compassion is the prerogative of the human being alone. A beast would have great difficulty surrendering to it.

Or we can approach the matter from the other end. Life, our very existence, is not dedicated to destruction. Could our whole life be reduced to an existence dedicated to destruction? Not at all! We do not exist to destroy, any more than we exist to suffer! Then do you not find that whether our lives are constructive or destructive lies in our own hands?

If we could be gifted with true discernment, and we could surround ourselves with loyal friends, we would have a life of great meaning: it would be constructive. It is important for us, then, to reform our mind by examining it in great detail. We ought to develop its goodness and its usefulness by reducing its harmful aspects. Is that not the essential?

To be sure, one could ask what we mean by 'good' and 'bad'. Suffering designates something 'bad', something undesirable. Suffering is a source of unpleasantness. It is happiness that we desire; happiness, then, will be our 'good'. We distinguish good and bad effects, those that are pleasant and those that are not, by considering their respective results. 'Bad' is the cause of suffering, and 'good' is the cause of well-being and what is authentically useful. When we have reformed our mind, our negative thoughts will diminish and our positive thoughts will increase. Then, we will suffer less and less of the 'bad', and grow more and more in the 'good'.

Peace of Mind and Happiness

Becoming rich and famous: is that really the essential goal of human life? Money is important. A 'name' is generally useful as well. But among those who have money, a name, and possessions— say, great wealth— we have seen more than one drowning in troubles and concerns. Others, by contrast, have neither name nor renown, they seem truly unfortunate from the material standpoint, but their minds seem at ease. Some have no money problems but are always having to take medicine. Yet others, even in the absence of all material comfort, feel physically well without having to take medicine.

What is their secret? When peace reigns in the mind, one is always happy, even if external conditions are not ideal. The body can gain health, but without peace of mind no happiness is possible, not even under the best conditions.

Then where is this secret? It is in our peace of mind. Would peace of mind come once one has wished for it? This would be very unlikely. The mere wish to know peace of mind cannot secure that peace. You know that one does not acquire money simply by wishing for it. One has to work to obtain it. Just so, peace is a possession of the mind, and this possession, this wealth, is not obtained simply by desiring it. Go to a big store in Paris, or even in New York. No one will sell you peace of mind.

Certain religious communities claim that their religions enable one to reach peace of mind instantly. But how could that be? I only know what I have studied, of course, but when I am told that it is possible to reach a certain peace of mind in no time at all, I become sceptical. It would be like asking your physician for an injection of peace of mind. I think the doctor would burst out laughing.

The Origin of the Dharma

Here, now, is how I am accustomed to explain the origin of the Dharma.

It was in the sacred city of Benares that the Instructor filled with goodness, expert in skillful methods, and overflowing with great compassion preached the Dharma for the first time. He set the wheel of the Dharma turning and taught the Four Noble Truths to the Five Good Ascetics. And so Buddhism began.

As you all know, the usual explanation is that there are two vehicles of Buddhism, the Lesser and the Greater, that is, the Vehicle of the Hearers and the eremitic Buddhas (Hinayana) and the Vehicle of the Bodhisattvas (Mahayana). The Greater Vehicle is in turn divided into the Greater Vehicle of the Sutras and the Greater Vehicle of the Tantras. The system of the Four Noble Truths, which forms all Buddhists' basic belief structure, necessarily follows this division into two vehicles.

The practice of the way as it is taught in the texts of the Lesser Vehicle constitutes the foundation of the Buddha's teachings. Without this foundation, it would have been very difficult for a 'greater' vehicle to appear. When, within Buddhism, adepts of the Greater Vehicle judge a teaching inferior because it belongs to the Lesser Vehicle, or adepts of the Lesser Vehicle doubt that the Greater Vehicle really flows from the Buddha, they are making these judgments out of Buddhism's essence, and this is a serious shortcoming. Without the practices associated with the Four Noble Truths, or the way of the thirty-seven aids of the

Awakening taught in the texts of the Lesser Vehicle, it is impossible to truly practice the spirit of Awakening of the Greater Vehicle, which is benevolence and compassion. I mean great compassion.

The same prejudices have occurred in Tibet between the Greater Vehicle of the Tantras and the Greater Vehicle of the Transcendences (the six transcendent virtues). The adepts of the transcendent virtues did not look favorably upon the tantras. For their part, the adepts of the tantras had scarcely any respect for the Vehicle of the Transcendences, especially where discipline was concerned. This prejudice was a defect and an error.

The levels of the vehicles are, then, Lesser Vehicle, Greater Vehicle of the Transcendences, and Greater Vehicle of the Tantras. The fruit of the more humble vehicles is easily attained by following their practices. Nevertheless it is impossible, without mastery of these 'lower' practices, to reach the fruit of the higher vehicles. Why? Because these lesser vehicles are the foundations upon which the greater take form. Among the teachings of the Buddha that have been preserved in all their integrity in Tibet, the Land of Snows, we find the practices of the Lesser and the Greater Vehicles, including the aggregate of the tantras. For me, this is an important fact.

The Three Cycles of the Buddha's Teachings

In the philosophical systems of the Greater Vehicle, what was taught by the Buddha in the texts of the Lesser Vehicle advances in breadth and depth. For example, the texts of the Lesser Vehicle concern only our Instructor Shakyamuni. In the first part of his life, he is said to have been an ordinary person and bodhisattva. Then, it is said, on the Diamond Throne (in Bodh Gaya, India), he undertook the way of juncture; and he became an authentic and perfect Buddha as he emerged from this diamond-like contemplation, or way of cessation. These texts teach that it was only during the second part of his life that he was a Buddha. However this may be, here it is a matter simply of what is called a supreme body of apparition, not other bodies of the Buddha. In the Greater Vehicle, the system of three or four bodies of the Buddha prevails.

In the Greater Vehicle of the Transcendences, the Buddha will teach the system of the four bodies. He will explain how the four bodies are realized in the tantras. Likewise, when he teaches the different ways or paths, and the meditations proper to each one, the Buddha does not limit himself to the way of the thirty-seven aids of the Awakening, and especially not to the way of the nonexistence of the individual self.

When the moment of the Greater Vehicle had come, the cycle of universal insubstantiality acquired its breadth. All the theories, such as the system of the ten earths, have constantly broadened since then. In the Vehicle of the Transcendences, the Buddha taught the practice of the six transcendent virtues and declared that the way was to be followed by combining method and knowledge itself. In the tantras an eminently sublime thing is taught: the extraordinary union of practice and knowledge.

And so, once he had deepened and broadened his teachings on the Four Noble Truths, the Buddha turned the wheel of the intermediate Dharma, that of the Greater Vehicle, on the peak of the Voutours. He then pronounced the sutras of Transcendent Knowledge. In these sutras the Buddha minutely studies the noble truth of the cessation of suffering that he had taught with the other three truths at Benares. In the third cycle of his teachings, he taught a variety of sutras that, like the principal sutras explicit in Continuity Unexcelled, such as the *Sutra of the Potential of the Buddha*, deal exclusively with the clear natural light of the mind.

In a word, it was fitting that, with a view to ultimate intellectual comprehension, the truth of the way, otherwise known as the sublime wisdom, be manifested. From then on the mind could attain to an ultimate state absolutely free of the two veils. And at the moment of the last cycle of teachings, when he pronounced texts like the principal sutras on which Continuity Unexcelled is founded, the Buddha taught the ultimate point of the clear light as the nature of the mind. This is the real sense of this kind of text, although certain sutras of the last cycle use a different language.

What the Buddha had first taught was found here more clearly and more profoundly. Later, in the Greater Vehicle of the Tantras, he taught extraordinary things such as the living practice of the 'clear natural light of the mind.' Indeed, this was the occasion on which he taught these things in their ultimate depth and immensity. Were not the deepening and broadening of what he had taught at the beginning only a natural sumptuousness and refinement? No. If the Buddha had restricted himself to his first teachings, he would have committed an error and his teachings would have gone against logic.

I repeat: the later teachings of the Buddha are more profound and clearer than the first. Were not these 'deepening' and clarifications only manners of digression? A luxury that would not be considered indispensable? I think not, for the teachings of the Buddha cannot ever be reduced to his first teachings.

Teachings of Provisional and Definitive Meaning

Let us clarify. One does not judge the definitive or provisional character of a declaration of the Buddha on the basis of its mere formulation— the letter. It is essentially its meaning—its spirit— that must be considered. So we will give the name sutras of definitive meaning to the texts that show forth absolute reality. Those whose content must be interpreted will then be sutras of provisional meaning.

So what is meant by *definitive meaning* and *provisional meaning*? Relative truth and absolute truth, it is explained, obey respectively the provisional meaning and the definitive meaning. We regard the definitive meaning as absolute truth, and absolute truth is the ultimate mode of everything. This ultimate constitution, being absolute truth, is called thusness, so that absolute truth designates the ultimate reality of everything, whatever it is. When one can no longer be drawn anywhere else, one can speak of an absolute, an ultimate. Such is the definitive meaning of the words of the Buddha. So the designation 'sutra of definitive meaning' will attach to the sutra that shows forth, before all else, this absolute truth.

Relative truth, and the texts of provisional meaning, present the wealth and variety of a thousand and one metamorphoses of a most brilliant appearance. Yet this is not to be confused with the ultimate mode of each thing. One can take these relative truths literally. The spirit of Awakening, for example, which is benevolence and compassion, or indeed karmic causality—all of this must be taken literally.

And so, based on the foundation of the first teachings, the subsequent teachings become clearer and broader. We now discover things more profound and vaster. This is the great sublimity of these texts. We cannot say that these teachings are eminently sublime simply because they differ from what already existed, but rather because they deepen and clarify. They are treated in all of their breadth, as we have seen.

Method and Knowledge

Let us now consider methods. The division into Greater and Lesser Vehicles, and within the Greater Vehicle into sutras and tantras, is a way of understanding the methods. In the Lesser Vehicle of the Hearers and eremitic Buddhas, the principal practice of compassion is not without power, surely, but it demands only that one not harm others and that one be helpful to them. In the Greater Vehicle, by contrast, committing oneself to the realization of the happiness of all animate beings and the abolition of their sufferings implies a desire for the omniscience necessary to accomplish this intent. So the differentiation into Greater and Lesser Vehicles only follows greatness or smallness of thought.

Let us move on to the difference between the sutras and the tantras. Scholars all have their own ways of expounding this difference, but it is essentially the differences between the various aspects of the way—methods of accomplishing Buddhahood—that constitute this distinction.

From the standpoint of knowledge, at present we hear it explained that Buddhists have four philosophical systems. Just as thought broadens in terms of method, in terms of knowledge it goes deeper. For example, the four philosophical systems of Buddhism admit insubstantiality. Now, while this insubstantiality has the same sense in the minds of the Vaibhashikas and the Sautrantikas, this is not the case for the Madhyamikas and Chittamatrins. The latter do not restrict themselves to the insubstantiality of the individual but teach the insubstantiality of all phenomena.

The difference between the Madhyamikas and the Chittamatrins with regard to the insubstantiality of all phenomena is a subtle matter. And analytical reasoning enables us to recognize the depths attained by these two philosophical systems. But it is wrong to say that the Buddha has given only these latter teachings, which are far more profound than the former. Why? Because both the latter and the former flow from him. And since they have their common emanation from the Buddha, some cannot be better than the others.

Can one readily gain certitude about these truths by examining them rationally, without also rendering oneself vulnerable to objections arising from analytical reasoning? For example, defending the unreality of the individual self without speaking of the insubstantiality of things—or maintaining that everything really exists, that the subject and object are not empty, and that everything is real—this is something that reason can invalidate.

If certain theses are not invulnerable to the reasoning of higher systems, if they yield to logic, it will be necessary to interpret the text in which they appear—the words of the Buddha—and place them among the declarations of provisional meaning that he pronounced with a precise intention. The profound teachings (those describing universal emptiness), it is explained, are logical to the point that no reasoning can invalidate them.

In all the declarations of the Teacher, one can find many points of seeming or actual contradiction. Yet they have all been pronounced by the same Teacher. How can this be? The Teacher has adapted them to the different constitutions and aspirations of his disciples. This being the case, I find it profitable to know with certitude that these full and disparate teachings are truly useful to a wide spectrum of constitutions and aspirations.

The Necessity of the Four Noble Truths

But let us come to an explanation of the system of the Four Noble Truths. We shall first have to define them, then show their importance, and finally practice them along the way they inspire. This is tantamount to saying that they must be understood from within. Now the differentiation into four truths obeys a deepening of our view. We shall analyze them, then, by seeking to see which proposition (in the very proclamation of the Four Noble Truths) is not invulnerable to reason and which will be proved by reasoning.

If I say that the Four Noble Truths are true because they have been formulated by the Buddha, I shall have the problem that we have just seen. One cannot decide that certain philosophical points taught by the Buddha are correct and others not. At this level, the distinction into correct and false can only result from analytical reasoning.

I want to insist on this point. Logic invalidates all that does not exist in reality and is but a mental creation. Actually, when one takes an unreal object for a reality, the reality is vulnerable to reasoning. And what is explained on the basis of this reality must be sought by reasoning on the real existence of the object in question. Because this object is invalidated, it is impossible that anything at all really exists on the basis of this object.

So logic invalidates theories founded on the thesis of real existence. What do we mean when we speak of irrefutability by reasoning? We mean something that actually is, something fundamental that must be known as it is, something that logic cannot refute. Not to know how something is that is—this is what can produce useless concepts that do not stand up to reasoning. It is important, then, to establish the real mode (absolute truth) of every object. Knowledge of this real mode forms the basis on which one can explain what ought to be adopted and reject by reference to this object what should not be adopted.

Then let us come to the Four Noble Truths taught by the Buddha. Suffering is something we do not want, and it must be repelled. To eliminate suffering, one must eliminate its cause. Once this cause is eliminated, one is necessarily delivered from suffering. This is surely how things should be explained, and I have no doubt about it.

If, then, we wonder whether it is possible to eliminate the origin of suffering, we must delve more deeply—think with more depth. In order to know with certitude what we should accept and reject, it is important to know the real nature of the cause of suffering.

The Two Fundamental Truths

Among Buddhists, all schools, beginning with the Vaibhashikas, hold that there are two levels of truth. Still, concerning the essential points of the practice of the two truths, we shall refer in a general way to the philosophical systems of the Greater Vehicle, and in particular to the texts of the Middle Way.

Among the texts of the Middle Way, the theory of the two truths defended by Nagarjuna and his spiritual descendants Buddhapalita, Chandrakirti, and Shantideva proves very profound. It will be necessary, then, to understand the fundamental state of things on the basis of the explanation of these two truths as they are expounded by the sublime bodhisattva Nagarjuna and his heirs.

In order to explain the two truths, we must add the word *fundamental*. The two truths, which describe the fundamental real state of things, are not creations of the karma of ordinary beings, or discoveries subsequent to Buddhahood, but something that one bears within.

In the context of the provisional and definitive meanings of the declarations of the Buddha, we have seen that the texts of definitive meaning express absolute truth, emptiness, and that the texts of provisional meaning concern relative truth. How, then, are we to define the two truths? Theories limited to the functions that operate on the mere level of appearances do not permit analysis to attain their durable situation, or their real mode.

On the level of mere appearances, one finds a variety of objects— in brief, the whole spectrum of perceptions designating the objects of the six senses, that is, forms, sounds, smells, tastes, textures, and intelligible phenomena. Nor is it a matter of something one finds by looking for it when one is unsatisfied by mere appearance. Under the aspect of mere appearances, we distinguish an ultimate situation and a temporary situation. The temporary situation is the apparent temporary, or conventional, mode: what the mind finds there is qualified as relative truth.

Now, when one has studied, or sought, what might be the durable, absolute situation, or the essence of all of this variety of things, without limiting oneself to their appearance—when, unsatisfied by mere appearances, one seeks their durable situation— what one finds is the ultimate meaning of each of these things. One speaks of 'meaning found by analytical reasoning on the ultimate truth of phenomena.' And so, what analytical reasoning on the ultimate discovers is nothing other than absolute truth, and what analytical reasoning on the conventional discovers is relative truth.

Mistaken prejudices generally lead to nothing. Falsified consciousness believes that what is not, and that what is not is, and this belief comes from the depths of the person. Not only has the falsified consciousness slighted itself but it is *distorted*. Now, the distorted consciousness cannot accomplish anything constructive, either in the Dharma or in the profane world. It is important, then, to establish the real mode of things. This quest for the real mode of the things that exist is the same as that undertaken at universities.

Under the aegis of the Prasangika Chandrakirti, adepts of the Middle Way declare that nothing really is, that nothing has being in itself, that no phenomenon exists on its own. These declarations permit in various ways the suppression of the negative emotions.

One may read in *The Two Truths of the Middle Way* the words of the Svatantrika master Jnanagarbha:

If things are as they appear,
It is unnecessary to analyze them.

You, down there: your various silhouettes appear the same way to me as our forms here must appear to you. Things are indeed as they appear to us. And as they appear to us, they obey their conventional mode. This, then, is the extent of their being on the conventional level. It is impossible to analyze them, but their objective existence appears as an existence imputed to a particular conventional designation that suits them. Things are as they appear, then, and it is unnecessary to analyze them.

This kind of objective existence of things as they appear is hardly a postulate flowing from the perception of a sound consciousness. Would it then be possible under another mode—an extraordinary one? No, says Jnanagarbha. Then, he continues, what appears to us really exists. What he is trying to say is that, when we consider that an object is as it appears, two possibilities present themselves: either the object is good and attractive, and the mind moves near and meets it, or it is repugnant, and the mind withdraws. When something good or bad appears that exists objectively, two movements are possible: approach to the desirable and retreat from the undesirable. For Jnanagarbha, there is no negative emotion here. These movements of the mind are not distortions.

For Buddhapalita and Chandrakirti, it is the very possibility of asserting that these appearances of objects really exist that is incorrect. Nothing, they say, appears to us as it actually is. What appears to us appears to exist objectively because we are accustomed to regard it so, but it is not as it appears. Objective existence, then, is manifested in the objects of our six consciousnesses, but these objects are scarcely as they appear. To be sure, we clearly see that they are there, but they are not actually as we perceive them.

Something good presents itself, we approach it; something bad, we withdraw from it. This itself, say the Prasangikas, is the irruption of the negative emotions, attachment and hatred. For the Svatantrikas and the lower systems, these movements of the mind are in accord with their objects, and this group sees no distorted consciousnesses or negative emotions here. Note that, on the conventional level, the negative emotions are classified as gross or subtle in terms of realities judged attractive or repugnant. The Prasangikas' definition of the negative emotions permits one to identify the more subtle emotions. But then, how shall one decide that something exists or not, as it appears? For this, one must follow the reasoning of the Middle Way.

If the object is as it appears, it will surely have to be found at the end of a process of analytical reasoning. Whatever object of the six consciousnesses presents itself to the mind, it is perceived as if it existed objectively. If it is really as it appears, we shall necessarily find it when we look for it. If this search is unsuccessful, we shall have the proof that the object does not exist objectively. Reasoning will invalidate its objective existence by proving that it does not exist objectively. The mistake, then, will consist in perceiving the object as if it had an objective existence. For it is not thus that it actually exists. Once we know that things are not really as they appear, we only have to accustom ourselves to this recognition for the power of the subtle negative emotions to diminish.

The manner of establishing the real mode of phenomena, that is, their emptiness, will then be subtle or gross. It is a matter of something that goes ever deeper, and whose ultimate state, formulated in the texts of the Middle Way, absolutely cannot be invalidated by reasoning. The very thing that reasoning proves when it comes to ultimate nature—this explanation of the truth of cessation according to the Middle Way—is, then, what we must concentrate on.

It would seem that the four philosophical systems of Buddhism are in agreement on the noble truth of cessation. In the Madhyamika, and more precisely the Prasangika, approach to this truth answers an extremely profound necessity. It is in terms of the differences of subtlety in philosophical vision, then, that one will likewise observe differences in subtlety when one proceeds to the identification of the negative emotions, which constitute the truth of the origin of suffering. If we can establish this difference among the negative emotions that are at the origin of suffering, the truth of suffering, too, will be subtle, or gross. The truth of cessation, which designates the exhaustion of suffering, and of the origin of suffering, considered in this way, will also be subtle or gross.

As the thesis of emptiness can be subtle or gross, when we come to know the principles of subtle emptiness we observe the differences of subtlety in the theses on emptiness, and in the manners of its perception. In terms of this essential point, there are various ways of defining the truth of cessation, which is the very essence of emptiness. Besides, the distorted perception of emptiness gives rise to a theory of the subtle negative emotions from which flows a subtle truth of suffering. So it is a difference of depth in the approach to emptiness that entails different manners of posing the principles of the Four Noble Truths.

Thus, in order to understand a detailed exposition of the Four Noble Truths, it is necessary to know with precision the system of the two fundamental truths. It is likewise necessary to know the subtle theory of the two truths.

Asanga's Ornament of Perfect Realization addresses the instructions on the meditation of the spirit of Awakening. An explanation of the two truths is followed by the principles of the Four Noble Truths in relation to the two truths and, finally, the three refuges (the Buddha, the Dharma, and the Sangha (Community)) in relation to the Four Noble Truths. The relationship between the two fundamental truths and the Four Noble Truths, and that between the Four Noble Truths and the three refuges, is addressed in great detail in Chandrakirti's Explication of the Stanzas of the Middle Way.

Recognizing That We Can End Our Suffering

How are the Four Noble Truths produced? What one does not desire is suffering. What one desires is pleasure. The undesirable, suffering, depends on causes and conditions. The desirable, pleasure, also comes from causes and conditions. Pleasure, here, or well-being, designates not only pleasant sensations but a lasting happiness, freed from all suffering; but this happiness also depends on causes and circumstances.

Suffering is what we do not want and what we seek to eliminate. The causes and effects of suffering constitute an ensemble, and those of lasting happiness, since they are that which must be brought about, form another ensemble.

Asanga, protege of Maitreya, proposes the following analogy. Let us say that the pains of a disease known to us represent the truth of the suffering; that the germs provide the truth of the origin of the suffering; that liberation from the disease thanks to the elimination of the germs represents the truth of cessation; and that, finally, the medicine providing for the defeat of the germs represents the truth of the way.

When we do not notice that we were sick in the first place, we cannot notice any longer being sick. One who suffers from a sickness must first have a consciousness of it. Some who are ill claim not to be, and it is absolutely impossible to make them take medicine. And so one must recognize that one is ill. And so, when he taught the Four Noble Truths, the Buddha declared that it was necessary to come to a consciousness of suffering.

Once the suffering is recognized, we tell ourselves that we want nothing of this illness and that we are truly miserable. Then we seek the cause of the illness, and in recognizing it understand that we have fallen ill for a certain reason, under certain circumstances, and that it can be treated. We may even tell ourselves that we shall soon recover.

It is in terms of the practice of the Four Noble Truths, then, that he declared that it was necessary

← 4 noble Truths

1. To recognize suffering.
2. To eliminate its origin.
3. To bring about its cessation.
4. To meditate on the way.

What Is the 'Self'?

What is the person who must recognize suffering, eliminate its origin, and bring about the way like? This person 'who wishes to be happy and does not wish to suffer, this 'I,' this self, must be examined in all of his or her depth. What we call 'I,' the 'self,' or the 'individual' is what survives from one life to another, to credit the texts of non-Buddhist Indians who consider that an entity or being must exist that has come from a former life into this one and will depart for the next. But when one perceives something that is not what comes from the previous life and will depart for the next life, one is obliged to posit a self, an 'I,' or a person different from the five aggregates. Certain adepts of the self (or atmari), then, maintain that the self is different from the aggregates.

Accordingly, to limit ourselves to the framework of a single life, it is essentially in relationship to our aggregates that we say that we are young, adult, or old. A person may say: I was small—at least for my teachers, for example, or for those who cared for me; then I was young; I gradually traversed the stage of maturity; then my hair turned gray, then it was white, then I lost my teeth, and now I am all wrinkled. When I say, alluding to my old body, 'I have grown old,' it seems necessary for me to have had an 'I' from the first instant of my life.

Certain champions of the self, then, explain that the self is different from the aggregates, and that something like an 'I' exists from the first instant of life. To explain things in terms of current biological knowledge: we certainly know that the particles constituting the body change from moment to moment. From this standpoint, the aggregates are pure change. We must think, then, that if one has an 'I' from the beginning of this life, it will inevitably be different from the aggregates. If an 'I' exists that is different from the aggregates, when one has understood the five aggregates—in other words, the body and the mind—there will have to be something remaining once the body and the mind have been detached from each other. But since there is nothing else to be found, there are no aggregates apart from the self.

The self is different from the aggregates, we hear it explained. It is immutable and abiding, unique and independent. In this case, the 'I' of childhood and the 'I' of old age constitute something unclassifiable, traced on the movements of the aggregates and therefore of a changing nature. Consequently, all Buddhists agree that no such thing as this substantial, abiding, unique, and independent individual exists.

SEVEN

THE BUDDHA*

As human beings we are fortunate to have the ability to achieve these goals. The state of enlightenment that we seek is freedom from the burden of disturbing emotions. The intrinsic nature of the mind is pure; the disturbing emotions that afflict it are only temporary flaws. However, we cannot eliminate negative emotions by removing certain brain cells. Even the most advanced surgical technology cannot perform this task. It can be achieved only by a transformation of the mind.

Buddhism teaches that the mind is the main cause of our being reborn in the cycle of existence. But the mind is also the main factor that allows us to gain freedom from this cycle of birth and death. This liberation is achieved by controlling negative thoughts and emotions and by promoting and developing those that are positive. It is important to realize that this task entails years of perseverance and hard work. We cannot expect instant results. Think of all the great adepts of the past. They willingly faced tremendous hardship in their quest for spiritual realization. The story of Buddha Shakyamuni is one of the best examples of this.

Motivated by compassion for all sentient beings, Buddha Shakyamuni was born more than twenty-five hundred years ago in India. He took birth as a prince. Even as a child he was mature in terms of both his knowledge and his compassion. He saw that by nature we all want happiness and do not want suffering. Suffering is not something that always comes from the outside. It does not only involve problems like famine and drought. If this were the case we could protect

---

* From *The Joy of Living and Dying in Peace*, the Library of Tibet series published by Thorsons, an Imprint of HarperCollins*Publishers*, 1998.

ourselves from suffering, for example, by storing food. But sufferings like sickness, ageing, and death are problems related to the very nature of our existence, and we cannot overcome them by external conditions. What is more, we have within us this untamed mind, susceptible to all kinds of problems. It is afflicted with negative thoughts like doubt and anger. As long as our minds are beset by this host of negative thoughts, even if we have soft, comfortable clothes and delicious food to eat, they will not solve our problems.

Buddha Shakyamuni observed all these problems, and he reflected on the nature of his own existence. He found that all human beings undergo suffering, and he saw that we experience this unhappiness because of our undisciplined state of mind. He saw that our minds are so wild that often we cannot even sleep at night. Faced with this host of sufferings and problems, he was wise enough to ask whether there is a method to overcome these problems.

He decided that living the life of a prince in a palace was not the way to eliminate suffering. If anything, it was a hindrance. So he gave up all the comforts of the palace, including the companionship of his wife and son, and embarked on the homeless life. In the course of his search he consulted many teachers and listened to their instructions. He found that their teachings were of some use, but they did not provide an ultimate solution to the problem of how to eliminate suffering. He undertook six years of strict asceticism. By giving up all the facilities that he had enjoyed as a prince and engaging in strict ascetic practice, he was able to strengthen his meditative understanding. Seated beneath the Bodhi tree, he overcame the obstructive forces and attained enlightenment. Subsequently he began to teach, to turn the wheel of doctrine, based on his own experience and realization.

When we talk about the Buddha, we are not talking about someone who was a Buddha from the beginning. He began just like us. He was an ordinary sentient being who saw the same sufferings we do: birth, old age, sickness, and death. He had various thoughts and feelings, happy feelings and feelings of pain, just as we do. But as a result of his strong and integrated spiritual practice, he was able to achieve the various levels of the spiritual path culminating in enlightenment.

We should look to him as an example. We have entered this life as free and fortunate human beings and, although we are subject to a variety of sufferings, we possess human intelligence. We have a discriminative awareness. We have encountered the Buddha's vast and profound teaching and, what is more, we have the capacity to understand it. From the time of Buddha Shakyamuni up to the present day, Buddhist practitioners have taken him and subsequent sublime teachers as their inspiration.

Even though we have been born as ordinary people, we must try to use this precious opportunity before we die to gain a secure realization of the Dharma, the teachings of the Buddha. If we can do that, we will not have to fear death. A good practitioner can die peacefully without regret because his or her human potential is fulfilled. On the other hand, if, as human beings, we are unable to leave any positive imprint on our minds and only accumulate negative activities, our human potential will have been wasted. To be responsible for the pain and destruction of humans and other sentient beings is to be more like an evil force than a human being. Therefore, make this human life worthwhile, not something destructive.

In this world, people sometimes wage war in the name of religion. This happens when we take religion to be merely a label but do not actually put its meaning into practice. Spiritual practice is something with which to discipline our unruly minds. If we let ourselves be led by negative thoughts, never making an effort to transform them, and we use the Dharma to strengthen our pride, it can become a cause of war. On the other hand, if we use spiritual practice to transform our minds, there will be no chance of its becoming a cause of conflict.

Too many people have the Dharma only on their lips. Instead of using the Dharma to destroy their own negative thoughts, they regard the Dharma as a possession and themselves as the owner. They use the Dharma to wage war and for other destructive activities. Whether we profess to be Buddhist, Hindu, Christian, Jewish, or Muslim, we should not simply be satisfied by the label. What is important is to extract the message contained in these different religious traditions and to use it to transform our undisciplined minds. In short, as Buddhists we should follow the example of Buddha Shakyamuni himself.

Sometimes when I reflect on the life of Buddha Shakyamuni, I have a sense of unease. Although Buddha Shakyamuni's teaching can be interpreted on various levels, it is evident from the historical account that Buddha Shakyamuni underwent six years of hard practice. This shows that the mind cannot be transformed merely by sleeping and relaxing and enjoying all of life's comforts. It shows us that only through working hard and undergoing hardship over a long period of time will we be able to attain enlightenment. It is not easy to attain all the spiritual levels and realizations within a short time without making any effort. Even the Buddha, the proponent of the teaching we are following, had to undergo such hardship. How, then, can we expect to attain spiritual heights and become enlightened merely by performing certain so-called practices and having a relaxing time? If we read the stories of the great spiritual teachers of the past, we find that they have attained spiritual realization through a great deal of meditation, solitude, and practice. They did not take any shortcuts.

If we really take refuge in the Buddha from the depths of our heart, we are bound to look to him as an example. When it comes to making the effort and undergoing hardship, the important thing is to know how to go about it. It is not as if we will be able to attain enlightenment merely by undergoing hardship and making the effort. In the Buddhist tradition, we need faith and devotion, but they must be coupled with intelligence and wisdom. Of course, we may be able to achieve a certain spiritual development through devotion and faith, but to attain nirvana and enlightenment will require wisdom as well.

In order to cultivate those positive qualities that we do not now have and to strengthen and develop those that we have already cultivated, it is important to understand the various levels of wisdom. It is important to be able to focus our intelligence and wisdom on the right subject. If a person with great intelligence is deprived of the opportunity, he or she will not be able to focus his or her intelligence on the right topic. In order to develop wisdom, we need to find the opportunity to apply our intelligence to a suitable aspect of the teaching. Therefore, Buddha Shakyamuni did not ask us simply to have faith in him. He did not solve all our problems by saying, 'Have faith in me.' He started by teaching the Four Noble Truths, on the basis of which he gave various levels of teaching, laying out the stages of the path to be followed.

Even the collection of the Buddha's words that were translated into Tibetan fills more than 108 volumes, which illustrates how extensively he taught. Besides these there were many teachings of the Buddha that were not translated into Tibetan. Authentic faith and wisdom are the fruit of proper study. We should try to understand and practise these teachings, which will help us develop our wisdom, assisted by the practice of compassion. Gradually we will be able to discipline our minds. In Buddhist philosophy we do not believe that things are created or motivated by some external factor. Nor do we believe that things arise from permanent causes. We relate the experiences of happiness and suffering and their causes to our own actions. And the quality of our action depends on the state of our mind—whether it is disciplined or undisciplined.

Problems and sufferings arise because of an undisciplined state of mind. Therefore, our own happiness is in fact in our own hands. The responsibility rests on our own shoulders; we cannot expect someone to simply bring us happiness. The way to experience happiness is to identify its causes and cultivate them, and to identify the causes of suffering and eliminate them. If we know what is to be practised and what is to be given up, we will naturally meet with joy.

The root of suffering is ignorance, which here means the misconception of self. All the myriad sufferings we encounter arise because of this misconception, this wrong understanding. Therefore, when it is said that the Buddha discarded all wrong views out of compassion, it means that he had the compassion to work for the benefit of all sentient beings. In order to benefit sentient beings he gave various levels of teachings that are free from wrong views and negative thoughts. Therefore, those who follow these teachings, by understanding the right view and putting it into practice, will be able to eliminate suffering. We pay homage to Buddha Shakyamuni because he gave such sublime teachings.

The Buddha is a reliable object of refuge because he initially developed compassion and then spent his whole life generating, cultivating, and nurturing compassion. In ordinary life too, whether a particular person is trustworthy or not depends upon whether he or she possesses compassion. If someone lacks compassion, we are unlikely to rely on them, even if they are intelligent and highly educated. Education alone is not enough; the basic quality that makes people helpful to other sentient beings is compassion. If someone possesses compassion or displays a mind wishing to benefit other sentient beings, we can confidently entrust ourselves to them. The most important quality of the Buddha is the mind wishing to benefit other sentient beings—compassion. Because he developed those positive qualities in himself, he has the power and the capacity to explain their importance. We can entrust ourselves to such a teacher because he has experience of these qualities.

Buddha Shakyamuni, the propounder of Buddhism, is a valid person, an infallible person, on whom we can safely rely. Still, it is not enough that he is infallible; we should know how to follow his example. We need to know how to discard the wrong path and how to cultivate and follow positive paths. Even without direct experience of these teachings, if we simply have some understanding of these things, we are in a better position to face sufferings and problems when we encounter them.

We can imagine that when two individuals encounter the same problem, depending on whether they have an understanding of the spiritual path or not, their attitudes and manners of coping with the situation will be completely different. Instead of alleviating sufferings and problems, the person with no spiritual understanding is likely to make them worse through anger, jealousy, and so forth. The person with some spiritual insight and understanding, because of his or her mental attitude, will be able to respond more openly and candidly to the situation. With some understanding of the teachings of the Buddha as well as some experience of these teachings, although we may not be able to stop suffering, we will be in a better position to deal with our problems. Therefore, we will actually derive benefit from the teachings in our daily lives.

The realms of the cycle of existence are impermanent like autumn clouds. The coming and going of sentient beings can be understood as scenes in a drama. The way sentient beings are born and die is similar to the way characters go on and off stage. Because of this impermanence, we have no lasting security. Today, we are fortunate to live as human beings. Compared to animals and those living in hell, human life is very precious. But even though we regard it as precious, life finally concludes with death. Reflecting on the whole process of human existence from beginning to end, we find that there is no lasting happiness and no security.

EIGHT

FOUR NOBLE TRUTHS*

In order to build a solid aspiration for liberation from the cycle of existence, we must thoroughly examine our condition and consider the reasons for wanting to escape. The first thing to recognize is that our bodies and minds are predisposed to suffering. The Four Noble Truths—the Buddha's first teaching—address this issue directly. These truths are the truth of suffering, the truth of the origin of suffering, the truth of the cessation of suffering, and the truth of the path leading to cessation. The Buddha's decision to teach the truths in this sequence has great significance for our practice. In order to underline the importance of understanding that what we ordinarily regard as happiness is in fact suffering, the Buddha taught the truth of suffering first.

The Truth of Suffering

In order to understand the first truth, that of suffering, one must meditate on suffering. We see ourselves as the most precious thing in the universe, and we treat ourselves as though we are more precious than a Buddha. But that kind of clinging has still not led to perfect happiness. Since beginningless time we have gone through the cycle of existence and had an infinite number of lives. From childhood till now, we have gone through ups and downs, all kinds of frustrations and confusions. Our lives are beset by problems, sufferings, miseries, frustrations. Eventually this life will end with death, and after that we have no certainty where it will lead us. We should really examine whether there is a way to free

---

*From *The Way to Freedom*, the Library of Tibet series published by HarperCollins*Publishers*, 1995.

ourselves from this unsatisfactory existence. If life were such that it arose independent of causes and conditions and ended without further continuity, we would be helpless to escape. And if that were true, we should live by hedonistic principles. But we know that suffering is something we really do not desire and that if it is possible to obtain total freedom from it, that this freedom is worth achieving.

Karmic actions of body, speech, and mind are what bind us to the cycle of existence and suffering. As we know, we can accumulate these actions even within a moment, and that moment can throw us into a lower realm. This bondage is rooted in the untamed mind and caused by our own ignorance, our own misunderstanding of the self. This instinctive notion of a kind of independent, isolated self prompts us to indulge in all sorts of negative actions, which result in suffering. This self-centered attitude has long been our master; we have always obeyed its order. We should realize that we have not benefited from following its advice. As long as we do so there is no chance for happiness. At this juncture we should examine whether or not it is possible to overcome this delusion.

Then there is the suffering of ageing. Ageing comes about gradually; otherwise we would not be able to bear it at all. When we become old, we lose the suppleness we had when we were young; we cannot digest the food we once enjoyed. We are unable to recall the names of people or things that we used to remember vividly. Gradually our teeth fall out, our hair falls out, and we lose our eyesight and hearing. Eventually we reach a stage of decline at which people begin to find the mere sight of us repulsive. When you have reached a stage when you need the assistance of others, people will shy away from you.

Next, there is the suffering of illness. Physical suffering and mental anxiety increase, and you have to spend days and nights wracked by illness. Sickness prevents you from eating the food that you really like, and you are prevented from doing the things that you love to do. You have to take medicines that taste awful. Next is the suffering of death. You will part from your precious belongings, and you will part from your own loved ones, and you will part from your own physical body that has accompanied you throughout your life. The suffering of death is very obvious to us; there is no need to explain it further.

Then there is the suffering of meeting with the unwanted, such as enemies. Within this lifetime, many experiences take place against our wishes. We Tibetans have lost our freedom; this is the suffering of meeting with the unwanted.

Another perspective on suffering is to contemplate the suffering of uncertainty. In this cycle of existence, over the course of many rebirths, and sometimes within a single lifetime, everything changes. Our parents will turn into enemies, our relatives will turn into enemies, our enemies will turn into friends, our parents will be born later as our own children. There is no certainty. Tsong-kha-pa says that we should try to prevent the kind of emotional fluctuations that we have toward other people, based on the discrimination or classification of some as enemies and some as relatives or friends. We should reflect upon the uncertainty of the entire life within this cycle of existence and try to develop some sense of aversion for samsara.

There is also the suffering of lack of contentment. If we really consider how much food we have eaten over the course of one life, then we feel depressed and wonder what use we have made of it. If that is the case with this lifetime, what if we consider all of our past lifetimes—the amount of milk we have drunk from our mothers as children, for example? It is beyond our imagination. You should reflect upon all sorts of prosperity and suffering in this cycle of existence and think that there is no kind of experience that you have not already undergone in samsara. We try to enjoy ourselves in order to have some kind of mental satisfaction, but the pleasure and happiness of samsara are such that no matter how much we try to enjoy them, there is no sense of contentment; it is just endless. You should reflect upon this lack of contentment, which in itself is a great suffering. We have gone through all these experiences and ups and downs in samsara infinite numbers of times. Reflecting upon the pointlessness of such experiences, you should determine that if you do not put a stop to this vicious circle now, there is no point in going on at all. Thus we should develop a deep sense of aversion toward the entire range of experience within this cycle of existence.

There is the suffering of having to discard the body again and again. Up to now we have lived so many lives and had so many bodies, and still we have not been able to make use of them in a meaningful

71

way. We have achieved nothing simply by taking on these countless bodies. We have had to undergo conception again and again. The Buddha said that if we were to count our mothers by setting aside pebbles, with each one representing our mother, there would be no end to this counting.

Reflect upon the fact that all the prosperity within samsara ends in some kind of misery and frustration. As the texts say, the end of gathering is depletion, the end of high status is downfall, the end of meeting is separation, and the end of living is death. In short, all experiences, pleasure, and happiness within this cycle of existence, no matter how forceful and how great they appear, end with misery.

Finally, a further perspective is provided by the three types of sufferings. The first type is called the suffering of suffering, the obvious experiences of physical and mental pain that we ordinarily identify as suffering. The second type is called the suffering of change. Because all worldly pleasures and happiness eventually turn into sufferings, they are called sufferings of change. Sufferings of change are misidentified as experiences of happiness. For example, if you have a fever or you feel very hot and cool water is thrown on your body, you feel a kind of pleasure. This is what we regard as happiness. Or if you have been walking for a long time and after a while you get a chance to sit down, at that moment it seems really very blissful. However, in actual fact it is not a blissful experience; what you are actually experiencing is a gradual cessation of the earlier suffering. If sitting down were a true pleasure, then going on sitting should cause you the same pleasure, but if you continue sitting, after a while you will get tired and will want to stand up.

The third type of suffering is the suffering of pervasive conditioning, the fact that our minds and bodies are so conditioned as to be capable of undergoing suffering at any moment. The three types of suffering can be illustrated in this way. If you have a burn and you apply an ointment that gives you some kind of feeling of protection and pleasure, that is like the suffering of change, because although that is momentarily pleasurable, the pleasure will not last. Then if someone touches it accidentally or hot water is splashed on it, you really feel acute pain. That is obvious suffering, the suffering of suffering. What makes these two sufferings possible is that we have that burn in the first place. If we had not been burned, we would not have the subsequent experiences. The burn provides the condition for further suffering, just as our possession of a body and mind predisposes us to further suffering. And the nature of the body itself provides the condition to be burned. It is predisposed to suffering. This is the suffering of pervasive conditioning.

We should recognize that the sufferings of animals, hungry ghosts, and hell- beings can also occur among humans. In Tibet many people died of starvation after the Chinese occupation began. It seems that they sometimes had to eat the leaves of trees and also some insects and worms. These are very similar to the experiences of hungry ghosts. The same suffering is occurring now in Africa, where millions of people are starving because of famine. When countries are at war, due to political differences, the people suffer almost as they do in the realms of hell. When Stalin came to power, he ruled the Soviet Union in an authoritarian and inhuman way. It is said that before the Second World War, 14.5 million people lost their lives under Stalin's rule. They were Russian peasants, many of whom died of starvation or torture. The Communist parry members had access to good food and a good life. When they had lunch they had to be protected by guards because of the danger that the peasants might riot and take the food.

Even the gods suffer. They are able to foresee their deaths before they die, so they suffer mentally. It is said that their flower garlands wilt and their clothes and bodies begin to stink. After having experienced all the pleasures of heaven, they have exhausted the entire potential of their positive actions. As a result, when they die they will go straight to the lower realms of existence. Tsong-kha-pa says that having thus reflected upon the general sufferings of all of samsara in general and also the specific sufferings of each of the realms of existence; we should develop a deep sense of aversion for all experience within samsara and develop deep renunciation. Then we will begin to really examine exactly what the causes are that lead to such miseries and frustrations. Therefore the question of the second truth, the truth of the origin of suffering, comes next.

THE ESSENTIAL DALAI LAMA

The Truth of Origin

Delusion is the chief cause of rebirth in samsara. Without delusions karmic actions would not have the power to produce rebirth; they would be like seeds that have been burned. It is very important to seek the antidotes to the delusions, and that in turn depends upon whether or not you have identified the delusions properly. Therefore, we should be very clear about the general and individual characteristics of the delusions. As the First Dalai Lama said, tame the one enemy within, which is delusion. External enemies might seem very harmful, but in future lives they could turn into our friends. Even now they provide us with the opportunity to practise patience and compassion because we are all basically the same: we all want happiness and do not want suffering. But the inner enemy, the enemy of delusion, has no positive qualities; it is only to be fought and destroyed. We thus have to identify the enemy properly and see how it operates. Any mental state that destroys calmness of mind and brings about mental misery, which upsets, afflicts, and torments the mind, is said to be a delusion.

Let us identify some of the chief delusions. First, there is attachment, which is the strong desire for beautiful persons, beautiful things, or pleasurable experiences. Attachment is very difficult to get rid of; it is as if your mind has become fixed to the object. Another delusion is anger. When people become angry, we can immediately see that they lose their composure; their faces become red and wrinkled, and even their eyes become red. The object of anger, whether animate or inanimate, is something found to be undesirable and repulsive. Anger is a very untamed state of mind, very rough and uneven. Another delusion, pride, is a state of mind in which one feels conceited about one's own status, position, and knowledge, based on a self-centered attitude. Regardless of whether one has really achieved something or not, one feels inflated. Someone who has very deep pride is very pompous and appears very inflated. Next is ignorance, which misconceives the Identity of the Four Noble Truths, the law of karma, and so forth. In this particular context, ignorance refers to a mental factor that is totally ignorant of the nature of the Three Jewels and the law of karma. The delusion of doubt is wavering thought concerning whether there are

74

Four Noble Truths or not, whether there is a law of karma or not.

Another category of delusions is wrong views, active misconceptions about the nature of reality. The first of these is a state of mind that focuses on one's self and misconceives it to be truly or substantially existent— to imagine that within our impermanent bodies and minds there is some kind of permanent, autonomous self. Other types of wrong view would hold that there is no life after death, no law of karma, and no Three Jewels. Based on the mistaken view of self, the other delusions arise. For example, if there is a coiled rope and it is a little dark, you might misidentify that coiled rope as a snake. Then the mistaken idea that the rope was a snake would set off all kinds of reactions in your mind, such as fear, and would lead to all sorts of actions, such as running out of the house or trying to kill the snake, all based on a simple misapprehension. In the same manner, we mistakenly believe that the body and mind possess some kind of self, and as a result all the other delusions, like desire and anger, follow. Due to this self-centered attitude, this misconception of self, we discriminate between ourselves and others. Then, based on how others treat us, we hold some to be dear and feel attachment for them and hold others to be distant and classify them as enemies. We then have experiences of anger and hatred, and, focussed upon ourselves, we become inflated and proud. Then, if the grip of the misconception of self is very strong, we may begin to question the validity of the Buddha himself who taught selflessness. We therefore may begin to doubt the law of karma, the Four Noble Truths, the Three Jewels. These wrong views lead to doubts. All of this arises because of the mistaken belief in an intrinsically existent self.

The Truth of the Path

Having seen that all experience in the cycle of existence has a nature of suffering, we should develop a genuine wish to gain liberation from it. Motivated by that wish, we should enter the path of the three trainings: the trainings of morality, concentration, and wisdom. Among these three, the antidote that will eliminate the delusions is the wisdom realizing selflessness. For that purpose, we first require the mental stability of concentration as the basis, and that in turn depends upon the observance

75

of pure morality. Therefore, we need training in morality as well. At the initial stage, the first priority should be given to the practice of morality; that is the immediate need.

Tsong-kha-pa says that mindfulness and introspection are the foundation of the entire Dharma. In order to have a pure observance of morality, the faculties of introspection and proper mindfulness are required. For laymen and laywomen the observance of pure morality, refraining from the ten negative actions, is the foundation of the practice of the path leading to enlightenment. If we do not consider practical needs, like the observance of morality, but instead go in search of more sophisticated practices, our practice will be simply a sham and not really very serious. With the practice of these three trainings, we should work for the achievement of liberation, not just for ourselves alone but also for other sentient beings.

Human existence is said to be the best form of existence to practice the Dharma and try to bring an end to this cycle. Among human beings, the life of laypeople is beset with all sorts of troubles and problems, and they are more involved with worldly activities that are not very conducive to the practice of the Dharma. Life as a monk or nun is said to be far more conducive to the practice of the Dharma, to put an end to this cycle of existence. Tsong-kha-pa says that to reflect upon the faults and the disadvantages of lay life and the advantages of monks' and nuns' lives reinforces your commitment to such a life if you already are a monk or nun. If someone has not yet chosen such a way of life, such reflection leaves a very strong karmic imprint on one's mind so that later one will have the chance to lead such a life. In lay life, if you are too wealthy, your life will be beset with problems and worries about protecting your wealth; if you are poor, then your life will just be involved in searching for material sustenance. To have many material possessions and not be content is not the way of life for a monk or nun. Monks and nuns should not be involved in business unless they have fallen into some kind of debt. Doing business and having too much involvement in trying to raise money when you have sufficient provisions should really be avoided. If you do not live according to the monastic way of life, with modesty and contentment, there is hardly any difference between laypeople and monks and nuns apart from the mere external appearance of different types of clothes.

There was a monk from Ganden monastery who was a very serious meditator. He had taken a pledge never to live under a roof and had done that for many years. He told me that one day he was meditating when a big snake crawled in front of him and just gazed at him. The meditator looked back at the snake and started to say some religious words. I found it quite funny, because it seemed as if the meditator was giving teachings to the snake. He told me that the snake looked at him for a long time and then went gently away.

The importance of moral discipline was emphasized by the Buddha himself. When he was passing away, the Buddha was asked who would succeed him, and he said that the practice of morality should be the guide and the master of the entire Buddhist doctrine. He named moral discipline as his successor.

Whatever realization you gain from your practice of the Dharma should be valued and judged on the basis of whether your commitment to the law of karma has increased and, as a result, whether your practice of morality has become pure and whether the force of delusions, like ignorance, hatred, and desire, has decreased within you. If you notice that as a result of your practice you have managed to change your mind and have overcome some of the gross manifestations of the delusions, like anger, hatred, ignorance, and desire, that really is a great achievement. As Shantideva says, ordinary heroes who kill their enemies are not really heroes because the people they kill would have died sooner or later; they are actually killing corpses. But someone who is fighting the delusions and is able to kill that enemy is a hero in the true sense of the word.

~

KARMA*

Categories of Karmic Action

What is the definition of karma? We should remember to situate karma within the context of the wider Buddhist understanding of the natural laws of causality. Karma is one particular instance of the natural causal laws that operate throughout the universe where, according to Buddhism, things and events come into being purely as a result of the combination of causes and conditions.

Karma, then, is an instance of the general law of causality. What makes karma unique is that it involves intentional action, and therefore an agent. The natural causal processes operating in the world cannot be termed karmic where there is no agent involved. In order for a causal process to be a karmic one, it must involve an individual whose intention would lead to a particular action. It is this specific type of causal mechanism which is known as karma.

So within the general field of karmic action we can talk about three different types of actions which produce corresponding effects. Actions which produce suffering and pain are generally considered negative or non-virtuous actions. Actions that lead to positive and desirable consequences, such as experiences of joy and happiness, are considered to be positive or virtuous actions. The third category includes actions which lead to experiences of equanimity, or neutral feelings and experiences; these are considered to be neutral actions, and are neither virtuous nor non-virtuous.

---

* From *The Heart of the Buddha's Path*, published by Thorsons, an Imprint of HarperCollins*Publishers*, 1995.

In terms of the actual nature of karmic actions themselves, there are principally two different types: mental acts—actions that are not necessarily manifested through physical action—and there are physical acts, which include both bodily and verbal acts. Then, from the point of view of the medium of expression of an action, we distinguish actions of the mind, actions of speech, and actions of the body. Furthermore, in the scriptures we also find discussions about karmic actions which are completely virtuous, completely non-virtuous, and those which are a mixture of the two. I feel that for many of us who practice the Dharma, most of our actions may be a mixture of the two.

If we analyze a single karmic action, we can see that there are several stages within that event. There is a beginning, which is the stage of the motivation or intention; there is the actual execution of the act; and then there is the culmination or completion of the act. According to the scriptures, the intensity and force of a karmic action vary according to the way each of these stages is carried out.

Let us take the example of a negative action. If, at the stage of motivation, the person has a very strong negative emotion like anger, and then acts on an impulse and carries out the action, but immediately afterwards feels deep regret for the action he has committed, all three stages would not be completely fulfilled. Consequently, the action would be less powerful compared to an instance where the person has acted out all stages completely—with a strong motivation, actual execution, and a sense of taking pleasure or satisfaction from the act committed. Similarly, there could be cases where the individual may have a very weak motivation but circumstances force him or her to actually commit the act. In this case, although a negative act has been committed it would be even less powerful than in our first example, because a strong motivating force was not present. So depending on the strength of the motivation, of the actual act, and of the completion, the karma produced will have corresponding degrees of intensity.

On the basis of these differences, the scriptures discuss four types of karma: karma which is carried out but not accumulated, karma which is accumulated but not carried out, karma where the act is both carried out and accumulated, and karma where there is an absence of both accumulation and the actual execution of the act. It is important to understand the significance of this point, and to appreciate that since there are different stages to every act, karmic actions themselves are composite, and their quality can be characterized as the cumulative result of each of their composing factors.

Once you appreciate this, then whenever you have the opportunity to engage in a positive action as a Dharma practitioner, it is important to ensure that at the initial stage your positive motivation is very strong, and that you have a strong intention to engage in the act. Then, while you are actually carrying out the act, you should ensure that you have given it your best, and you have put all your effort into making the action successful. Once the action is performed, it is important to ensure that you dedicate the positive karma that you have thereby created towards the well-being of all beings as well as your own attainment of enlightenment. If you can reinforce that dedication with an understanding of the ultimate nature of reality, it would be even more powerful.

Karma and the Person

How does a Buddhist practitioner actually go about trying to lead a moral life? A person's ultimate aspiration is to attain liberation from samsara, to attain spiritual freedom or enlightenment, so one of his or her principal tasks is to gain victory over the kleshas. However, there is no way that a practitioner can directly combat negative emotions and thoughts at the initial stage, so the sensible way to proceed is simply to find a way of containing the expression of the negative actions of our body, speech and mind. The first step, then, is to guard our body, speech and mind from engaging in negative actions so that we don't give in to the power and domination of our negative thoughts and emotions.

Once you have achieved this first stage, you can proceed to the second stage and tackle the root cause—the fundamental ignorance of which we spoke earlier. At this stage you are able to counteract the forces of the kleshas directly. Once you can do that, the third stage consists not simply of gaining victory over them, but also of rooting out all the propensities and imprints they have left within the psyche. This is why Aryadeva states in *Four Hundred Verses on Madhyamaka* that a true spiritual aspirant must first overcome negative behaviour, in the middle phase must counter any grasping at self, and in the final stage should overcome all the views that bind us within the samsaric realm.[2]

As we have already seen, Buddhism explains how the environment and the sentient beings living in that environment are produced as a result of fundamental ignorance, particularly the karma which arises from ignorance. However, we should not think that karma produces these things from out of nowhere. This is not the case. Karma is not like an eternal cause. We should realize that in order for karma to operate, and in order for it to have the potential to create its consequences, it must have a basis on which to do so. It follows that there exists a continuum of both the physical and the mental worlds. We can trace the continuum of the physical world to the beginning of a particular universe, and then we can even trace that 'beginning' to empty space. Buddhism accepts the existence of what are known as 'space particles' *(namkhai dut)*, and asserts there is a stage of empty space in which the source of the material universe is in some sense contained. In the case of the mental world, we cannot say that the continuum of consciousness in sentient beings is a result of karma. Neither can we say that the unending process of the continuity of both matter and mind results from karma.

If this is the case, if the basic continuum is not produced by karma, then where does karma fit in? At what point does karma play a causal role in producing sentient beings and the natural environment in which they live? Perhaps we can say that there is a natural process in the world and at a certain point when its evolution has reached a stage where it can affect the experiences of beings—giving rise to either painful experiences of suffering or joyful experiences of happiness—that is the point where karma enters the picture. After all, the karmic process only makes sense in relation to the experience of sentient beings.

So if we were to ask whether consciousness is produced by karma, or whether sentient beings are produced by karma, it seems the answer should be 'no'. But on the other hand, if we ask whether the human body and the human consciousness are products of karma, then the answer is 'yes' because both result from virtuous actions. This is because, when we talk about the human body and human consciousness, we are referring to a state of existence which is directly related to the painful and pleasurable experiences of an individual. Finally, if we were to ask whether or not our natural instinct to seek happiness and overcome suffering is a product of karma, it seems the answer would again be 'no'.

Karma and the Natural World — 5 elements

At this point I feel that unless we complement the general explanation of the karmic process found in the Buddhist literature[3] with points from the Vajrayana literature, our understanding will not be complete. The Vajrayana explains that both the physical world and the bodies of living beings are composed of the five elements: earth, water, fire, wind, and space. Space here should be understood in terms of vacuum, of empty space, rather than as space in the technical sense of absence of obstruction. The Vajrayana literature discusses these in terms of external elements and internal elements, and shows how they are related to each other at a very profound level. Through understanding this relationship, our insight into the way karma affects the world is a much deeper one.

As we discussed earlier, the fact that consciousness exists is a natural fact. Consciousness exists; that is it. Similarly, the continuum of consciousness is also a natural principle: consciousness maintains its continuity. To this we must add that in Buddhism, there is an understanding that consciousness cannot arise from nowhere or without a cause; and, at the same time, that consciousness cannot be produced from matter. This is not to say that matter cannot affect consciousness. However, the nature of consciousness is sheer luminosity, mere experience; it is the primordial knowing faculty, and therefore it cannot be produced from matter whose nature is different. It follows that since consciousness cannot arise without a cause, and since it cannot arise from a material cause, it must come from a ceaseless continuum. It is on this premise that Buddhism accepts the existence of (beginningless) former lives.

We have seen that the origin of suffering lies in both karma and ignorance, but actually ignorance is the principal origin.

Karma and the Emotions

There are differences in the way each school of Buddhism understands the nature of the kleshas, corresponding to their various interpretations of the doctrine of anatman, or no-soul theory. For example, certain states of mind, and certain thoughts and emotions which, according to the Madhyamaka-Svatantrika and Chittamatra schools, may be considered non-delusory, are seen as delusory from the point of view of the Madhyamaka-Prasangika school. This is a very complex point, of course, and would require a lot of study.

The most important thing for us to know is that afflictive emotion is our ultimate enemy and a source of suffering. Once it develops within our mind, it immediately destroys our peace of mind, and eventually destroys our health and even our friendships with other people. All negative activities such as killing, bullying, cheating and so forth, stem from afflictive emotion. This, therefore, is our real enemy.

An external enemy may be harmful to you today, but tomorrow could become very helpful, whereas the inner enemy is consistently destructive. Moreover, wherever you live the inner enemy is always there with you, and that makes it very dangerous. In contrast, we can often keep an external enemy at some kind of distance. In 1959, for example, we escaped from Tibet since escape was a physical possibility; but in the case of this inner enemy, whether I am in Tibet, or in the Potala, or in Dharamsala, or here in London, wherever I go it follows me. I think the inner enemy is even there in meditation; and even if I visualize a mandala, I may still find this enemy in its very centre! So this is the main point we have to realize: the real destroyer of our happiness is always there within us.

So what can we do about it? If it is not possible to work on that enemy and to eliminate it, then I think we had better forget the spiritual path and rely on alcohol and sex and other such things to improve our lives! However, if there is a possibility of eliminating the inner enemy, then I think we should take the opportunity of having a human body, a human brain and a good human heart, and combine these strengths to reduce and ultimately uproot it. This is why human life is considered to be so precious according to the Buddhist teachings, for it alone enables a being to train and transform the mind, mainly by virtue of intelligence and reasoning.

Buddhists distinguish between two kinds of emotion. One type is without reason, and is just based on prejudice. Hatred is one of these. This sort of emotion will rely on superficial reasons, of course, such as 'this person has hurt me terribly', but deep down, if you pursue that reasoning further, you find it does not go very far. Emotions without proper reason are what we call negative emotions. The other kind of emotion, which includes compassion and altruism, is emotion with reason because through deep investigation you can prove it is good, necessary and useful. Furthermore, although by nature it is a type of emotion, it is actually in accord with reason and intelligence. In fact, it is by combining our intelligence and emotion that we can change and transform our inner world.

So long as the inner enemy is there, and so long as we are under its control, there can be no permanent happiness. Understanding the need to defeat this enemy is true realization, and developing a keen desire to overcome it is the aspiration to seek freedom, technically called renunciation. Therefore this practice of analyzing our emotions and our inner world is very crucial.

The scriptures say that so far as the desire to overcome the first level of suffering is concerned, the 'suffering of suffering', even animals have it naturally. And so far as the aspiration to free oneself from the second level of suffering is concerned, the 'suffering of change', this is not something that is unique to the Buddhist path. Many ancient Indian non-Buddhist paths were similar, seeking inner tranquility through samadhi. However, the genuine aspiration to seek complete liberation from samsara can only arise from a recognition of the third level of suffering, the 'suffering of conditioning', where we realize that so long as we remain under the control of ignorance we will be subject to suffering, and there will be no room for lasting joy and happiness. It may be said that the recognition of this third level of suffering is unique to the Buddhist path.

Questions

Q: Could Your Holiness please explain why the result of karma is sometimes instant and why on other occasions we have to wait lifetimes before the causal effect occurs?

His Holiness: One factor would be the intensity of the karmic action itself. Another factor is the extent to which the various other conditions that are necessary for that karma to ripen are complete, and this is dependent, in turn, on other karmic actions. Vasubandhu addressed this issue in the Abhidharmakosha, in which he states that, generally speaking, the karmic actions which are the most forceful tend to produce their effects first. If the intensity of a karmic action is equal to that of another karmic action, then the result of the action with which the individual is most familiar tends to ripen first. However if two karmic actions are equally forceful and equally familiar, then the one that is committed earlier tends to produce its result first.

Q: Is there a difference between thought and action with regard to karmic effects? In other words, can a thought cause an action and vice versa?

His Holiness: As I explained, the Buddhist concept of karma is not confined to bodily action alone; it also embraces mental acts or, we could say, emotional acts. For example, when we talk about an act of covetousness, or a harmful intention, these are not necessarily manifest in behaviour. One could think such thoughts fully and in detail without expressing them in action at all, so a certain completion of these acts does happen on the mental level.

Furthermore, there are certain types of actions which do not necessarily have an immediate motivation or intention, but because of the conditioning from past karmic actions, one could have a propensity to act in a certain way. This means that some actions can arise not as a result of motivation, but as a result of karmic tendencies.

TEN

~

THE BODHISATTVA IDEAL*

Being content with the achievement of liberation from the cycle of
existence is not enough. Even speaking from the viewpoint of your
own aims, it is the omniscient state of Buddhahood that is the complete
fulfillment of your own welfare. After having developed the wish to
achieve liberation and having undertaken practice of the three trainings,
instead of being concerned with the achievement of your own personal
liberation, it is better for intelligent practitioners to meditate on the
altruistic aspiration to Buddhahood, called bodhichitta, right from the
outset and enter the Mahayana, the Great Vehicle. If you see people
who are under the constant sway of delusions and undergoing suffering,
yet you do not work for their benefit, it is really very unfair and
disappointing. You should not be content with working for your own
personal benefit alone. You should think in broader terms and try to
work for the benefit of many people. This is what distinguishes human
beings from animals, because the wish to work for the benefit of oneself
and one's relations is something that even animals do. The unique feature
of human beings is that they work for the benefit of others, not being
concerned with their own welfare alone. That is the beauty and the
specialty of a human being.

People like the American president Lincoln and the Indian leader
Mahatma Gandhi are regarded as really great men because they did
not think of themselves alone but worked for the benefit of the people.
They thought of the entire human society, and they struggled and fought
for the rights of the poor. Take the example of Mahatma Gandhi: after
gaining Indian independence he just remained as an ordinary citizen,

* From *The Way to Freedom*, HarperCollins*Publishers*, 1995.

never taking any position, such as prime minister. That is the mark of a distinguished person. Mao at first worked very hard for the rights of the masses, but after gaining power, he himself became a member of the very same class he had fought against. He succumbed to power and became utterly totalitarian, taking even the slightest dissent as a great personal offence. Once Mao was praised, but now that people have become disillusioned, more and more things are revealed.

When the sun shines, it shines without any discrimination; it shines on every point of the country, every nook and corner. We should be like that. We practitioners of the Mahayana should not be concerned with our own benefit but with a single-pointed mind should develop the courageous altruistic attitude, taking upon our own shoulders the responsibility of working for all sentient beings.

Bodhichitta, the compassionate wish to achieve Buddhahood for the sake of others, is the entrance to the Mahayana path. When you cultivate bodhichitta, even though you might not make any further progress on the path, you become a Mahayanist, but the moment bodhichitta degenerates, even though you might have very high realizations, you fall from the ranks of the Mahayana. Shantideva says that the moment you develop bodhichitta, even though you might be living in a lower realm of existence, you will be called a bodhisattva, a child of the Buddhas. As a result of bodhichitta, you will be able to purify negativities very easily and be able to fulfill your aims. You will be invulnerable to interferences and harm, because if you have this faculty of bodhichitta, you regard other people as more important and precious than your own life. When harmful spirits realize this, they hesitate to harm you. As a result of bodhichitta, if you are able to purify negativities and accumulate great stores of merit, you will encounter favorable circumstances that are necessary for making speedy progress on the path. Bodhichitta and compassion are the very sources and foundations of all the goodness in this world and nirvana. You should regard bodhichitta as the essence of your practice and should not leave it only at an intellectual level; you should not be satisfied with your practice of bodhichitta if it consists merely of the recitation of a few verses at the beginning of a meditation session. You should try to generate it through experience.

Tsong-kha-pa says that if you have an authentic aspiration to enlightenment, then any act of goodness, even something minor like giving grain to a crow, becomes a bodhisattva deed. However, if you lack this motivating factor, even though you might make offerings of an entire universe filled with jewels to other sentient beings, it will not be the deed of a bodhisattva. If your practice of bodhichitta is not successful, no matter how long you try to practice the Dharma, it will be a very slow and laborious process, like cutting grass with a blunt tool. But if you have a perfect and successful realization of bodhichitta, even though it may take some time to make that your primary motive, all of your practices will be very powerful. If you do not repeatedly reinforce your compassion, improving and enhancing it, there is a great danger of losing your courage and becoming depressed, because sentient beings are infinite. There are many hostile sentient beings who, instead of repaying your kindness, will try to harm you. Therefore, you should not be satisfied with a single experience of compassion but should really work to enhance it to the point where your compassion is deeply rooted. If that happens, you will not care much about hardships, and as a result you will never be depressed by circumstances when you work for the benefit of others. It is because of the force of compassion that the Buddhas remain committed to working for the benefit of other sentient beings. The Buddha said that bodhisattvas do not need to be concerned with many aspects of the path; they need not practice many other things. It is by one practice alone that Buddhahood will be in the palm of your hand. That one practice is great compassion, meaning the desire to become enlightened in order to liberate all other sentient beings. In order to generate this aspiration to enlightenment it is not enough to have great compassion and love, wishing sentient beings to be free of suffering. In addition, what is required is the sense of personal responsibility to shoulder the task of freeing them from sufferings and providing them with happiness.

When we reflect upon the suffering nature of sentient beings, we might be able to develop the wish that they be free from such sufferings. In order to discover a warm and kind heart that is forceful, stable, and firm, it is very important first of all to have an affectionate attitude toward sentient beings, regarding them as precious and dear. The more affection you feel toward other sentient beings and the more you hold them dear, the better you will be able to develop genuine compassion for them. Normally, when we let our natural reactions follow their own course, we find it unbearable to see the sufferings of our relatives and friends. We tend to delight in the misfortunes and failures of our enemies, and we tend to remain indifferent to people we do not know. Our emotions fluctuate in relation to these different people. The more we regard a person as close and dear to us, the stronger our feeling of being unable to bear it when that person suffers.

In order to equalize your feelings, visualize three people in front of you: a very close friend, an enemy, and a neutral person. Having visualized these three people let your mind react naturally. You will find that your mind reacts in an unbalanced way. You find yourself attached to the friend and repelled by the enemy, and your attitude to the third person is totally indifferent. Then, examine why you react in such a manner. Friends might be friends now, but they may have been our enemies in the past, and they could be our enemies in the future. Those whom we call enemies now may have been our best friends or relatives in the past and could also turn out to be the same in the future. What is the point of making such discriminations? Friends are those whom we wish to have happiness and to enjoy life. We wish them happiness and success because they are our relatives and friends and have been good to us. But in the future they could turn out to be our enemies, and even in this life they could turn against us. Similarly, when we react to our enemies, we tend to react in a very negative manner, wishing instinctively, deep down, that they face misfortune, hardship, and failure. We react like that because we think that they have harmed us. But even though they might actually be harmful at present, they could turn out to be our friends in the future. There is no certainty, no totally reliable or permanent friend or enemy. Likewise, although the neutral person is totally unconcerned with us and we are indifferent to him or her in turn, in the past that person may have been either our friend or enemy. If you train your mind this way, you will come to see all people in the same light, and gradually such a drastic discrimination among the three types of people will begin to fade. You should extend this practice to include everyone, eventually encompassing all sentient beings. That is how you develop equanimity. This is not to suggest that we do not have friends and enemies. What we are concerned with here is to offset our drastic, imbalanced emotional reactions to others. This equanimity is very important; it is like first levelling the ground before cultivating it. Although equanimity itself is not a great realization, if you have that foundation, further practices become very successful.

After developing equanimity, the first of the cause-and-effect precepts for creating the aspiration to enlightenment is the recognition that all sentient beings have been our mother in a past life. This is because there is no beginning to the cycle of existence. Because life in the cycle of rebirth is beginningless, our own lives are also beginningless. Life and death succeed each other without any interruption. Whenever we take on a body, we require a mother. Since the cycle of existence has no beginning, there is no sentient being we can point to and say, 'That person has not been my mother .in the past.' Not only have they been our mothers in the past, but also they will be our mothers in the future. If you are able to develop deep conviction in this fact, it will be quite easy to recollect and reflect upon their great kindness and then develop the wish to repay their kindness. Although it is usually recommended that you see all sentient beings as your mother, you should do this meditation according to your own experience. For example, some people feel closer to their father. The person to whom you feel closest and regard as most kind should be taken as the model. There is not a single sentient being who has not been either our mother or father or relative in the past. The fact that we do not remember or recognize them does not mean that they have not been our mothers. For example, even in this lifetime there are cases of parents and children being separated when the children are very young. Later, these children are unable to recognize their parents.

The next precept is to reflect on the kindness of all sentient beings. This meditation is said to be most successful if, after having recognized all the other sentient beings as your mother, you recollect their kindness, taking your own mother as an example. Visualize your mother in front of you, and reflect that she has been your mother not only in this lifetime but also numerous times in the past. Then think of how kind she has been to you, how she has protected you from danger and how she has helped you, how in this life she first conceived you and even during the pregnancy she took great care of you. She looked after you with no sense of hesitation. She was willing to give up her possessions for your sake, and she was willing to use devious and irreligious means to obtain what you needed with no care for the hardships it caused her. Her commitment and love for her child was such that she would prefer to fall ill herself rather than have her child become sick. You should single-pointedly meditate on her great kindness. When you develop a deep feeling of indebtedness to your mother for her great kindness by reflecting this way, you should apply the same method to other people who have been kind to you, such as your friends and relatives. Eventually you can extend it to include neutral persons. If you are able to develop that same kind of feeling for neutral persons, shift it to your own enemy as well. Gradually include all other sentient beings within the sphere of your recognition of kindness.

Next is meditation on repaying their kindness. You should understand that it is only because of our constantly changing lives that we are not able to recognize that all sentient beings have been our kind mothers, parents, and relatives. Now they are without protectors, they have no refuge. If we see their suffering and their helplessness and then still work for our own benefit and personal liberation alone, we will not only be acting unfairly, but also extremely ungratefully. You should develop a deep sense of commitment that you will never abandon them but will instead repay their kindness. Even in a worldly sense, if someone does not repay the kindness of people but acts against them, he or she is regarded as a very bad and ungrateful person. How then can a Mahayana practitioner completely neglect the welfare of other sentient beings and not think of repaying their kindness?

Imagine your mother, mentally unstable, blind, and without any guide, walking toward a cliff. She calls out to her own child nearby, her only refuge, in whom she places her hopes. If her own child does not help her, who is going to? We should reflect on the idea that since the beginning of time sentient beings have been mentally unstable because they have been slaves of delusion, they lack the eye of wisdom to see the path leading to nirvana and enlightenment, and they lack the necessary guidance of a spiritual teacher. Moment by moment they are indulging in negative actions, which will eventually bring about their downfall. If these mothers cannot seek help from their children, in whom can they place their hope? Feeling a sense of responsibility, you should repay the great kindness of the mother.

Next is the meditation on love. The Buddhist definition of love is the wish that all sentient beings may enjoy happiness and never be parted from happiness. It is said that meditation on love even for a moment far exceeds the merits accumulated through making infinite offerings to infinite Buddhas. It was by the power of meditation on love that the Buddha defeated the hosts of demons who tried to keep him from his goal. Meditation on love is the supreme protection. The actual sequence of meditation on love is that first you should cultivate love directed toward your own friends and relatives, then you should shift that attention to neutral persons, then on to your enemies as well. Then gradually include all other sentient beings whom you encounter.

Next is meditation on compassion. There are two types of compassion; one is just a wish that sentient beings be free of suffering, and the other is more powerful: 'I shall take the responsibility for freeing sentient beings from suffering.' First you should meditate on your own parents, friends, and relatives and then shift that attention to neutral persons and eventually to your enemies, so that eventually all sentient beings you encounter will be a part of your meditation. This has great significance because when you are able to extend your meditation to all sentient beings, your compassion and love will become so pervasive that the moment you see suffering, compassion will spontaneously arise. Otherwise, if you try to meditate on compassion and love for all sentient beings, thinking about 'all sentient beings' without first identifying them individually, your idea of 'all sentient beings' will be very vague, and your compassion will not be very strong and firm. When you meet with certain individuals, you will begin to doubt whether you really wish them to enjoy happiness. On the other hand, if you cultivate compassion in a gradual process, first of all picking out individual categories of people and making a very special effort to cultivate that kind of love and compassion focussed on your enemy, who is the most difficult object, then having love and compassion toward others will become very easy, and your compassion will be able to withstand any circumstances you might meet.

In the actual meditation you should contemplate how sentient beings, like yourself, rotate in the cycle of existence tormented by all types of sufferings. To be successful in developing love and compassion, it is very important to understand and realize the faults and defects of the cycle of existence. If you are able to do that in terms of your own observations, you can extend your understanding to other sentient beings through experience. Otherwise, if you have not developed renunciation yourself and a sense of aversion for the entire range of experience within this cycle of existence, there is no way you can cultivate compassion. Renunciation is indispensable for the cultivation of compassion. Compassion and renunciation differ only in their object: renunciation is focussed upon yourself; it is the wish that you be liberated from suffering. Compassion is directed toward other sentient beings; it is the wish that all beings be liberated from suffering.

It is very important to study and understand the many types of sufferings. Having gained extensive knowledge by reading many texts and thinking a lot, you should contemplate the faults and defects of the cycle of life and death and how sentient beings in this cycle of existence spin through this chain reaction. For example, in scientific laboratories, guinea pigs are tortured with all sorts of equipment. To understand how the brain operates, scientists have to experiment on animals. It is a very strange situation, because their primary aim is to help and prolong the life of human beings. In a way it is a noble aim, but it is also difficult to justify. Although they may use tranquilizers, scientists do these kinds of experiments without any sense of compassion or mercy for the animals. In the West there are groups who protest against such treatment of animals, not out of religious sentiments but out of their compassionate attitude toward animals. I support this effort.

Initially it might prove quite difficult to generate any experience of compassion for all beings, but once you begin to develop it, it will become firm, genuine, and unshakable, because it is based on a firm foundation of knowledge and reason. If you have some experience of compassion, it is really important to try to stabilize it by reinforcing it with reasons and extensive understanding. Merely depending upon some kind of intuition alone is not very reliable, because there is a danger that afterward that kind of experience will disappear without a trace. This is true not only of meditation on compassion and love, but for all the other practices as well.

As a result of your continuous meditation and contemplation, your feeling of compassion toward other sentient beings will become as intense as the love of a mother toward her only child when she sees him or her suffering from an illness. The child's suffering would cause her worry and pain, and day and night she would have the natural wish that her son or daughter be well.

If your attitude toward any other sentient being is such that, regardless of whether or not they are related to you, the moment you see any suffering you are able to develop an equally intense compassion toward all other sentient beings without partiality, that is the sign of having achieved and developed compassion. This applies to love as well. Such love and compassion will lead naturally, without any effort, to the superior attitude of taking upon your own shoulders the responsibility of working for the benefit of other sentient beings, which in turn leads to the eventual realization of the aspiration to enlightenment.

In meditating on repaying kindness you have reflected on the great kindness of the mother sentient beings and on the necessity of working for their benefit. Here the primary concern is to cultivate a deep-felt sense of responsibility to work for their benefit and shoulder the task of relieving sentient beings of suffering and providing them with happiness. Throughout your daily life and activities, wherever the occasion arises, you should immediately seize that opportunity to train in this meditation. Only then can you begin to hope for progress in the realization. The Indian poet Chandragomin (sixth century CE) said that it is stupid to expect to change the taste of a very sour fruit simply by adding one or two drops of cane sugar. In the same way, we cannot expect the taste of the mind, which is so contaminated with the sour flavor of delusion, to be instantly changed into the sweet taste of bodhichitta and compassion, just by one or two meditations. Sustained effort and continuity are really very important.

In the last step, the actual development of bodhichitta, the mind aspiring to achieve enlightenment for others, you should not be satisfied by seeing the importance of enlightenment for the sake of others alone.

There is no way to fulfill that ultimate aim without your achievement of the omniscient state of Buddha-hood, from which you can best benefit others. You should develop a very deep, heartfelt faith in the enlightened state, and that will lead to a genuine aspiration to achieve it. Generally speaking, there are many causes and conditions for the cultivation of bodhichitta, but chief among all of them is compassion.

We should realize that the purpose of taking birth in this world is to help others. If we cannot do that, at least we should not harm other living beings. Even people who are opposed to religion speak highly of the altruistic attitude. Although the Chinese Communists are ideologically opposed to religion, they talk of the wish to work for the welfare of the masses. If these people truly had an altruistic attitude, they would be able to fulfill the wish for a perfect socialist state. On the other hand, if they continue to use violent methods to enforce a totalitarian system, there is no way that they can bring about what they are looking for. Nations have diverse political systems, but an essential factor in most societies is the altruistic attitude—the wish to work for others, for the welfare of the majority. The altruistic attitude is the root of happiness within the human community. All the major religions of the world encourage cultivation of an altruistic attitude, irrespective of their different philosophical systems. In short, if you cultivate the altruistic attitude, it not only helps you by providing peace of mind, it also creates a peaceful atmosphere around you. That is one of the practical results that you can see. The ultimate purpose of cultivating the altruistic attitude is to achieve the enlightened state so that you will be able to work for the total fulfillment of the wishes of other beings. Therefore, the Buddha has not left the importance of cultivating bodhichitta as a matter of simple advice; he has also shown the techniques and means by which we can develop such an altruistic aspiration.

The practice of bodhichitta is indispensable for someone who wishes to achieve enlightenment. All the Buddhas and bodhisattvas of the past have achieved these high realizations by cultivating this altruistic attitude. Some ideologies lose their relevance as time passes. The Buddha taught that life is our most cherished possession and that we should treat the lives of others as more important and precious than our own. This kind of message and teaching retains its relevance throughout the ages. In this modern age when there is a great danger of the destruction of the entire world, we find the message of the Buddha more and more relevant.

The other method for developing the altruistic aspiration to enlightenment is the equalizing and exchanging of self and others. The first step in this practice is to recognize the advantages of exchanging oneself for others and the disadvantages of not doing so. All the good qualities in this universe are the product of cherishing the welfare of others, and all the frustrations and confusions and sufferings are products and consequences of selfish attitudes. But is it possible to exchange oneself for others? Our experience testifies that we can change our attitude toward certain types of people whom we formerly found repulsive and fearful, that when we get closer to such persons and understand them, we can change our attitude. Exchanging self and others does not mean that you physically change yourself into others but rather that the attitude that you have about yourself is applied to others. The strong cherishing that you feel for yourself should now be shifted to others, so that you will have a natural tendency to work for the welfare of others instead of yourself.

Therefore, we should decide, 'From now on I shall dedicate myself, even my body, for the welfare of others. From now on, I will not work for my own happiness but rather for the happiness of others. From now on others are like my master; my body will obey and take orders from others instead of myself.' Reflecting upon the great disadvantages and harms of the selfish attitude, you should develop a strong determination, saying to the self-cherishing attitude, 'Your domination of my mind is a thing of the past. From now on I will not obey your orders. You have only done me great harm by your devious means. From now on do not pretend that you are working for my own happiness, because I have realized that you are the great enemy and the source of all my frustrations and sufferings. If I do not abandon you and work for others, you will again plunge me into the sufferings of unfortunate rebirth.' Understand that a self-centered attitude is the source of all suffering, and concern for others is the source of all happiness and goodness.

ELEVEN

INTERDEPENDENCE*

In a discussion of interdependence, interconnectedness and the nature of reality, the first question is: What is time? We cannot identify time as some sort of independent entity. Generally speaking, there are external matters and internal feelings or experiences. If we look at the external things, then generally there is the past, the present and the future. Yet if we look closely at 'the present', such as the year, the month, the day, the hour, the minute, the second, we cannot find it. Just one second before the present is the past; and one second after is the future. There is no present. If there is no present, then it is difficult to talk about the past and the future, since both depend on the present. So if we look at external matters, it would seem that the past is just in our memory and the future is just in our imagination, nothing more than a vision.

But if we look at our internal experiences or states of consciousness, the past is no longer there and the future has not yet come: there is only the present. So things become somewhat complicated when we think along these lines. This is the nature of interdependency, the Sanskrit word *pratityasamutpada*. This is a very useful idea and it is one of my favourite subjects.

There are two levels of interdependency: a conventional level and a deeper level. First I will deal with the conventional level. When we speak of the Buddhist principle of interdependence, which is often referred to as 'interdependent origination', we must bear in mind that there are many different levels of understanding of that principle. The more superficial level of understanding of the principle is the

* From *The Heart of the Buddha's Path*, Thorsons, an Imprint of HarperCollins*Publishers*, 1997.

interdependent nature or relationship between cause and effect. The deeper level of understanding of the principle is much more pervasive and, in fact, encompasses the entire spectrum of reality. The principle of interdependent origination in relation to cause and effect states that nothing can come about without the corresponding causes and conditions; everything comes into being as a result of an aggregation of causes and conditions.

If we consider the law of nature, we see it is not created by karma or by Buddha, it is just nature. We consider that Buddhahood developed according to natural law. Therefore, our experiences of pain and suffering, pleasure and joy, depend entirely on their own causes and conditions. Because of this natural relationship between causes and their effects, the Buddhist principle states that the greater your undesirability of a particular experience, event or phenomenon, the greater effort you must put into preventing the aggregation of its causes and conditions, so that you can prevent the occurrence of that event. And the greater your desirability of a particular event, outcome or experience, the greater attention you must pay to ensure that these causes and conditions are accumulated so that you can enjoy the outcome.

I personally believe that the relationship between a cause and an effect is also a sort of natural law. I don't think that one could come up with a rational explanation as to why effects necessarily follow concordant causes and conditions. For instance, it is stated that afflictive emotional states like anger and hatred lead to undesirable consequences and according to the Buddhist scriptures, one consequence of hatred and anger is ugliness. But there is not a full, rational account as to how ugliness is a consequence of that particular afflictive emotion. Yet in a way one can understand it, because when you experience very intense anger or hatred, even your facial expression changes and you assume a very ugly face. Similarly, there are certain types of mental and cognitive emotional states which bring about almost instantaneous positive changes in your facial expression. These states bring you presence of mind, calmness and serenity and such an emotional state or thought could lead to a more desirable outcome. So one can see a type of connection, but not a full rational explanation.

Now if you understand the importance of appreciating the

relationship between cause and effect, then you will appreciate the teachings on the Four Noble Truths. The entire teaching on the Four Noble Truths is based on the principle of causality. When the causal principle that is implied in these teachings is elaborated, you read Buddha's doctrine of the Twelve Links of Dependent Origination. In that teaching he stated that, because there is a particular cause, its effects follow; because the cause was created, the effect came about; and because there was ignorance, it led to action or karma.

So here you find three statements: one is that because the cause exists, the effect follows; because the cause was created, the effect was produced; and because there was ignorance, it led to the action. Now the first statement indicates that, from an affirmative point of view, when causes are aggregated, effects will naturally follow. And what is also implied in that statement is that it is due to the mere aggregation of the causes and conditions that the effects come into being, and that, apart from the causal process, there is no external power or force such as a Creator and so forth which brings these things into being.

The second statement again points out another important characteristic of dependent origination, which is that the very cause which brings about the effects must itself have a cause. If the cause is an eternally existing, permanent absolute entity, then such an entity could not be itself an effect of something else. If that is the case, then it will not have the potential to produce an effect. Therefore, first of all there must be a cause; second, that very cause must itself have a cause.

And the third statement points out another important characteristic of the principle of dependent origination. It is that the effect must be commensurate with the cause—there must be a concordance between the two. Not just anything can produce anything; there must be a sort of special relationship between cause and effect. Buddha gave an example of ignorance leading to action. Here the implication is, 'Who commits that action?' It is a sentient being—and by committing an act motivated by an ignorant state of mind that being is in a way accumulating his or her own downfall. Since there is no living being that desires unhappiness or suffering, it is due to ignorance that the individual engages in an act which has the potential to produce undesirable consequences.

So we find that the entire Twelve Links of Dependent Origination fall into three classes of phenomena. First, there are afflictive emotions and thoughts; second, there is the karmic action and its imprints; and third, there is its effect: suffering. So the principal message is that suffering is something that we all do not desire, but it is a consequence or an effect of ignorance. Buddha did not state that suffering is an effect of consciousness, because if that was the case, then the process of liberation or the process of purification would necessarily involve putting an end to the very continuum of consciousness. One moral that we can draw from this teaching is that the sufferings which are rooted in afflictive and negative emotions and thoughts can be removed. This ignorant state of mind can be dispelled, because we can generate insight which perceives the nature of reality. So we see that the principle of dependent origination shows how all these 12 links in the chain of dependent origination which forms an individual's entry into the cycle of existence are inter-connected.

Now if we were to apply this inter-connectedness to our perception of reality as a whole, then we could generate a great insight from it. For instance, we would then be able to appreciate the interdependent nature of one's own and others' interests: how the interests and well-being of human beings is dependent upon the well-being of animals living on the same planet. Similarly, if we develop such an understanding of the nature of reality, we would also be able to appreciate the inter-connectedness between the well-being of human beings and the natural environment. We could also consider the present, the future and so forth. We would then be able to cultivate an outlook on reality which is very holistic and has very significant implications.

So in a few words, you can see that there are no independent causes of one's own happiness. It depends on many other factors. So the conclusion is that in order to have a happier future for yourself, you have to take care of everything which relates to you. That is, I think, quite a useful view.

So far, I have spoken about the principle of dependent origination from the perspective of the first level of understanding. We can see in the Buddhist scriptures the importance of understanding this level of the dependent origination. In fact, one of the Mahayana texts known as *Compendium of Deeds*, in which Shantideva quotes heavily from

Buddha's sutras, points out the need to first of all appreciate the inter-connectedness of all events and phenomena: how, due to the causal and conditional process, phenomena and events come into being; and how crucial it is to respect that conventional reality, because it is at that level that we can understand how certain types of experiences lead to certain types of undesirable consequences, how certain causes, certain types of aggregation of causes and conditions can lead to more desirable consequences, and so forth; how, in fact, certain events can directly affect our well-being and experience. Because there is that sort of relation, it is very crucial for practising Buddhists to first develop a deep understanding of the perspective of the first level. Then Buddha states that one should go beyond that understanding and question the ultimate nature of the things that relate to each other in this inter-connected way. This points towards the Buddha's teachings on Emptiness.

In the teachings on the Twelve Links of Dependent Origination, the Buddha states that, although sentient beings do not desire suffering and dissatisfaction, it is through ignorance that they accumulate karmic actions which then lead to undesirable consequences. Now the question then is: what exactly is the nature of that ignorance? What is the mechanism that really leads an individual to act against what he or she fundamentally desires? Here Buddha points to the role of afflictive emotions and thoughts, like anger, hatred, attachment and so forth, which blind the person's understanding of the nature of reality. If we were to examine the state of mind at the point when an individual experiences an intense emotion like hatred, anger or extreme attachment, we would find that, at that point, the person has a rather false notion of self: there is a kind of unquestioned assumption of an independently existing 'I' or subject or person which is perceived, not necessarily consciously, as a kind of a master. It is not totally independent from the body or mind, nor is it to be identified with the body or mind, but there is something there which is somehow identified as the core of the being, the self, and there is a strong sort of grasping at that kind of identity or being. Based on that, you have strong emotional experiences, like attachment towards loved ones, or strong anger or hatred towards someone whom you perceive as threatening, and so forth.

We find in Nagarjuna's own writings extensive reasoning to refute the validity of our notion of self and negate the existence of self or person as we falsely perceive it. He argues that if the self or person is identical with the body, then just as the body is momentary, transient, changing every day, the self or the person should also be subject to the same law. For instance, a human being's bodily continuity can cease and, if the self is identical with the body, then the continuum of the self will also cease at that point. On the other hand, if the self is totally independent of the body, then how can it make sense to say, when a *person* is physically ill, that the person is ill, and so forth? Therefore, apart from the interrelationships between various factors that form our being, there is no independent self.

Similarly, if we extend the same analysis to external reality, we find that, for example, every material object has directional parts, certain parts facing towards different directions. We know that so long as it is an entity it is composed of parts and that there is a kind of necessary relationship between the whole and its parts, so we find that apart from the interrelationship between the various parts and the idea of wholeness, there is no independent entity existing outside that interface. We can apply the same analysis to consciousness or mental phenomena. Here the only difference is that the characteristics of consciousness or mental phenomena are not material or physical. However, we can analyse this in terms of the various instants or moments that form a continuum.

Since we cannot find the essence behind the label, or since we cannot find the referent behind the term, does it mean that nothing exists? The question could also be raised: Is that absence of phenomena the meaning of the doctrine of Emptiness? Nagarjuna anticipates the criticism from the realists' perspective which argues that if phenomena do not exist as we perceive them, if phenomena cannot be found when we search for their essence, then they do not exist.

Therefore, a person or self would not exist. And if a person does not exist, then there is no action or karma because the very idea of karma involves someone committing the act; and if there is no karma, then there cannot be suffering because there is no experience, then there is no cause. And if that is the case, there is no possibility of freedom from suffering because there is nothing from which to be freed. Furthermore, there is no path that would lead to that freedom. And if that is the case, there cannot be a spiritual community or sangha that would embark on the path towards that liberation. And if that is the case, then there is no possibility of a fully perfected being or Buddha. So the realists argue that if Nagarjuna's thesis is true, that the essence of things cannot be found, then nothing will exist and one will have to deny the existence of *samsara* and Nirvana and everything.

Nagarjuna says that such a criticism, that these consequences would follow from his thesis, indicates a lack of understanding of the subtle meaning of the doctrine of Emptiness, because the doctrine of Emptiness does not state or imply the non-existence of everything. Also the doctrine of Emptiness is not simply the thesis that things cannot be found when searched for their essence. The meaning of Emptiness is the interdependent nature of reality.

Nagarjuna goes on to say what he means by the claim that the true meaning of Emptiness emerges from an understanding of the principle of dependent origination. He states that because phenomena are dependent originations, because phenomena come about as a result of interdependent relationships between causes and conditions, they are empty. They are empty of inherent and independent status. An appreciation of that view is understanding of the true Middle Way. In other words, when we understand dependent origination, we see that not only the existence of phenomena, but also the identity of phenomena, depend upon other factors.

So dependent origination can dispel extremes of both absolutism and nihilism, because the idea of 'dependence' points towards a form of existence which lacks independent or absolute status, therefore it liberates the individual from extremes of absolutism. In addition, 'origination' frees the individual from falling to the extremes of nihilism, because origination points towards an understanding of existence, that things do exist.

I stated earlier that the unfindability of phenomena or entities when we search for their essence is not really a full meaning of Emptiness, but at the same time it indicates that phenomena lack intrinsic reality, they lack independent and inherent existence. What is meant by this is that their existence and their identity are derived from mere interaction of

THE ESSENTIAL DALAI LAMA

various factors. Buddhapalita, one of the disciples of Nagarjuna, states that because phenomena come about due to interaction of various factors, their very existence and identity are derived from other factors. Otherwise, if they had independent existence, if they possessed intrinsic reality, then there would be no need for them to be dependent on other factors. The very fact that they depend on other factors is an indication that they lack independent or absolute status.

So the full understanding of Emptiness can come about only when one appreciates the subtlety of this principle of dependent origination—if one concludes that the ultimate nature is that phenomena cannot be found if we were to search for their essence. Nagarjuna states that if the principle or doctrine of Emptiness is not valid, if phenomena are not devoid of independent and inherent existence and intrinsic reality, then they will be absolute; therefore there will be no room for the principle of dependent origination to operate and there will be no room for the interdependent principle to operate. If that is the case, it would not be possible for causal principles to operate and therefore the holistic perception of reality also becomes a false notion. And if that is so, then the whole idea of the Four Noble Truths will be invalid because there is no causal principle operating. Then you will be denying the entire teachings of the Buddha.

In fact, what Nagarjuna does is to reverse all the criticisms levelled against his thesis, by stating that in the realists' position all the teachings of the Buddha would have to be denied. He sums up his criticism by saying that any system of belief or practice which denies the doctrine of Emptiness can explain nothing coherently, whereas any system of belief or thought which accepts this principle of interdependent origination, this doctrine of Emptiness, can come up with a coherent account of reality.

So what we find here is a very interesting complementary relationship between the two levels of understanding of dependent origination I spoke of earlier. The perspective of the first level really accounts for much of our everyday existence or everyday world of experience, where causes and conditions interact and there is a causal principle operating. That perspective of dependent origination, according to Buddhism, is called the correct view at the worldly level.

The greater your appreciation of that perspective, the closer you will be able to come to the deeper level of understanding of dependent origination, because your understanding of the causal mechanism at that level is used to arrive at an understanding of the empty nature of all phenomena. Similarly, once your insight into the empty nature of all phenomena becomes deep, then your conviction in the efficacy of causes and effects will be strengthened, so there will be a greater respect for the conventional reality and relative world. So there is a kind of interesting complementary relationship between the two perspectives.

As your insight into the ultimate nature of reality and Emptiness is deepened and enhanced, you will develop a perception of reality from which you will perceive phenomena and events as sort of illusory, illusion-like, and this mode of perceiving reality will permeate all your interactions with reality. Consequently, when you come across a situation in which you generate compassion, instead of becoming more detached from the object of compassion, your engagement will be deeper and fuller. This is because compassion is ultimately founded upon a valid mode of thought and you will have gained a deeper insight into the nature of reality. Conversely, when you confront situations which would normally give rise to afflictive, negative emotions and responses on your part, there will be a certain degree of detachment and you will not fall prey to the influences of those negative and afflictive emotions. This is because, underlying those afflictive emotions and thoughts, such as desire, hatred, anger and so forth, there is a mistaken notion of reality, which involves grasping at things as absolute, independent and unitary. When you generate insight into Emptiness, the grip of these emotions on your mind will be loosened.

At the beginning of my talk I gave an example of our concept of time: ordinarily we presume there is a kind of an independent existent or independent entity called 'time' present or past or future. But when we examine it at a deeper level, we find it is a mere convention. Other than the interface between the three tenses, the present, future and past, there is no such thing as an independently existing present moment, so we generate a sort of dynamic view of reality. Similarly, when I think of myself, although initially I might have an unquestioned assumption of there being an independent self, when I look closer I will find that, apart from the interface of various factors that constitute my being and various moments of the continuum that form my being, there is no such thing as an absolute independent entity. Since it is this mere conventional 'self', I or person that goes towards the attainment of liberation or eventually transforms into Buddha, even Buddha is not absolute.

~

TWELVE

DEPENDENT ORIGINATION[*]

At a public talk I gave in Japan a few years ago, I saw some people coming toward me carrying a bunch of flowers. I stood up in anticipation of receiving their offering, but to my surprise, they walked straight past and laid the flowers on the altar behind me. I sat down feeling somewhat embarrassed! Yet again I was reminded that the way in which things and events unfold does not always coincide with our expectations. Indeed, this fact of life—that there is often a gap between the way in which we perceive phenomena and the reality of a given situation—is the source of much unhappiness. This is especially true when, as in the example here, we make judgments on the basis of a partial understanding, which turns out not to be fully justified.

Before considering what a spiritual and ethical revolution might consist in, let us therefore give some thought to the nature of reality itself. The close connection between how we perceive ourselves in relation to the world we inhabit and our behaviour in response to it means that our understanding of phenomena is crucially significant. If we don't understand phenomena, we are more likely to do things to harm others and ourselves.

When we consider the matter, we start to see that we cannot finally separate out any phenomena from the context of other phenomena. We can only really speak in terms of relationships. In the course of our daily lives, we engage in countless different activities and receive huge sensory inputs from all that we encounter. The problem of misperception, which, of course, varies in degree, usually arises because of our tendency

---

[*] From *Ethics for the New Millennium*, Riverhead Books, Penguin Putnam Inc., 1999.

to isolate particular aspects of an event or experience and see them as constituting its totality. This leads to a narrowing of perspective and from there to false expectations. But when we consider reality itself we quickly become aware of its infinite complexity, and we realize that our habitual perception of it is often inadequate. If this were not so, the concept of deception would be meaningless. If things and events always unfolded as we expected, we would have no notion of illusion or misconception.

As a means to understanding this complexity, I find the concept of dependent origination (in Tibetan, *ten del*), articulated by the Madhyamika (Middle Way) school of Buddhist philosophy, to be particularly helpful. According to this, we can understand how things and events come to be in three different ways. At the first level, the principle of cause and effect whereby all things and events arise in dependence on a complex web of interrelated causes and conditions is invoked. This suggests that no thing or event can be construed as capable of coming into, or remaining in, existence by itself. For example, if I take some clay and mold it, I can bring a pot into being. The pot exists as an effect of my actions. At the same time, it is also the effect of a myriad of other causes and conditions. These include the combination of clay and water to form its raw material. Beyond this, we can point to the coming together of the molecules, the atoms, and other minute particles, which form these constituents (which are themselves dependent on innumerable other factors). Then there are the circumstances leading up to my decision to make a pot. And there are the cooperative conditions of my actions as I give shape to the clay. All these different factors make it clear that my pot cannot come into existence independently of its causes and conditions. Rather it is dependently originated.

On the second level, *ten del* can be understood in terms of the mutual dependence which exists between parts and whole. Without parts, there can be no whole; without a whole, the concept of parts makes no sense. The idea of 'whole' is predicated on parts, but these parts themselves must be considered to be wholes comprised of their own parts.

On the third level, all phenomena can be understood to be dependently originated because, when we analyze them, we find that, ultimately, they lack independent identity. This can be understood from the way in which we refer to certain phenomena. For example, the words 'action' and 'agent' presuppose one another. So do 'parent' and 'child.' Someone is a parent only because he or she has children. Likewise, a daughter or son is so called only in relation to them having parents. The same relationship of mutual dependence is seen in the language we use to describe trades or professions. Individuals are called farmers on account of their work on the land. Doctors are so called because of their work in field of medicine.

In a more subtle way, things and events can be understood in terms of dependent origination when, for example, we ask, what exactly is a clay pot? When we look for something we can describe as its final identity, we find that the pot's very existence—and by implication that of all other phenomena— is to some extent provisional and determined by convention. When we ask whether its identity is determined by its shape, its function, its specific parts (that is, its being compounded of clay, water, and so on), we find that the term 'pot' is merely a verbal designation. There is no single characteristic which can be said to identify it. Nor indeed does the totality of its characteristics. We can imagine pots of different shapes that are no less pots. And because we can only really speak of it existing in relation to a complex nexus of causes and conditions, viewed from this perspective, it has no one defining quality. In other words, it does not exist in and of itself, but rather it is dependently originated.

As far as mental phenomena are concerned, we see that again there is dependence. Here it lies between perceiver and perceived. Take, for example, the perception of a flower. First, in order for the perception of a flower to arise, there must be a sense organ. Second, there must be a condition—in this case the flower itself. Third, in order for a perception to occur, there must be something, which directs the focus of the perceiver to the object. Then, through the causal interaction of these conditions, a cognitive event occurs which we call the perception of a flower. Now let us examine what exactly constitutes this event. Is it only the operation of the sense faculty? Is it only the interaction between that faculty and the flower itself? Or is it something else? We find that in the end, we cannot understand the concept of perception except in the context of an indefinitely complex series of causes and conditions.

If we take consciousness itself as the object of our investigation, although we tend to think of it in terms of something intrinsic and unchangeable, we find that it, too, is better understood in terms of dependent origination. This is because apart from individual perceptual, cognitive, and emotional experiences, it is difficult to posit an independently existing entity. Rather, consciousness is more like a construct which arises out of a spectrum of complex events.

Another way to understand the concept of dependent origination is to consider the phenomena of time. Ordinarily, we suppose that there is an independently existing entity which we call time. We speak of time past, present, and future. However, when we look more closely, we see that again this concept is merely a convention. We find that the term 'present moment' is just a label denoting the interface between the tenses 'past' and 'future.' We cannot actually pinpoint the present. Just a fraction of a second before the supposed present moment lies the past; just a fraction of a second after it lies the future. Yet if we say that the present moment is 'now,' no sooner have we spoken the word than it lies in the past. If we were to maintain that nevertheless there must be a single moment which is indivisible into either past or future, we would, in fact, have no grounds for any separation into past, present, and future at all. If there is a single moment which is indivisible, then we would have only the present. But without a concept of the present, it becomes difficult to speak about the past and the future since both clearly depend on the present. Moreover, if we were to conclude from our analysis that the present does not then exist, we would have to deny not only worldly convention but also our own experience. Indeed, when we begin to analyze our experience of time, we find that here the past disappears and the future is yet to come. We experience only the present.

Where do these observations leave us? Certainly, things become somewhat more complex when we think along these lines. The more satisfactory conclusion is surely to say that the present does indeed exist. But we cannot conceive of it doing so inherently or objectively. The present comes into being in dependence on the past and the future.

How does this help us? What is the value of these observations? They have a number of important implications. Firstly, when we come to see that everything we perceive and experience arises as a result of an indefinite series of interrelated causes and conditions, our whole perspective changes. We begin to see that the universe we inhabit can be understood in terms of a living organism where each cell works in balanced cooperation with every other cell to sustain the whole. If, then, just one of these cells is harmed, as when disease strikes, that balance is harmed and there is danger to the whole. This, in turn, suggests that our individual well-being is intimately connected both with that of all others and with the environment within which we live. It also becomes apparent that our every action, our every deed, word, and thought, no matter how slight or inconsequential it may seem, has an implication not only for ourselves but for all others, too.

Furthermore, when we view reality in terms of dependent origination, it draws us away from our usual tendency to see things and events in terms of solid, independent, discrete entities. This is helpful because it is this tendency, which causes us to exaggerate one or two aspects of our experience and make them representative of the whole reality of a given situation while ignoring its wider complexities.

Such an understanding of reality as suggested by this concept of dependent origination also presents us with a significant challenge. It challenges us to see things and events less in terms of black and white and more in terms of a complex interlinking of relationships, which are hard to pin down. And it makes it difficult to speak in terms of absolutes. Moreover, if all phenomena are dependent on other phenomena, and if no phenomena can exist independently, even our most cherished selves must be considered not to exist in the way we normally assume. Indeed, we find that if we search for the identity of the self analytically, its apparent solidity dissolves even more readily than that of the clay pot or the present moment. For whereas a pot is something concrete we can actually point to, the self is more elusive, its identity as a construct quickly becomes evident. We come to see that the habitual sharp distinction we make between 'self' and 'others' is an exaggeration.

One of the most promising developments in modern science is the emergence of quantum and probability theory. To some degree at least, this appears to support the notion of the dependent origination of phenomena. Although I cannot claim to have a very clear understanding of this theory, the observation that at the subatomic level it becomes difficult to distinguish clearly between the observer of an object and the object itself seems to indicate a movement toward the conception of reality I have outlined. I would not wish to emphasize this too strongly, however. What science holds to be true today is liable to change. New discoveries mean that what is accepted today may be doubted tomorrow. Besides, on whatever premise we base our appreciation of the fact that things and events do not exist independently, the consequences are similar.

THIRTEEN

AWARENESS OF DEATH*

Just as when weaving
One reaches the end
With fine threads woven throughout,
So is the life of humans.

—Buddha

It is crucial to be mindful of death—to contemplate that you will not remain long in this life. If you are not aware of death, you will fail to take advantage of this special human life that you have already attained. It is meaningful since, based on it, important effects can be accomplished.

Analysis of death is not for the sake of becoming fearful but to appreciate this precious lifetime during which you can perform many important practices. Rather than being frightened, you need to reflect that when death comes, you will lose this good opportunity for practice. In this way contemplation of death will bring more energy to your practice.

You need to accept that death comes in the normal course of life. As Buddha said:

A place to stay untouched by death
Does not exist.
It does not exist in space, it does not exist in the ocean,
Nor if you stay in the middle of a mountain.

---

* From *Advice on Dying and Living a Better Life* by the Dalai Lama, translated and edited by Jeffrey Hopkins, published by Rider and reprinted by permission of The Random House Group Ltd.

If you accept that death is part of life, then when it actually does come, you may face it more easily.

When people know deep inside that death will come but deliberately avoid thinking about it that does not fit the situation and is counterproductive. The same is true when old age is not accepted as part of life but taken to be unwanted and deliberately avoided in thought. This leads to being mentally unprepared; then when old age inevitably occurs, it is very difficult.

Many people are physically old but pretend they are young. Sometimes when I meet with longtime friends, such as certain senators in countries like the United States, I greet them with, 'My old friend,' meaning that we have known one another for a long period, not necessarily physically old. But when I say this, some of them emphatically correct me, 'We are not old! We are longtime friends.' Actually they are old—with hairy ears, a sign of old age—but they are uncomfortable with being old. That is foolish.

I usually think of the maximum duration of a human life as one hundred years, which, compared to the life of the planet, is very short. This brief existence should be used in such a way that it does not create pain for others. It should be committed not to destructive work but to more constructive activities—at least to not harming others, or creating trouble for them. In this way our brief span as a tourist on this planet will be meaningful. If a tourist visits a certain place for a short period and creates more trouble that is silly. But if as a tourist you make others happy during this short period, that is wise; when you yourself move on to your next place, you feel happy. If you create problems, even though you yourself do not encounter any difficulty during your stay, you will wonder what the use of your visit was.

Of life's one hundred years, the early portion is spent as a child and the final portion is spent in old age, often just like an animal feeding and sleeping. In between, there might be sixty or seventy years to be used meaningfully. As Buddha said:

Half of the life is taken up with sleep. Ten years are spent in childhood. Twenty years are lost in old age. Out of the remaining twenty years, sorrow, complaining, pain, and agitation eliminate much time, and hundreds of physical illnesses destroy much more.

To make life meaningful, acceptance of old age and death as parts of our life is crucial. Feeling that death is almost impossible just creates more greediness and more trouble—sometimes even deliberate harm to others. When we take a good look at how supposedly great personages—emperors, monarchs, and so forth— built huge dwelling places and walls, we see that deep inside their minds was an idea that they would stay in this life forever. This self-deception results in more pain and more trouble for many people.

Even for those who do not believe in future lifetimes, contemplation of reality is productive, helpful, scientific. Because persons, minds, and all other caused phenomena change moment by moment, this opens up the possibility for positive development. If situations did not change, they would forever retain the nature of suffering. Once you know things are always changing, even if you are passing through a very difficult period, you can find comfort in knowing that the situation will not remain that way forever. So, there is no need for frustration.

Good fortune also is not permanent; consequently there is no use for too much attachment when things are going well. An outlook of permanence ruins us: Even if you accept that there are future lives, the present becomes your preoccupation, and the future takes on little import. This ruins a good opportunity when your life is endowed with the leisure and facilities to engage in productive practices. An outlook of impermanence helps.

Being aware of impermanence calls for discipline— taming the mind—but this does not mean punishment, or control from the outside. Discipline does not mean prohibition; rather, it means that when there is a contradiction between long-term and short-term interests, you sacrifice the short-term for the sake of long-term benefit. This is *self*-discipline, which stems from ascertaining the cause and effect of karma. For example, for the sake of my stomach's returning to normal after my recent illness, I am avoiding sour foods and cold drink that otherwise appear to be tasty and attractive. This type of discipline means protection. In a similar way, reflection on death calls for self-discipline and self-protection, not punishment.

Human beings have all the potential to create good things, but its full utilization requires freedom, liberty. Totalitarianism stifles this growth. In a complementary way, individualism means that you do not expect something from the outside or that you are waiting for orders; rather, you yourself create the initiative. Therefore, Buddha frequently called for 'individual liberation,' meaning self-liberation, not through an organization. Each individual must create her or his own positive future. Freedom and individualism require self-discipline. If these are exploited for the sake of afflictive emotions, there are negative consequences. Freedom and self-discipline must work together.

Disadvantages of Not Being Mindful of Death

It is beneficial to be aware that you will die. Why? If you are not aware of death, you will not be mindful of your practice, but will just spend your life meaninglessly not examining what sorts of attitudes and actions perpetuate suffering and which ones bring about happiness.

If you are not mindful that you might die soon, you will fall under the sway of a false sense of permanence 'I'll die later on, later on.' Then, when the time comes, even if you try to accomplish something worthwhile, you will not have the energy. Many Tibetans enter a monastery at a young age and study texts about spiritual practice, but when the time comes to really practice, the capacity to do so is somehow lacking. This is because they do not have a true understanding of impermanence.

If, having thought about how to practice, you make a decision that you absolutely have to do so in retreat for several months or even for many years, you have been motivated by your knowledge of impermanence. But if that urgency is not maintained by contemplating the ravages of impermanence again and again, your practice will peter out. This is why some people stay in retreat for years but experience no imprint on their lives afterward. Contemplating impermanence not only motivates your practice, but also fuels it.

If you have a strong sense of the certainty of death and of the uncertainty of its arrival, you will be motivated from within. It will be as if a friend is cautioning, 'Be careful, be earnest, another day is passing.'

You might even leave home for the monastic life. If you did, you would be given a new name and new clothing. You would also have fewer busy activities; you would have to change your attitude, directing your attention to deeper purposes. If, however, you continued busying yourself with the superficial affairs of the moment—delicious food, good clothing, better shelter, pleasant conversation, many friends and acquaintances, and even making an enemy if someone does something you do not like and then quarrelling and fighting—you would be no better off than you were before you entered the monastery, and perhaps even worse. Remember, it is not sufficient to withdraw from these superficial activities out of embarrassment or fear of what your friends who are also on the path might think; the change must come from within. This is true for monks and nuns as well as lay people who take up practice.

Perhaps you are beset by a sense of permanence, by thinking that you will not die soon and that while you are still alive, you need especially good food, clothing, and conversation. Out of desire for the wondrous effects of the present, even if they are of little meaning in the long run, you are ready to employ all sorts of shameless exaggerations and devices to get what you want—taking loans at high interest, looking down on your friends, starting court proceedings—all for the sake of more than adequate provisions.

Advantages of Being Mindful of Impermanence

However, if you do not wait until the end for the knowledge that you will die to sink in, and you realistically assess your situation now, you will not be overwhelmed by superficial, temporary purposes. You will not neglect what matters in the long run. It is better to decide from the very beginning that you will die and investigate what is worthwhile. If you keep in mind how quickly this life disappears, you will value your time and do what is valuable. With a strong sense of the imminence of death, you will feel the need to engage in spiritual practice, improving your mind, and will not waste your time in various distractions ranging from eating and drinking to endless talk about war, romance, and gossip.

All beings want happiness and do not want suffering. We use many levels of techniques for removing unwanted suffering in its superficial and deep forms, but it is mostly humans who engage in techniques in the earlier part of their lives to avoid suffering later on. Both those who do and do not practice religion seek over the course of their lives to lessen some sufferings and to remove others, sometimes even taking on pain as a means to overcome greater suffering and gain a measure of happiness.

On the other hand, if you do not think about death and simply try to forget it, you will involve yourself only in activities concerned with this life. Even if you pretend to practice the Dharma, you will do it mainly for the benefits of this life. So, not remembering death leads to a very limited kind of existence. But thinking about death reminds us of the next life, which reduces our emphasis on the things of this life. Of course, we have to work to maintain our livelihood, but we will not forget the next life. We need to think about death and impermanence because we are too attached to the goods of this life: our possessions, relatives, and so forth. Fear of death, to one who practices the Dharma, does not mean fear of becoming separated from relatives, wealth, or one's own body. From that point of view, fear is pointless because sooner or later we have to die. A more useful fear is the fear of dying too soon, without having been able to do what is necessary to ensure a better future life.

It is common knowledge that death is certain and that no one can avoid it. Instead of disregarding it, it is better to prepare beforehand. Numerous scriptures explain the advantages of remembering death and disadvantages of ignoring it. If we prepare for the eventuality through meditation, when it strikes it will not come as such a shock or be so hard to cope with. If we anticipate trouble in the future, we take precautions. When we are mentally prepared for what might happen, we are not caught unawares when calamity actually befalls us. Thus we meditate on death, not in order to create terror or unhappiness for ourselves, but to equip ourselves to face it when it comes. As long as we remain in the cycle of existence, we will not be free from sickness, old age, or death. Therefore, it is wise to prepare ourselves for what is inevitable. We need to make ourselves familiar with the process by which death occurs and the intermediate state between lives that follows it. If we do so, when we encounter these different events we will be able to face them with determination and courage.

As I said above, in reflecting on death there are three major points to remember. These are that death is certain, that the time of death is unpredictable and that at the time of death nothing will help except our understanding of the Dharma. The inevitability of death is obvious and goes without saying. Nevertheless, we should reflect on how death occurs in relation to time and place. Not a single individual will avoid death. Death is a universal condition. This has been true in the past, remains so at present, and will continue to be true in the future. Whatever physical existence we adopt will not be immune to death. Even Buddhas have left their bodies behind, so what can be said of ordinary beings?

In terms of place, there is nowhere that can be regarded as a death-free zone. Wherever we stay we cannot avoid death. We cannot hide in the mountains; we cannot remain in space beyond death's reach. Death comes upon us like the falling of a huge mountain from which there is no escape. We may be brave, cunning, and clever, but whatever tactics we use, there is nowhere to escape from death, not high in the mountains, deep in the sea, in the densest forest, or in the crowded city. There is not a single person in history who has not had to die. Even the most spiritually evolved have passed away, not to mention the most powerful kings and the bravest warriors. Everyone, rich and poor, great and small, man and woman, has to die.

When meditating on death, we should pay closest attention to its unpredictability. The uncertainty about when death will strike actually impedes our spiritual endeavours. We accept that death will definitely come one day, but since its time of arrival is not fixed, we tend to think of it always as being some way off. This is an illusory notion. As a matter of fact, we are constantly racing toward our death without stopping even for a moment.

We may be alive today, but sometimes death overtakes us without our finding the time to practice the Dharma. We cannot add anything to lengthen our lives. Life continuously and uninterruptedly declines. Years are consumed by months, months are consumed by days, and the day is consumed by hours. Our lives are destroyed as quickly as a drawing on the surface of water. Just as the shepherd drives his flock to the fold, old age and sickness drive us toward death. Because of our physical structure, we are unlikely to live longer than a hundred years. Our life span is defined by our karma. It is not easily extended. Of course, prayers for long life, longevity empowerments, and so forth might enhance one's life to some extent, but it is very difficult to prolong or add to it. Things we did just a few days ago now exist only in our memories. We cannot have these experiences back. This is true even of the experiences we had this morning. Since then, a few hours have passed, which means that our lives are a few hours shorter. Life is ebbing away with every tick of the clock.

As each week follows another, we fail to notice time passing. Sometimes, when I have a vivid recollection of my life in Lhasa, it seems I experienced it only a few days ago. We have been in exile over thirty years, but it is only when we meet old friends from Lhasa or their children that we realize what a long time it has been. We have a tendency to think of the past as something that happened quickly and the future as stretching out into the distance. Consequently, we always tend to think that we still have a lot of time to practice. We think of it as a future project. We are deceived by this negative tendency.

Even while we are alive, we do not have much time to practise the Dharma. Half our lives we spend asleep. The first ten years we are merely children, and after twenty we begin to grow old. Meanwhile, our time is taken up with suffering, anxiety, fighting, sickness, and so forth, all of which limit our ability to practice.

One hundred years from today, not one of us, except the one or two born in the last few days, will still be alive. We have a strange habit of talking about someone dying in a certain place, without thinking that the same death will overpower us. It never occurs to us that we too will die. The television reports people being killed, but we always remain the viewers, not the ones who are going to die. Therefore, thinking about the inevitability of death, we should determine to practise the Dharma, to cease procrastinating by starting today. Of the many levels of practice, meditation on the awakening mind is the most important, so we should resolve to do that now.

In Buddhist cosmology, our planet is referred to as the Southern

World. Since we inhabit this world, our lifespan is extremely uncertain, whereas the lifespan of beings in the Northern World is said to be definite. It is difficult to take the scriptural description of these worlds literally. What is important about the Buddha's teaching is his explanation of the Four Noble Truths and his instructions on how to transform the mind. Sometimes I lightheartedly tell people that the Buddha did not come to India to draw the map of the world. When there is a contradiction between the scientific account and the Buddhist scriptural description of the universe, we should accept what can be observed to be true. There is no need to be dogmatic or narrow-minded about it. This is not to disparage the Buddha's fundamental teachings. Reflecting on these, we can appreciate the vast profundity of the Dharma. What the scriptures do say is that the lifespan of the beings of our world is extremely unpredictable. Sometimes people die when they are still very young, and sometimes they live into ripe old age.

In our meditation on death we should consider the factors that bring it about. The conditions that sustain life are limited. Ironically, sometimes even these cause death. Food and shelter are among our basic needs, but occasionally bad food or overeating can be fatal. Our bodies are composed of elements, which are by nature opposed to each other. When we talk about good health, we mean that these opposing elements are in proper balance. When that balance is disturbed, we suffer from different ailments. On the outside our bodies seem to be solid and strong, but the human metabolism is so subtle and complex that if something happens to one part of the body it can disrupt the functions of the other organs. The body is like a machine with many delicate components. The heart, for instance, has to beat twenty-four hours a day. It could stop at any time. Then what would we do?

Even at the best of times there is no guarantee that we will not die tomorrow. We may believe that because someone is in perfect health, she will not die for a long time. We may think that because someone else is weak and ill, he will die soon. But these are mere assumptions. There are so many causes and conditions for dying that we do not know when death will strike. You may think that, in the event of an earthquake, you have a very solid house. You may think that, if a fire breaks out, your feet are swift and you will be able to run away. Still, we do not have any guarantee that we can protect ourselves against every eventuality. Therefore, we should take every precaution and prepare to face this unknown situation. We can be sure that our deaths will come; we are only unsure when.

Finally, at the time of death, nothing can help except your Dharma practice. When you die, you have to go alone, leaving everything behind. You may have many wonderful friends and relatives, but at that time none of them can help you. Whoever is dearest to you is absolutely helpless. You may be rich, but wealth cannot help you at the time of death. You cannot take a single penny with you. Instead, it is more likely to be a cause of worry. Your best friend cannot accompany you to your next life. Even a spiritual master cannot take his or her most devoted disciples to the next world. Every one of us has to go alone, propelled by the force of our karma.

I often reflect on my own situation as the Dalai Lama. I am sure there are people who are prepared to sacrifice their lives for me. But when my death comes, I have to face it alone. They cannot help me at all. Even my own body has to be left behind. I will travel to the next life under the power of my own actions. So what is it that will help us? Only the imprints of positive actions left on our minds.

Both positive and negative karmic imprints are deposited on the subtle consciousness. This subtle consciousness is known as the primordial consciousness or clear light, which has no beginning or end. This is the consciousness that came from previous lives and goes on to the next. It is the karmic imprints upon it that give rise to experiences of pain and happiness. When you come to die, only the imprints of your positive deeds will help you. Therefore, while you are alive, and especially when you are young, your mind is fresh, and you are able to do a systematic practice, it is important that you prepare yourself for death. Then you will be able to face it properly when the time comes.

The process of death takes place through the gradual dissolution of your internal elements. If you have made your mind familiar with this process, at the time of death when it actually takes place you will be able to handle it. Similarly, if you have become familiar with meditation on love and compassion and exchanging your happiness for the suffering of other sentient beings, these practices will help you. If you have been a real Dharma practitioner, you will face death contentedly.

Of course, if you believe we have only this present life, then at death everything comes to an end. But if you accept the possibility of future lives, then death is just like changing your clothes. The continuity of the mind goes on. However, as we have no idea what the future holds, it is necessary to engage now in practices that will help us then. Even in this world we need friends and support in times of difficulty. When we have to face the unknown alone we will have only our previous practice to support us.

III

PRACTICE

~

FOURTEEN

CREATING THE PERSPECTIVE FOR PRACTICE*

Life as a free and fortunate human being is referred to here as something precious. Such a human life is found rarely, but individuals who possess it can achieve great things because of it. Yet it is not enduring but fragile and extremely transient. It is important that we are aware of these characteristics of our lives and then prepare ourselves for making the best use of them. It is easy to see that human potential far exceeds the abilities of other living creatures in the world. The human mind has far-reaching vision. Its knowledge is boundless. Because of the power of the human mind, new discoveries and inventions abound on our planet. But the crucial thing is that all these innovations should promote happiness and peace in the world. In many instances this is not the case. Unfortunately, too often human ingenuity is used in a misguided way to create disturbances, disunity, and even war.

The achievements of human intelligence are obvious. The ideas and activities of even a single individual can have far-reaching benefits for millions of people and other living creatures. When our human skills are channeled in the right direction, motivated by a proper attitude, wonderful things happen. Therefore, the value of human life is inestimable. From a more strictly spiritual perspective, it is on the basis of a human life that we can develop different types of insight and realization. Only the human mind can generate infinite love and

---

* From *Awakening the Mind, Lightening the Heart*, HarperCollins *Publishers*, 1995.

compassion. Being more concerned about other sentient beings than ourselves and working tirelessly in their interest are among the noble attributes of human nature.

Life as a human being is extremely valuable in terms of achieving both our temporary and ultimate goals. In this context, the temporary goal refers to attaining higher rebirth, and the ultimate goal refers to nirvana and full enlightenment. These goals are precious and difficult to attain. To do so, individuals must be in a position to practice and to accumulate the necessary causes. Only human beings are endowed with the opportunity and intelligence to achieve these goals. If we are to be reborn in the higher realms, we need to refrain from unwholesome actions and practice virtues like generosity and patience. When we engage in right practices, we have the potential to achieve nirvana and Buddhahood.

Once we have gained some conviction that life as a free and fortunate human being is rare and precious, we should reflect that it is not permanent. Although life as a human being has such potential, it is short-lived and does not last. According to the textual instruction, we should meditate here on three fundamental topics: the certainty of death, the uncertainty of when it will occur, and that when death does take place, only the individual's spiritual realization will be of any help. These points can be easily understood and present no intellectual challenge. However, we must meditate on them over and over again until we are deeply convinced. Everyone agrees that sooner or later we all have to die. So the certainty of death is not in question. Rich or poor, young or old, all must die one day. Death is uniform and universal, and no one can either deny or defy this fact of life.

What fools us is the uncertainty of the time of death. Even though we know very well we have to die, we assume that it will be after some time. We all think that we are not going to die soon, and we cling to a false belief that death will not occur for years and years. This notion of a long and indefinite future stretching out ahead of us deters us from serious spiritual endeavor. The whole purpose of meditation on impermanence and death is to move us to engage actively in spiritual practices.

Let me lay out some general guidelines that can help to make our spiritual practice productive and fruitful. Our spiritual pursuit consists, as I have already explained, of meditation sessions and the postmeditation period. People often have the impression that spiritual practices are done only during meditation sessions; they ignore the need for practice during the postmeditation period. It is important to realize that this approach is mistaken. Practice during the postmeditation period is equally important. Therefore, we need to understand how the two kinds of practice complement each other. Spiritual understanding gained in meditation should enhance our understanding during the postmeditation period and vice versa. As a result of the inspiration gained during the meditation sessions, we can develop many virtues like compassion, benevolence, respecting others' good qualities, and so forth. During the session, it is much easier to assume a certain degree of piety. But the real test is when we are faced with the outside world. Therefore, we must be diligent in our practices during the postmeditation period.

When we sit and do our prayers and meditation, we certainly find some peace of mind. We are able to generate compassion toward the poor and needy and feel more tolerant toward our rivals. The mind is more relaxed and less aggressive. But it is really difficult to maintain this momentum when we are confronted with the circumstances of real life. Meditation is like training ourselves for the real world. Unless we engage in a harmonious blend of our experiences of the meditation and postmeditational periods, our spiritual endeavor will lose its much-needed effect. We can be kind and compassionate during our meditation, but if someone harasses us on the road or insults us in public; it is very possible we will become angry and aggressive. We might even retaliate on the spot. If that happens, all the kindness, patience, and understanding we developed in our meditation instantly vanish. Of course, it is very easy to be compassionate and altruistic when we are sitting comfortably on our seats, but the test of the practice is when we encounter a problem. For example, when we have the opportunity to fight and we refrain from fighting, that is Dharma practice. When we have the power to bully someone and we refrain from doing so, that is Dharma practice. So, the real Dharma practice is to control ourselves in such circumstances.

To make our spiritual practice stable and enduring, we must train consistently. A fair-weather practitioner has little hope of achieving his or her goal. It is extremely important to practice the teachings day after day, month after month, and year after year. Anyone who practices consistently can develop spiritual realizations. Since every impermanent phenomenon changes, one day our wild and rough minds will become disciplined and wise, fully relaxed and peaceful. Such wonderful mental qualities can be developed simply by seeing the advantage of virtuous thought and action and the drawbacks of delusion. Nevertheless, it is vital that the practitioner learns the proper technique and method. In the quest for spiritual realization, we do not have to use brute force.

When I was receiving teachings from Khun-nu Lama, he told me a story of someone in Lhasa doing circumambulations. Someone else was meditating there, and the one circumambulating asked, 'What are you doing?' The other replied, 'I am meditating on patience.' The first retorted, 'Eat shit!' and the meditator jumped up, shouting in anger. This clearly shows that the real test of practice is whether we can apply it when we encounter disturbing situations. I feel that practice after the session is probably more important than the practice we do during the session. During the session we are actually refuelling or recharging our energy to be able to do the practice after the session. Therefore, the more we are able to mold the mind during the session, the better we will be able to face difficulties afterward.

The text explains the nature of the special kind of human life that has the freedom to practise the Dharma. Individuals who have the freedom and opportunity to do Dharma practice are not encumbered by wrong views. They are free from the constraints of birth as an animal, a hungry spirit, or a hell being. They have avoided being born in a place where the Buddha's teaching does not prevail or in a remote barbaric land. Nor have they been born dumb or stupid.

Imagine being born as a bird, concerned only with finding food. We would have no opportunity to practice the Dharma. Fortunately, we have not been born as birds or animals but as human beings. But, even as human beings, we could have been born in a remote land where the Buddha's teaching was unheard of. Wealth and intelligence would make no difference; we would not be able to practice the Dharma. My Western friends come from places where there used to be no practice of Buddhism. But, because of their positive instincts and the changing times, we have been able to meet and share the teachings. At one time, Western lands would have been called remote lands where people were not free to practice. We should appreciate not only that we have been born as human beings, but also that we all now have the conditions necessary for putting the Dharma into practice.

Life as a human being is the most suitable basis for attaining nirvana and Buddhahood. Since we have found such a great opportunity, nothing could be worse than failing to put it to good use. We have found this precious human birth as a result of accumulating great virtue in the past. We must put it to good effect now by continuing to practice the Dharma. Otherwise we will be like the merchants of old who went to great lengths to cross the ocean in search of jewels, only to return empty-handed. This human body is likened to a ship in which we can cross the ocean of suffering of the cycle of existence. Having found it, we have no time to sleep and not do the practice.

It is important to understand what is meant by practice of the teachings. Different modes and procedures are aimed directly or indirectly at molding the unruly mind and disciplining it, subduing negative aspects of the mind and enhancing its positive aspects. For example, we recite prayers and do meditation. Such practices should promote goodness of heart and foster virtues like kindness and patience. They should subdue and eliminate negative aspects of the mind like animosity, anger, and jealousy, because these are a source of disturbance and unhappiness for ourselves and others. This is why practice of the Dharma is beneficial.

This automatically leads to the question: Is it possible to practise the teachings? The answer is an emphatic yes. At this juncture we have obtained this human life. We have the fortune to have met appropriate spiritual masters who are compassionate and capable in guiding us on the proper path. We also have freedom and opportunity to engage in spiritual practice.

We should not think of postponing our practice of Dharma until the next life. This is a mistake, because it will be difficult to be born as a human being in the future. Nor should we think that we will put off our practice until next year or even next month. That we will die is inevitable, but we do not know when it will be. Of the many practices open to us, generating the awakening mind is the most important.

It is important to remember that everyone innately possesses Buddha nature and that disturbing emotions are only temporary afflictions of the mind. By properly practising the Dharma, these disturbing emotions can be completely removed, and our Buddha nature will be revealed in all its potential.

All our spiritual practices should be directed toward developing the altruistic thought of the awakening mind. In order for this sublime thought to arise, it is essential to understand sentient beings' plight. This helps us to generate kindness and compassion for others. Unless we have some experience of suffering, our compassion for others will not amount to very much. Therefore, the wish to free ourselves from suffering precedes any sense of compassion for others. The goal of all our spiritual practices should be the awakening mind. This is the supreme and most precious of all the Buddha's teachings. In order that our sense of the awakening mind be effective and powerful, meditate on death and the law of cause and effect.

Meditate, in addition, on the vicious nature of the cycle of existence and the benefits of nirvana. All these practices are complementary because they each serve to provoke us into developing the awakening mind.

The second step in developing the awakening mind is to think about death and the impermanent nature of things as well as the disadvantages of not doing so. Thinking about death and impermanence opens the door to achieving excellent qualities in this life and the next. Meditation on death and miseries of the lower realms of existence is of primary concern to those practitioners who are trying to ensure the welfare of their own future lives. They aim to achieve their goals by taking refuge in the Three Jewels and observing the law of cause and effect. Such practitioners principally abstain from the ten unvirtuous actions.

Through the process of meditation, individuals seeking a happy rebirth come to realize that the body is impermanent and subject to decay. It is under the sway of disturbing emotions and past actions, both of which ultimately stem from the ignorant conception of true existence. Whatever arises because of ignorance is miserable by nature. Practitioners, who merely seek a happy rebirth, chiefly meditate on coarse impermanence, observing that we all die, flowers wither, and houses collapse. Those who seek the peace of nirvana meditate on subtle impermanence, observing that all phenomena are subject to momentary change.

Now when we talk about Dharma practice, people sometimes misunderstand what it means. So let me put it in perspective. Practising the Dharma does not mean you have to give up your profession or do away with your possessions. There are various levels of practice according to individual ability and mental disposition. Everyone cannot renounce the world and meditate in the mountains. This is not practical. How long could we survive? We would soon starve. We need farmers to grow food, and we need as well the support of the business community. These people also can practise the teachings and integrate their lives within the bounds of the Dharma. Business people must make profit to earn their living, but the profit should be moderate. Similarly, people in other trades and professions can work honestly and conscientiously without contradicting the Dharma. In this way they can serve the community and help the overall economy.

I usually advise people to devote half their time to the affairs of life and half their time to the practice of the teachings. This, I think, is a balanced approach for most people. Of course, we need the real renunciates who dedicate their whole lives to practice. They are worthy of our respect and veneration. We can find them among all traditions of Tibetan Buddhism. There are many meditating in the Himalayas.

After our deaths we do not disappear; we take rebirth. But we cannot be confident that our rebirths will not be in miserable circumstances. We do not take birth voluntarily; we are compelled to do so through the force of our actions. Our actions are of two kinds, positive and negative. If we are to ensure our future well-being, it is important to cultivate wholesome actions. Because existence as an animal, hungry spirit or inhabitant of hell is extremely miserable, practitioners aspire to attain a more fortunate rebirth. The principal way to fulfill this wish is to abstain from the ten unvirtuous actions. These ten misdeeds include three physical activities— taking life, taking what is not given, and abusive sexual behaviour; four verbal activities—lying, slander, harsh words, and idle gossip; and three mental activities— covetousness, malice, and wrong view. Abandoning these ten is crucial if we want to achieve a fortunate rebirth.

The practice of this kind of morality should be understood within the context of the law of karma or action. Every action is bound to produce results. This means that whatever positive or negative activities you do, you will experience similarly positive and negative results. Whatever actions you do will follow you just like the shadow of a bird flying in the sky. Actions also have the potential to increase and multiply. Even if you do a small positive or negative action, the eventual result can be tremendous. You should not think that a particular misdeed is insignificant and will not harm you in the future. Just as a large vessel is filled by drops of water, even minor negativities will harm you later. If you have not performed an action, you will not have to face its result, yet once an action has been done, its effects will never merely disappear. This means that you will have to face its results.

Now, the subtlest workings of actions and their results or karma are extremely difficult for the human mind to understand. Ordinary people like us cannot comprehend such extremely obscure phenomena either by direct perception or by way of reasoning. No amount of analysis and examination can help us here. We have to depend on someone who has knowledge and experience of these phenomena, such as Buddha Shakyamuni. We do not do so merely by saying that he is great or he is precious. We depend on his words. This is justified because a Buddha does not lie; he possesses great compassion and the omniscient mind, which is the result of eradicating all mental defilements and obstructions. The Buddha's loving-kindness is unconditional and universal. His sole mission is to help sentient beings in whatever way is useful. In addition to his universal compassion, the Buddha is endowed with the wisdom directly apprehending emptiness. These attributes of compassion and wisdom qualify the Buddha as an authentic teacher. He is someone on whom we can rely when our own reason fails.

The Communist Chinese are against religion in general and Buddhism in particular. They denounce religion as a poison, claiming that it harms economic growth and is a tool of exploitation. They even say that religion is an empty and meaningless pursuit. Tibetans, on the other hand, believe in the Buddha's teaching and see it as a source of peace and happiness. Broadly speaking, Tibetans are indeed happy, peaceful, and resilient in the face of difficulties. Those who oppose religion tend to be more anxious and narrow-minded. It is also noticeable that Tibetans do well without having to work so hard, while the Chinese struggle much harder to survive.

Positive, meritorious activity results in happiness and success. The forces involved in the law of cause and effect are not physical entities, but if we observe them carefully we can learn how they operate. When we Tibetans became refugees, our lives were initially very hard. We possessed not an inch of land and had to depend on others for support. In the course of time, our situation improved. This is our good karma coming to fruition. Similarly, in ordinary life some people are more successful than others for no obvious reason. We just say that he or she is lucky, but these are instances of the working of positive karma.

~

FIFTEEN

REFUGE: THE THREE JEWELS*

From the outset of the Buddhist path, the connection between our understanding of the way things are and our spiritual behaviour is important. It is through this relationship that we establish that we are followers of the Buddha. A Buddhist is defined as one who seeks ultimate refuge in the Buddha, in his doctrine known as the Dharma, and in the Sangha, the spiritual community that practises according to that doctrine. These are known as the Three Jewels of Refuge. For us to have the will to seek ultimate refuge in the Three Jewels, we must initially acknowledge a dissatisfaction with our present predicament in life; we must recognize its miserable nature. Based on a true, profound recognition of this, we naturally wish to change our condition and end our suffering. We are then motivated to seek a method for bringing this about. Upon finding such a method, we view it as a haven or shelter from the misery we wish to escape. The Buddha, Dharma and Sangha are seen to offer such shelter and are therefore apt providers of refuge from our suffering. It is in this spirit that a Buddhist seeks refuge in the Three Jewels.

Before we seek refuge from suffering, we must first deepen our understanding of its nature and causes. Doing so intensifies our wish to find protection from suffering. Such a mental process, which incorporates study and contemplation, must also be applied to develop our appreciation of the Buddha's qualities. This leads us to value the method by which he attained these qualities: his doctrine, the Dharma. From this ensues our respect for the Sangha, the spiritual practitioners engaged in applying the Dharma. Our sense of respect for this refuge is

---

* From *An Open Heart*, Little, Brown and Company, 2001.

strengthened by such contemplation, as is our determination to engage in a daily spiritual practice.

As Buddhists, when we take refuge in the Buddha's doctrine, the second of the Three Jewels, we are actually taking refuge in both the prospect of an eventual state of freedom from suffering and in the path or method by which we attain such a state. This path, the process of applying this doctrine through conscious spiritual practice, is referred to as the Dharma. The state of being free of suffering can also be referred to as the Dharma, as it results from our application of the Buddha's doctrine.

As our understanding and faith in the Dharma grows, we develop an appreciation for the Sangha, the individuals, both past and present, who have attained such states of freedom from suffering. We can then conceive of the possibility of a being who has attained total freedom from the negative aspects of mind: a Buddha. And as our recognition of the miserable nature of life develops, so does our appreciation of the Buddha, Dharma, and Sangha—the Three Jewels in which we seek shelter. This intensifies our quest for their protection.

At the outset of the Buddhist path, our need for the protection of the Three Jewels can, at most, be grasped intellectually. This is especially so for those not raised inside a faith. Because the Three Jewels have their equivalent in other traditions, it is often easier for those who have been raised inside such a tradition to recognize their value.

~

SIXTEEN

MEDITATION: A BEGINNING*

In this chapter we explore the techniques for changing our minds from our habitual ways to more virtuous ones. There are two methods of meditating that are to be used in our practice. One, analytical meditation, is the means by which we familiarize ourselves with new ideas and mental attitudes. The other, settled meditation focuses the mind on a chosen object.

Although we all naturally aspire to be happy and wish to overcome our misery, we continue to experience pain and suffering. Why is this? Buddhism teaches that we actually conspire in the causes and conditions that create our unhappiness, and are often reluctant to engage in activities that could lead to more long-lasting happiness. How can this be? In our normal way of life, we let ourselves be controlled by powerful thoughts and emotions, which in turn give rise to negative states of mind. It is by this vicious circle that we perpetuate not only our unhappiness but also that of others. We must deliberately take a stand to reverse these tendencies and replace them with new habits. Like a freshly grafted branch on an old tree that will eventually absorb the life of that tree and create a new one, we must nurture new inclinations by deliberately cultivating virtuous practices. This is the true meaning and object of the practice of meditation.

Contemplating the painful nature of life, considering the methods by which our misery can be brought to an end, is a form of meditation. This book is a form of meditation. The process by which we transform our more instinctual attitude to life, that state of mind which seeks only to satisfy desire and avoid discomforts, is what we mean when we use

---

* From *An Open Heart*, Little, Brown and Company, 2001.

the word *meditation*. We tend to be controlled by our mind, following it along its self-centered path. Meditation is the process whereby we gain control over the mind and guide it in a more virtuous direction. Meditation may be thought of as a technique by which we diminish the force of old thought habits and develop new ones. We thereby protect ourselves from engaging in actions of mind, word, or deed that lead to our suffering. Such meditation is to be used extensively in our spiritual practice.

This technique is not in and of itself Buddhist. Just as musicians train their hands, athletes their reflexes and techniques, linguists their ear, scholars their perceptions, so we direct our minds and hearts.

Familiarizing ourselves with the different aspects of our spiritual practice is therefore a form of meditation. Simply reading about them once is not of much benefit. If you are interested, it is helpful to contemplate the subjects mentioned, as we did in the previous chapter with the non-virtuous action of senseless talk, and then research them more extensively to broaden your understanding. The more you explore a topic and subject it to mental scrutiny, the more profoundly you understand it. This enables you to judge its validity. If through your analysis you prove something to be invalid, then put it aside. However, if you independently establish something to be true, then your faith in that truth has powerful solidity. This whole process of research and scrutiny should be thought of as one form of meditation.

The Buddha himself said, 'O monks and wise ones, do not accept my words simply out of reverence. You should subject them to critical analysis and accept them on the basis of your own understanding.' This remarkable statement has many implications. It is clear that the Buddha is telling us that when we read a text, we should rely not merely on the fame of the author but rather on the content. And when grappling with the content, we should rely on the subject matter and the meaning rather than on the literary style. When relating to the subject matter, we should rely on our empirical understanding rather than on our intellectual grasp. In other words, we must ultimately develop more than mere academic knowledge of the Dharma. We must integrate the truths of the Buddha's teaching into the depths of our very being, so that they become reflected in our lives. Compassion is of little value if it remains

139

an idea. It must become our attitude toward others, reflected in all our thoughts and actions. And the mere concept of humility does not diminish our arrogance; it must become our actual state of being.

Familiarity with a Chosen Object

The Tibetan word for meditation is gom, which means 'to familiarize.' When we use meditation on our spiritual path, it is to familiarize ourselves with a chosen object. This object need not be a physical thing such as an image of the Buddha or Jesus on the cross. The 'chosen object' can be a mental quality such as patience, which we work at cultivating within ourselves by means of meditative contemplation. It can also be the rhythmic movement of our breath, which we focus on to still our restless minds. And it can be the mere quality of clarity and knowing—our consciousness—the nature of which we seek to understand. All these techniques are described in depth in the pages that follow. By these means our knowledge of our chosen object grows.

For example, as we research what kind of car to buy, reading the pros and cons of different makes, we develop a sense of the qualities of a particular choice. By contemplating these qualities, our appreciation of this car intensifies, as does our desire to possess it. We can cultivate virtues such as patience and tolerance in much the same way. We do so by contemplating the qualities that constitute patience, the peace of mind it generates in us, the harmonious environment created as a result of it, the respect it engenders in others. We also work to recognize the drawbacks of impatience, the anger and lack of contentment we suffer within, the fear and hostility it brings about in those around us. By diligently following such lines of thought, our patience naturally evolves, growing stronger and stronger, day by day, month by month, and year by year. The process of taming the mind is a lengthy one. Yet once we have mastered patience, the pleasure derived from it outlasts that provided by any car.

We actually engage in such meditation quite often in our daily lives. We are particularly good at cultivating familiarity with unvirtuous tendencies! When displeased with someone, we are able to contemplate that person's faults and derive a stronger and stronger conviction of his or her questionable nature. Our mind remains focussed on the 'object' of our meditation, and our contempt for the person thereby intensifies. We also contemplate and develop familiarity with chosen objects when we focus on something or someone we are particularly fond of. Very little prodding is needed to maintain our concentration. It is more difficult to remain focussed when cultivating virtue. This is a sure indication of how overwhelming the emotions of attachment and desire are!

There are many kinds of meditation. There are some that do not require a formal setting or a particular physical posture. You can meditate while driving or walking, while on a bus or train, and even while taking a shower. If you wish to devote a particular time to more concentrated spiritual practice, it is beneficial to apply early mornings to a formal meditation session, as that is when the mind is most alert and clear. It is helpful to sit in a calm environment with your back straight, as this helps you remain focussed. However, it is important to remember that you must cultivate virtuous mental habits whenever and wherever possible. You cannot limit meditation to formal sessions.

Analytical Meditation

As I have said, there are two types of meditation to be used in contemplating and internalizing the subjects I discuss. First, there is analytical meditation. In this form of meditation, familiarity with a chosen object—be it the car you desire or the compassion or patience you seek to generate—is cultivated through the rational process of analysis. Here, you are not merely focusing on a topic. Rather, you are cultivating a sense of closeness or empathy with your chosen object by studiously applying your critical faculties. This is the form of meditation I shall emphasize as we explore the different subjects that need to be cultivated in our spiritual practice. Some of these subjects are specific to a Buddhist practice, some not. However, once you have developed familiarity with a topic by means of such analysis, it is important to then remain focussed on it by means of settled meditation in order to help it sink in more profoundly.

Settled Meditation

The second type is settled meditation. This occurs when we settle our minds on a chosen object without engaging in analysis or thought. When meditating on compassion, for example, we develop empathy for others and work at recognizing the suffering they are experiencing. This we do by means of analytical meditation. However, once we have a feeling of compassion in our hearts, once we find that the meditation has positively changed our attitude toward others, we remain fixed on that feeling, without engaging in thought. This helps deepen our compassion. When we sense that our feeling of compassion is weakening, we can again engage in analytical meditation to revitalize our sympathy and concern before returning to settled meditation.

As we become more adept, we can skillfully switch between the two forms of meditation in order to intensify the desired quality. 'Calm Abiding,' refers to the technique for developing our settled meditation to the point where we can remain focussed single-pointedly on our object of meditation for as long as we wish. As I've said, this 'object of meditation' is not necessarily something we can 'see.' In a sense, one fuses his or her mind with the object in order to cultivate familiarity with it. Settled meditation, like other forms of meditation, is not virtuous by nature. Rather, it is the object we are concentrated on and the motivation with which we engage in the practice that determine the spiritual quality of our meditation. If our mind is focussed on compassion, the meditation is virtuous. If it is placed on anger, it is not.

We must meditate in a systematic manner, cultivating familiarity with a chosen object gradually. Studying and listening to qualified teachers is an important part of this process. We then contemplate what we have read or heard, scrutinizing it so as to remove any confusion, misconceptions, or doubts we might have. This process itself helps affect the mind. Then, when we focus on our object single-pointedly, our minds become fused with it in the desired manner.

It is important that before we try to meditate on the more subtle aspects of Buddhist philosophy, we are able to keep our minds concentrated on simpler topics. This helps us develop the ability to analyze and remain single-pointedly focussed on subtle topics such as the antidote to all our suffering, the emptiness of inherent existence.

Our spiritual journey is a long one. We must choose our path with care, ensuring that it encompasses all those methods that lead us to our goal. At times the journey is steep. We must know how to pace ourselves down to the snail's pace of profound contemplation while also ensuring that we do not forget our neighbour's problem or that of the fish swimming in polluted oceans many thousands of miles away.

SEVENTEEN

~

TRANSFORMING THE MIND THROUGH MEDITATION*

Meditation is a *familiarization* of the mind with an object of meditation. In terms of how the mind is familiarized with the object, there are many types of meditation. In one type, the mind is generated into the entity of a particular type of consciousness, as in meditating compassion or meditating wisdom. In such meditation you are seeking to generate your own mind into a compassionate consciousness or a wisdom consciousness—compassion and wisdom not being the object on which you are meditating, but that entity into which you are seeking to transform your consciousness through a process of familiarization.

However, when you meditate on impermanence or on selflessness, impermanence and selflessness are taken as the objects of the mode of apprehension of the mind, and you are meditating *on* them. In another type of meditation, if you meditate on the good qualities of a Buddha wishing to attain them, these qualities are objects of wishing; this is called meditation in the manner of wishing. Then, another type of meditation is one in which you cause levels of the path to appear to the mind in the sense of taking to mind that there are such and such levels of realization; this is called reflective meditation.

In another way, meditation is divided into two types: analytical and stabilizing. In general, calm abiding (*shamatha, zhi gnas*) is stabilizing meditation, whereas special insight (*vipashyana, lhag mthong*) is analytical meditation.

With respect to objects of meditation, the objects of both stabilizing

---

* From *Kindness, Clarity, Insight*, Snow Lion Publications, 1984.

and analytical meditation can be either the final mode of being of phenomena or any among the varieties of phenomena. In general, emptiness is something found at the conclusion of analysis by reasoning investigating the final mode of being of objects; nevertheless, at the time of stabilizing meditation observing emptiness, the meditator fixes one-pointedly on the meaning of emptiness which has been ascertained and does not analyze. Thus, there is both stabilizing and analytical meditation observing emptiness. Similarly, both stabilizing and analytical meditation observing any of the varieties of phenomena can occur depending on how the mind is acting on the object.

Calm abiding, which is predominantly stabilizing meditation, is common to both non-Buddhist and Buddhists. Within Buddhism it is common to both the Low and Great Vehicles, and within the Great Vehicle is common to both the Sutra and Mantra Vehicles. I will explain in brief how to achieve calm abiding.

Our mind, as it is now, is completely scattered to external objects, due to which it is powerless. Our thought is like water running in every direction. But just as water, when channelized, becomes powerful, so it is with our minds.

How is the mind channelized? In the Mantra Vehicle in general and in Highest Yoga Mantra in particular, many techniques are described, but first I will describe the technique that is common to all vehicles. In order to set the mind steadily on an object of observation, it is necessary initially to identify an object of observation. Buddha described four types—objects for purifying behaviour, skillful objects, objects for purifying afflictions, and pervasive objects. For example, with regard to objects for purifying behaviour, no matter what afflictive emotion we predominantly engaged in earlier, its force remains with our mind now, and thus it is necessary to choose an object for meditation which will counter the force of that particular afflictive emotion. For someone who predominantly engaged in desire, the object of meditation is ugliness. From among the four mindful establishments this is explained in connection with mindful establishment on the body. Here, 'ugliness' does not necessarily refer to distorted forms; the very nature of our body—composed of blood, flesh, bone, and so forth—might seem superficially to be very beautiful with a good colour, solid and yet soft to touch, but when it is investigated, you see that its essence is things like bone. If I were wearing X-ray glasses, I would see a room full of skeletons as well as a skeleton that is talking from this podium. Thus, meditating on 'ugliness' means to investigate the nature of our physical body.

For someone who has predominantly engaged in hatred, the object of meditation is love. For someone who was predominantly sunk in obscuration, the meditation is on the twelve links of the dependent-arising of cyclic existence. For someone whose predominant afflictive emotion is pride, the meditation should be on the divisions of the constituents because, when meditating on the many divisions, you get to the point where you realize that there are many things you do not know, thereby lessening pride. For those dominated by conceptuality, the prescribed meditation is on observing the exhalation and inhalation of the breath. Those are the objects for purifying behaviour.

As mentioned earlier, the object of observation could also be emptiness. Also, you could take even a flower, and so forth, as the object. Still another is to take your own mind as the object of observation. Also, a Buddhist could meditate on Buddha's body; a Christian could meditate on Jesus or the cross.

No matter what the object is, this is not a case of meditating within looking at an external object with your eyes but of causing an image of it to appear to the mental consciousness. This image is called a 'reflection', and it is the object of observation.

Having identified the object, how do you set your mind on it? Initially, you have to hear about the object to be meditated on from a teacher; then, you gain ascertainment of it by thinking again and again on it. For instance, if you are to meditate on the body of a Buddha, first you need to come to know it through hearing it described or looking at a picture or statue and then get used to it so that it can appear clearly to the mind.

At that point, imagine it about four feet in front of you, at the height of your eyebrows. It should be meditated as clear, with a nature of light; this helps to prevent the onset of laxity.

Also, consider the imagined Buddha body to be heavy; this helps to prevent excitement. As much as you can reduce the size of the object, so much does it help in withdrawing the mind, channelizing it. Your physical posture also important.

For the object of observation it is also possible to use letters or drops of light at important places in the body. When meditating this way, the object must be tiny; the smaller the object is, the better. Once the object originally has been determined, you may not change its size, bigger or smaller; you must consider it to have been fixed for the duration of generating calm abiding.

First cause the object to appear to the mind. Then, hold it with mindfulness such that you do not lose it. Not losing the object through mindfulness acts as a cause of developing introspection.

While keeping on the object, your mind must have two qualities—(1) great clarity not only of the object but also of the consciousness and (2) abiding one-pointedly on the object of observation. Two opposing factors prevent these from developing—laxity and excitement. Laxity prevents the development of clarity, and excitement prevents the stability of staying with the object.

Laxity is a case of the mind's becoming too relaxed, too loose, lacking intensity—the tautness of the mind having become weak. A cause of laxity is lethargy, which is like having a hat on the head, a heaviness. As an antidote, you have to make the mind more taut.

When the mode of apprehension of the mind is tightened, there is less danger of laxity but more danger of generating excitement. Scatterings of the mind that are due to desire are called excitement; thus, scattering can be to any type of object whereas excitement is a scattering only to objects of desire. As an antidote to excitement and any other type of scattering, you need to lower the level of the mode of apprehension of the mind, making it less taut.

While holding the object of observation with mindfulness, investigate with introspection from time to time to see whether the mind has come under the influence of laxity or excitement. If through introspection you find that there is danger of laxity, you need to heighten the mode of apprehension; if there is danger of excitement, lower the mode of apprehension a little. Through experience, a sense of a moderate level of tautness of the mind will develop.

To heighten the level of the mode of apprehension of the mind, reflect on something that makes you joyous; to lower it, reflect on something that sobers the mind, such as suffering. When initially training this way, it is best to do frequent, short sessions of meditation, and because it is difficult initially to generate a deep state of meditation when in a busy, noisy city, you need complete isolation and tranquility. Without quiet, it is almost impossible to achieve a fully qualified state of calm abiding.

As you practice in this way, the mind gradually develops more and more stability, culminating in calm abiding. Through the power of stabilizing meditation in which the mind is set one-pointedly on its object of observation, mental pliancy is generated. In dependence upon that, physical pliancy is generated, leading to the bliss of physical pliancy. In dependence upon that, the bliss of mental pliancy is generated. At the point at which the bliss of mental pliancy becomes stable, calm abiding is attained. Among the four concentrations and four formless absorptions, this state— which is conjoined with physical and mental bliss—is the lowest of the preparations for the first concentration.

Special insight is attained in a similar way when the bliss of mental pliancy is induced, not by the power of stabilizing meditation, but by the power of analysis with investigatory wisdom. There are mundane and supramundane forms of special insight. The mundane is a case of viewing a lower level as gross and a higher level as peaceful, whereas supramundane special insight, if taken in a general way, has the aspect of the four noble truths. From the specific viewpoint of the Great Vehicle systems of tenets, supramundane special insight has the aspect of the selflessness of phenomena.

To induce meditative stabilization even faster, the mantra systems have special techniques revolving around deity yoga. The path of deity yoga brings about speedier progress to Buddhahood through special techniques for developing unified concentration and wisdom, these being the last two of the six perfections—giving, ethics, patience, effort, concentration, and wisdom—which are described in the Bodhisattva scriptural collections. If you do not have concentration in which the mind is unfluctuatingly stable and clear, the faculty of wisdom cannot know its object, just as it is, in all its subtleties. Therefore, it is necessary to have concentration. The reason for cultivating wisdom realizing the emptiness of inherent existence is that even though you have mere concentration, it cannot harm the misconception that objects exist in and of themselves. A union of concentration and wisdom is needed.

According to the *Vajrapañjara Tantra*, an explanatory tantra of the Guhyasamaja cycle, there are four divisions of the Mantra Vehicle—Action, Performance, Yoga, and Highest Yoga Tantras. Among these, the three lower tantras—Action, Performance, and Yoga—describe a mode of progressing on the spiritual path in terms of yogas with and without signs, these being yogas of the non-duality of the profound and the manifest. Meditative stabilization is achieved within taking—as the object of observation of the meditation—the clear appearance of your own body as the body of a deity. While observing your body clarified or visualized as a deity's body, you ascertain its absence of inherent existence, thus making a combination of manifestation in divine form and profound wisdom realizing the final nature of that body. Such profound realization and simultaneous divine appearance is the yoga of the non-duality of the profound and the manifest.

In Action Tantra during the yoga with signs the mode of generating or imagining yourself as a deity is by way of six steps called the six deities. The first is the *ultimate deity*, meditation on the emptiness of inherent existence equally of yourself and of the deity. The second is the *sound deity*, viewing an appearance of the natural form of emptiness as the reverberating sounds of the mantra of the particular deity in space.

The third is the *letter deity* in which the sounds of the mantra appear in the form of letters standing around the edge of a flat moon disc. The fourth is the *form deity*, a transformation of the moon and letters into the body of the deity.

The fifth is the *seal deity*, the blessing of important places of the divine body with hand gestures called 'seals'. Then, you set a white om at the crown of the head, a red ah in the throat, and a blue hum at the heart, symbolizing exalted body, speech, and mind, and concentrate on this divine body which now has all the qualifications or signs of a deity. This is the last step, the *sign deity*.

When some success is gained in visualizing yourself as a deity, the concentrations of abiding in fire and abiding in sound are used to enhance speedy development of meditative stabilization. After that, you cultivate the yoga without signs, the concentration bestowing liberation at the end of sound. This is cultivation of supramundane special insight observing the emptiness of inherent existence. Although deity yoga is still done, the main emphasis is on the factor of ascertaining the final nature of phenomena.

The explanation of the procedure of the path in Performance Tantra is roughly the same as in Action Tantra, but in Yoga Tantra it is slightly different. There, the bases of purification are explained as body, speech, mind, and activities, and as means of purification four seals are described for transforming these into the exalted body, speech, mind, and activities of the effect stage of Buddhahood. In this process the achievement of calm abiding is enhanced by meditation on a tiny hand symbol, such as a vajra, at the point of the nose, gradually increasing in number such that first your own body and then the surroundings are pervaded by the tiny hand symbol. The specific hand symbol is determined in accordance with the five Buddha lineages, the deities of which carry a special symbol in their hands; Vairochana, for instance, carries a wheel, Akshobhya a vajra. Meditation on such a tiny hand symbol helps in developing calm abiding due to the size of the object and helps in increasing meditative dexterity through the practice of dispersing and gathering many forms of the symbol.

Highest Yoga Tantras mainly explain a yoga of undifferentiable bliss and emptiness in terms of two stages of yoga—a stage of generation which is imaginary and fabricated and a stage of completion which is non-imaginary and non-fabricated. In both the stage of generation and the stage of completion in Highest Yoga Mantra the ordinary states of death, intermediate state, and rebirth are brought into the path to be transformed into the Three Bodies of a Buddha—Truth Body, Complete Enjoyment Body, and Emanation Body.

In Highest Yoga Mantra there are techniques for meditating on the inner channels, winds (energies), and drops of essential fluid. Presentations of the channels are given in two ways: one is a physical description whereas the other is merely for meditation. The latter description is for the sake of specific meditative effects, and thus exact physical correspondence is not the aim. The sought-after effects, however, are definitely produced.

A practitioner meditates on drops, light, or letters in these channel centres. Due to the special places where these are meditated and due to the force of initiation as well as of preliminary meditations called 'approximation to the state of a deity', and so forth, just stabilizing meditation is used in cultivating special insight realizing the emptiness of inherent existence. Also, it is possible to achieve calm, abiding and special insight simultaneously.

The technique of focusing on letters or light at important places within the body serves as a means of forcefully stopping conceptuality. The reason for stopping conceptuality is that within consciousness there are many levels from the gross to the most subtle, and in Highest Yoga Mantra the subtler levels of consciousness are transformed into path consciousnesses of wisdom. Normally, when we die, the grosser levels of consciousness cease, and the subtler levels become manifest, culminating in manifestation of the subtlest consciousness, the mind of clear light of death. An ordinary person has no awareness during this phase, being as if in a swoon. However, if while the body—the basis of the mind—has not degenerated a yogi withdraws the grosser levels of consciousness through the power of meditation, the subtler consciousnesses can be experienced in full awareness and clarity. Forcefully withdrawing the grosser and subtler levels of wind (energy) and mind, the yogi manifests the most subtle level, the mind of clear light. Used in the path process, this level of consciousness is particularly powerful and quick. To ripen the mind so that these levels of the path can be practised, it is necessary first to practise the stage of generation.

That is just a brief presentation; understanding these states and how they are achieved in sutra and mantra is very useful.

~

EIGHTEEN

ENVIRONMENT/SYMBOLS/POSTURE/ BREATHING*

For the beginner, the place (for meditation) is quite important. Once we have developed certain experiences, then external factors have very little effect. But generally speaking, the place for meditation should be quiet.

When we meditate on single-pointedness of mind, then we need a completely isolated place, one with no noise. That is very important. Then, for certain yoga practices, the altitude also makes a difference. A higher altitude is better; high mountains are the best place.

Also, there are sites where experienced meditators have lived before, and thus blessed and empowered the place. So later, persons of less experience are inspired by the place, get vibrations or blessings from the place. First one highly developed person blesses the place, and later these blessings are transmitted to other meditators.

When we clean and tidy up the room our wish should not be just to have a clean place, but to put our minds in order. When later we visualize deities, make offerings, and recite mantras, it is as if we had prepared to receive important guests. When we expect an invited guest, then first we clean and tidy up. It is not nice to invite a guest into an untidy place. In order to practice meditation, first clean your room. Your wish to do so should not be polluted by negative states of mind like attachment, aversion or similar attitudes.

There is a story about one of the great meditators in Tibet. One day

---

* From *Cultivating a Daily Meditation*, Library of Tibetan Works and Archives, 1991.

he arranged his offerings particularly well, then he sat down and thought, 'Why did I do that?'

He realized that he had done it because he wanted to impress one of his benefactors, who was going to come and see him on that day. He was so disgusted with his polluted motivation that he took a handful of dust and threw it over the offerings.

This meditator had once been a thief. Occasionally he would still be moved by the urge to steal. When once he visited a certain family, his right hand automatically reached out toward a beautiful object. With his left hand he caught it and called out, 'Here is a thief, here is a thief.' He could train himself in this way. This was really a very effective way of practising, because at every moment he implemented the right thing.

Similarly, when we clean or make some preparations, our motivation must be pure and sincere. Worldly concerns should be involved as little as possible.

Then the way in which the different objects of refuge should be arranged on the altar is explained (in the text). If you can afford to have all the required religious objects, then you should display them. If you cannot afford them, then no matter. The great meditator of Tibet, the yogi Milarepa, had nothing apart from some rolls of paper which contained instructions by his master Marpa, which he put up around the cave. He did not have anything in his cave, but one night a thief broke in. Milarepa laughed and said, 'Since I cannot find anything here during the day, what is there that you will find during the night?' It is said that a real meditator never feels the lack of external materials.

Symbols of Refuge

First the statue of the Buddha is explained.

The Sanskrit term 'Buddha' indicates a being whose mind is purified of faults and whose realizations have completely developed.

Buddha is also known as Tathagatha, the one who has entered into the nature of suchness and the one who arose from it.

When one explains the meaning of someone arising from the nature of suchness then one comes to the topic of the three bodies of a Buddha: Truth Body (*Dharmakaya*), Enjoyment Body (*Sambhogakaya*), and

Emanation Body (*Nirmanakaya*).

Detailed explanations of the three bodies of the Buddhas can be found throughout Mahayana literature.

According to this doctrine, when the Buddha came into this universe as Buddha Shakyamuni he assumed the Emanation Body from the Truth Body. Here all the great events in the life of the Buddha, starting from conception in the womb up to his *Parinirvana*, are regarded as deeds of the Buddha.

The Buddhas are also known as Gone to Bliss *(Sugata),* the ones who have passed into peace, the ones who have travelled the peaceful path into a peaceful state. This term includes peaceful realizations, peaceful abandonments or cessation, and the Buddhanature, the essence of Buddha that, according to Buddhist doctrine, is inherent in all sentient beings.

Generally the body, speech and mind of the Buddhas are explained as having different manifestations: the body as Avalokiteshvara, speech as Manjushri, and mind as Vajrapani. Avalokiteshvara, Manjushri, and Vajrapani are explained as the embodiments of compassion, wisdom, and energy of the Buddhas.

Avalokiteshvara and Manjushri appear as peaceful deities, whereas Vajrapani appears slightly wrathful.

Generally speaking, when someone has strong force of mind he can engage in actions more drastically and more forcefully, and this is the reason for having wrathful deities. According to highest yoga tantra, one calls this 'taking desire or anger into the path.'

Tara, another peaceful deity, is spoken of as the purifying aspect of the energy of the body. All the different qualities of the Buddha, including compassion, wisdom and power, depend on the moving factor, which is energy.

One can also say that Tara is the feminist deity. There is a legend according to which Tara, when she cultivated the aspiration to achieve enlightenment, made it a point to become enlightened in her female form.

As a representation of the speech of the Buddhas, we use a sacred text, if possible a copy of the *Perfection of Wisdom Sutra*, or *Prajnaparamitasutra*.

Prajnaparamita means the wisdom gone beyond. There are different types of wisdom, such as natural wisdom, the path which leads to it, and the resultant wisdom state. The *Perfection of Wisdom Sutra* explains these different types of wisdom.

This type of literature constitutes the main body of Mahayana scripture. In the Tibetan translation of the sacred Buddhist canon there are some twenty volumes of *The Perfection of Wisdom Sutra*, comprised of about twenty different texts. The most extensive text has one hundred thousand verses, the next twenty-five thousand, eight thousand, and so forth.

The shortest text consists of the letter *AH*. This is known as the *Perfection of Wisdom Sutra* of one letter. In Sanskrit, *AH* is the letter for negation because suchness, or the ultimate nature, as we already discussed, is the absence of independent existence; this is a negation.

The next symbol of refuge is the stupa. This represents the mind of the Buddhas. There exist eight different types of stupas, for example, those symbolizing victory over demons, enlightenment, *Parinirvana*, and so forth. When I look at these different kinds of stupas, I think that they were developed as a means of remembrance.

Next the offering of pure water, flowers, incense, light, and fruit is placed on the altar. This is modelled on the custom of how a guest was served in India at the time. If Buddha had taught Buddhism in Tibet he would have talked about offerings like butter and tsampa.

Physical Posture and Breathing

Next I will explain the physical posture during meditation. The meditation seat should be slightly raised at the back because that helps reduce tightness. The present seat on which I am sitting is springy; the front is actually higher than the back, just the opposite.

Sitting in vajra (cross-legged) position is very difficult, but if it causes no pain then that is the proper way. Or you can sit in half vajra (His Holiness demonstrated a very comfortable cross-legged position), or in Arya Tara's posture (again demonstrated), which is very comfortable.

In the correct hand mudra, the back of the right hand rests in the

155

palm of the left hand and the two thumbs stand up and touch one another, forming a triangle. This triangle has a tantric significance, symbolizing the Realm of Truth (*Dharmadhatu*), the reality source and also inner heat at the navel.

The arms should not touch the body. The head is slightly bent down, the tip of the tongue touching the palate, which prevents thirst and drooling when the meditator engages in deep, single-pointed concentration. Lips and teeth should be left in their natural position, eyes looking at the tip of the nose. This is no problem when one has a big, pointed nose, but when one has a small nose, looking at its tip sometimes causes pain. (Laughing) So this depends on the size of one's nose.

As to the position of the eyes, at the beginning it might give you a clearer visualization when they are closed, but in the long run this is not good; you should not close your eyes. Visualization is done on a mental and not a sensory level. If you train yourself to meditate with open eyes and become used to it, then even when an object comes in front of your eyes, you will not lose the mental image you are meditating on. On the other hand, if you train yourself and become used to meditating with closed eyes, you will lose the mental image the moment you open them.

During meditation your breathing should be natural. You should not breathe violently nor too gently. Sometimes if you are meditating in connection with tantric practices and do certain energy yogas, like the nine-round breathing practice, then it is different.

When you are in a fluctuating state of mind, like when you are angry or have lost your temper, then it is good to bring back calmness by concentrating on breathing. Just count the breaths, completely forgetting about anger. Concentrate on breathing and count in/out 'one, two, three,' up to twenty.

At that moment when your mind concentrates fully on breathing, the breath coming and going, the passions subside. Afterwards it is easier to think clearly.

Since all activities, including meditation, depend very much on the force of intention or motivation, it is important that, before you begin to meditate, you cultivate a correct motivation. We are engaged here in a practice which is connected with tantra, so the appropriate motivation is to avoid being distracted by concern for this life alone. Nor should our motivation be influenced by concern for perfection and happiness of samsaric life alone. The correct motivation is the altruistic attitude.

~

NINETEEN

THE NATURE OF THE MIND*

Let us examine what sort of characteristics constitute the mind. We surely do possess something called mind but how are we to recognize its existence? The real and essential mind is what is to be found when the entire load of gross obstructions and aberrations (i.e. sense impressions, memories, etc.) have been cleared away. Discerning this aspect of real mind, we shall discover that, unlike external objects, its true nature is devoid of form or colour; nor can we find any basis of truth for such false and deceptive notions as that the mind originated from this or that, or that it will move from here to there, or that it is located in such-and-such a place.

When it comes into contact with no object, mind is like a vast, boundless void, or like a serene, limitless ocean. When it encounters an object, it at once has cognizance of it like a mirror instantly reflecting a person who stands in front of it. The true nature of mind consists not only in taking clear cognizance of the object but also in communicating a concrete experience of that object to the one experiencing it. Normally, our forms of sense cognition, such as eye-consciousness, ear-consciousness, etc. perform their function on external phenomena in a manner involving gross distortion. Knowledge from sense cognition, being based on gross external phenomena, is also of a gross nature. When this type of gross stimulation is shut out, and when concrete experiences and clear cognizance arise from within, mind assumes the characteristics of an infinite void similar to the infinitude of space. But

---

* Extracted from *Opening the Mind and Generating a Good Heart* and *Universal Responsibility and the Good Heart Part 2*. Published by the Library of Tibetan Works & Archives.

this void is not to be taken as the true nature of mind.

We have become so habituated to consciousness of the form and colour of gross objects that, when we make concentrated introspection into the nature of mind it is, found to be a vast, limitless void free from any gross obscurity or other hindrances. Nevertheless, this does not mean that we have discerned the subtle true nature of the mind. What has been explained above concerns the state of mind in relation to the concrete experience and clear cognizance by the mind which are its function, but it describes only the relative nature of mind.

There are several aspects and states of mind. In other words there are many attributes related to it. Just as an onion consists of layer upon layer that can be peeled away, so does every sort of object have a number of layers; and this is no less true of the nature of mind as explained here—it, too, has layer within layer, state within state.

All compounded things are subject to disintegration. Since experience and knowledge are impermanent and subject to disintegration, the mind of which they are functions (nature) is not something that remains constant and eternal. From moment to moment, it undergoes change and disintegration. This transience of mind is one aspect of its nature. However, in its true nature, as we have observed, the mind has many aspects, including consciousness of concrete experience and cognizance of objects.

Now let us make a further examination in order to grasp the meaning of the subtle essence of such a mind. Mind came into existence because of its own cause. To deny that the origination of mind is dependent on a cause, or to say that it is a designation given as a means of recognizing the nature of mind aggregates, is not correct. To our superficial observance, mind, which has concrete experience and clear cognizance as its nature, appears to be a powerful, independent, subjective, complete, ruling entity. However, deeper analysis will reveal that this mind, possessing as it does the function of experience and cognizance, is not a self-created entity, but is dependent on other factors for its existence. Hence it depends on something other than itself. This non-independent quality of the mind substance is its true-nature which, in turn, is the ultimate reality of the self.

Of the other two aspects i.e. the ultimate true nature of mind and a knowledge of that ultimate true nature, the former is the base, and the latter is an attribute. Mind (self) is the basis, and all its different states are attributes. However, the basis and its attributes have, from the first, pertained to the same single essence. The non–self-created (depending on a cause other than itself) mind (basis) and its essence, shunyata, have unceasingly existed as the one, same, inseparable essence from beginningless beginning. The nature of shunyata pervades all elements. However, as we are now, since we cannot grasp or comprehend the indestructible, natural, ultimate reality (shunyata) of our own minds, we continue to commit errors and our defects persist.

Taking mind as the subject and mind's ultimate reality as its object one will arrive at a proper comprehension of the true essence of mind, i.e. its ultimate reality. And when, after prolonged, patient meditation one comes to perceive and grasp at the knowledge of mind's ultimate reality which is devoid of dual characteristics, one will gradually be able to exhaust the delusions and defects of the central and secondary minds such as wrath, love of ostentation, jealousy, envy, and so on.

Failure to identify the true nature of mind will be overcome through an acquisition of the power to comprehend its ultimate reality. This will, in turn, eradicate lust and hatred and all other secondary delusions emanating from the basic ones. Consequently, there will be no occasion for accumulating negative karma. By this means the creation of (evil) karma affecting future lives will be eliminated; one will be able to increase the quality and quantity of meritorious causal conditioning and to eradicate the creation of harmful causal conditioning affecting future lives-apart from the bad karma accumulated earlier.

In the practice of gaining a perfect knowledge of the true nature of mind, strenuous and concentrated mental efforts are required. In our normal condition as it is at present, when our mind comes into contact with something it is immediately drawn to it. This makes comprehension impossible. Therefore, in order to acquire this power, the maximum effort is the first imperative. For example, a big river flowing over a wide expanse of shallows will have very little force; but when it passes through a steep gorge, all the water is concentrated in a narrow space and therefore flows with great force. For a similar reason all the mental distractions which draw the mind away from the object of contemplation are to be avoided and the mind kept steadily fixed upon it. Unless this is done, the practice for gaining a proper understanding of the nature of mind will be a total failure.

To make the mind docile, it is essential for us to discipline and control it well. Speech and bodily activities which accompany mental processes must not be allowed to run on in an indiscreet, unbridled, random way. Just as a trainer disciplines and calms a wild and wilful steed by subjecting it to skilful and prolonged training, so must the wild, wandering, random activities of body and speech be tamed to make them docile, righteous, and skilful. Therefore the teachings of the Lord Buddha comprise three graded categories, that is, Shila (Training in Higher Conduct), Samadhi (Training in Higher Meditation) and Prajna (Training in Higher Wisdom), all of them for disciplining the mind.

A person so trained will be endowed with the wonderful quality of being able to bear patiently the miseries and suffering which are the fruit of his past karma. He will regard his misfortunes as blessings in disguise, for they will enlighten him as to the meaning of nemesis (karma) and convince him of the need to concentrate on performing only meritorious deeds. If his past (evil) karma has not as yet borne fruit, it will still be possible for him to obliterate this unripe karma by utilizing the strength of the four powers, namely: 1. Determination to attain the status of Buddhahood; 2. Determination to eschew demeritorious deeds even at the cost of his life; 3. The performance of meritorious deeds; and 4. Repentance.

Such is the way to attain immediate happiness, to pave the way for attaining liberation in future, and to help avoid the accumulation of further demerits. There are some who do not understand the Dharma, or who know a little but do not grasp the reasoning perfectly, who may think that the present mind depends simply on this body and that since past and future lives cannot be seen directly they do not exist. Such an opinion either maintains that if something exists it must be seen directly, or that the mind is produced in dependence on the body and that since the body is formed in dependence on the four elements, previous lives do not exist. It is thought that at the time of death the body reverts to the four principal elements, while the mind vanishes like a rainbow in the sky and that therefore future lives do not exist. Others, asserting that the mind is dependent on the body, consider that as the ability to intoxicate is an attribute of alcohol, so the mind is the attribute of the body. Others think that like the brightness of a lamp, the mind is a product of the body or that like a drawing on a wall the mind is a decoration of the body.

Essentially, all these views assert that in this life it is not necessary for the mind which is produced at the time of birth to be generated from a corresponding mind, because it is born from inanimate elements. By way of example, it is likewise thought that intoxication resulting from drinking alcohol and the fire produced with a magnifying glass, etc., are results which arise from incongruent causes. Similarly, some dialecticians assert the non-existence of causality based on incorrect reasoning, stating that there is no agent creating the roundness of peas, the sharpness of thorns, nor the splendour of a peacock's tail, while it may be observed that the miser who never gives becomes rich, that killers live long, and so forth.

Past and future lives certainly exist, for the following reasons: certain ways of thinking from last year, the year before that and even from childhood can be recollected now. This clearly establishes that there existed awareness previous to the present continuity of awareness of an adult. Likewise, the first instant of consciousness of this life is not produced without cause, nor is it born from something permanent, neither is it produced from a solid, inanimate, incongruent substantial cause, therefore it must surely be produced from a congruent substantial cause. In what way are they congruent? Since a moment of mind is an awareness which is clear and knowing, it is preceded by a similar moment of mind which was clear and knowing. It is not feasible that such a preceding awareness be produced other than on the basis of a previous birth. Otherwise, if the physical body alone were the substantial cause of mind, then the absurd consequences of a dead body having a mind and a change in the body necessitating a change in consciousness would also ensue.

The substantial cause of mind is that which is suitable to be transformed into the nature of mind. Although the physical body may act as an auxiliary cause of subtle change in the mind, it is impossible for it to be a substantial cause. Something inanimate can never transform into mind, nor can mind transform into something inanimate. As an illustration, it is impossible for what is not space to transform into space, or for space itself to change into that whose nature is not space, and the changes in a non-physical mind are similar. Thus, with reference to the present physical body and non-physical mind, the substantial cause of the body is the blood and semen produced by the parents, but the parents' minds can never be the substantial cause of the present mind. For example, it is possible for a dull and foolish child to be born to intelligent parents, no matter how educated they are.

Therefore, in reality the mind flowing from a previous life acts as the substantial cause of this mind and the blood and semen of our present parents act as the substantial cause of this body. As a relationship between the two was established by an action in former lives, a relationship exists between the mind and body of this life. Due to that, even a newborn baby or calf immediately after birth begins to eat or suck at the mother's breast without being taught. This is an indication of instincts left in the mind from previous lives.

TWENTY

PRACTICE OF CALM ABIDING*

Calm abiding meditation should be achieved first. Calm abiding is that mind which has overcome distraction to external objects, and which spontaneously and continuously turns toward the object of meditation with bliss and pliancy.

After properly fulfilling the preparatory practices, you should engage in the actual meditation, which consists of calm abiding and special insight. What is this calm abiding meditation? It is that state of mind that naturally attends to the object of meditation as a result of pacifying distraction to external objects.

Besides that, it gradually eliminates the defects of the body and mind due to its being free from mental dullness and excitement. 'With bliss and pliancy' refers to these physical and mental qualities that a meditator develops. In the process of meditation, mental pliancy is developed first and is followed by physical pliancy. Interestingly, physical bliss is generated after that, followed by mental bliss. When the mind is conjoined with bliss, it is known as calm abiding meditation. What is special insight?

That which properly examines suchness from within a state of calm abiding is special insight. *The Cloud of Jewels Sutra* reads, 'Calm abiding meditation is a single-pointed mind; special insight makes specific analysis of the ultimate.'

---

* From *Stages of Meditation* by HH The Dalai Lama, translated by Geshe Lobsang Jordhem, Losang Choephel Ganchenpa and Jeremy Russell, published by Rider and reprinted by permission of The Random House Group Ltd.

After developing the ability to engage in calm abiding meditation, the meditator does not single-pointedly place the mind on the object, but starts examining it. The object of meditation here is primarily ultimate truth, but conventional phenomena are not excluded. The concentration that generates physical and mental bliss by the force of analysing the object is special insight. Thereafter, a union of calm abiding and special insight is attained.

Calm abiding and special insight are not differentiated according to their objects of concentration. They can both take conventional and ultimate truth as objects. There is calm abiding meditation that focuses on the ultimate truth, and there is special insight that meditates on conventional truth. For instance, there is calm abiding meditation in which the mind is single-pointedly placed on emptiness. Special insight also meditates on conventional phenomena such as the subtle and grosser aspects of the meditative paths.

In general, the difference between these two types of meditation is that calm abiding is a concentrative meditation and special insight an analytical one. The Perfection Vehicle and the first three classes of tantra share this notion. According to the highest tantra, special insight is a concentrative meditation. This is a unique mode of understanding within the context of which special insight operates fully as a concentrative meditation. On the other hand, the Great Seal of Mahamudra of the Kagyu tradition and the Great Accomplishment, or Dzogchen, of the Nyingma tradition deal only with analytical meditation. Also, from the *Unraveling of the Thought Sutra*:

'Maitreya asked, 'O Buddha, how should (people) thoroughly search for calm abiding meditation and gain expertise in special insight?' The Buddha answered, 'Maitreya, I have given the following teachings to Bodhisattvas: sutras, melodious praises, prophetic teaching, verses, specific instructions, advice from specific experiences, expressions of realization, legends, birth tales, extensive teachings, established doctrine, and instructions.

'Bodhisattvas should properly listen to these teachings, remember their contents, train in verbal recitation, and thoroughly examine them mentally. With perfect comprehension, they should go alone to remote areas and reflect on these teachings and continue to focus their minds upon them. They should focus mentally only on those topics that they have reflected about and maintain this continuously. That is called mental engagement.'

In calm abiding meditation, you single-pointedly focus the mind on the essential and summary points of the teaching. The Buddha's teachings, as described in these twelve categories, are extensive and cover vast topics such as those concerning the mental and physical aggregates, elements, sources of perception, and so forth. In the context of calm abiding meditation, you are not to elaborate, but are to attend to the essential nature or the point of the teaching, whether it be emptiness or impermanence, and contemplate its nature. On the other hand, meditation on special insight is analytical. The meditator elaborates on the identity, origin, and other characteristics of the objects of meditation, such as the aggregates, elements, sources of perception, and so forth.

When the mind has been repeatedly engaged in this way and physical and mental pliancy have been achieved, that mind is called calm abiding. This is how Bodhisattvas properly seek the calmly abiding mind.

Through the process of meditation, the practitioner initially actualizes mental pliancy. This is preceded by a kind of heaviness of the brain that is in fact a sign of relinquishing the defects of the mind. After generating mental pliancy, physical pliancy is actualized. This is the direct opponent of the physical defects. Physical bliss is generated as a result, and from this mental bliss is generated.

When the Bodhisattva has achieved physical and mental pliancy and abides only in them, he eliminates mental distraction. The phenomenon that has been contemplated as the object of inner single-pointed concentration should be analyzed and regarded as like a reflection. This reflection or image, which is the object of single-pointed concentration, should be thoroughly discerned as an object of knowledge. It should be completely investigated and thoroughly examined. Practise patience and take delight in it. With proper analysis, observe and understand it. This is what is known as special insight. Thus, Bodhisattvas are skilled in the ways of special insight.

Generation of a positive motivation is crucial. The practitioner should recreate this positive attitude throughout the process of practice. Think, 'I shall listen to this holy text by the great Kamalashila in order to attain unsurpassed Buddhahood for the sake of all sentient beings as vast as space.' It is highly important that we realize the rarity and preciousness of the human life. It is on this basis that we can attain both temporary and ultimate goals. This life as a free and fortunate human being is a great occasion and we should take full advantage of it. The root and foundation for walking the ultimate goal of enlightenment is generation of the altruistic thought, and this in turn derives from compassion. Other complementary practices essential in this context are the practice of generosity and other meritorious deeds, and training in concentration, which is the union of calm abiding and special insight.

Before generating compassion for other sentient beings, the practitioner must think about the sufferings of cyclic existence in general, and in particular the sufferings of the different realms within the cycle of existence. Through this process of contemplation, the practitioner comes to appreciate the unbearable nature of the miseries of the cycle of existence. This naturally leads you to find out how to abandon them. Is there an occasion when we can be completely free of suffering? What methods need to be applied in order to relinquish suffering? When you earnestly engage in such an inquiry and examine the question well, you will realize what causes sufferings. The source of suffering is the mental defilement that arises from action and disturbing emotions. This is temporary and the mind can be completely separated from it. The practitioner comes to realize that the Noble Truth of cessation can be attained with the pacification, or elimination, of suffering and its causes. The corollary is that the individual develops renunciation, wishing for freedom from suffering and its causes. And when you wish for other sentient beings also to gain freedom from

167

suffering and its causes, you are taking a major step toward generating compassion.

First a practitioner should train in the stages of the common path and then gradually incorporate the stages of the greater path. This is a sound and correct mode of actualizing a spiritual career.

After having performed the preparatory practices, you undertake the training in the two types of awakening mind. These two are the conventional and ultimate awakening minds. With generation of the conventional awakening mind, a practitioner engages in the deeds of a Bodhisattva, which include the six perfections. Meditation on the ultimate awakening mind is done by generating a transcendental wisdom directly realizing emptiness. Such a wisdom is a meditative stabilization that is a union of calm abiding and special insight. This means that while focusing single-pointedly you can simultaneously analyse the nature of emptiness.

With respect to developing calm abiding meditation, the practitioner is at liberty to choose the object of meditation that he or she feels to be appropriate and comfortable. He or she should then concentrate the mind on the object, not allowing it to become distracted to external objects, nor letting it fall into the pits of dullness. He or she should aim to attain single-pointed concentration conjoined with sharp clarity.

Dullness occurs when the mind is dominated by laziness, and lacks alertness and sharpness. Even in everyday life we may describe our minds as 'unclear' or 'sluggish.' When dullness is present, the meditator is not holding firmly onto the object, and so the meditation is not effective.

If the mind is found to be dull due to sleepiness and mental torpor or if you fear that dullness is approaching, then the mind should attend to a supremely delightful object such as an image of the Buddha, or a notion of light. In this process, having dispelled dullness the mind should try to see the object very clearly.

Mental torpor and dullness occur in a mutual cause and effect relationship. When a meditator is beset by fogginess, the mind and body feel heavy. The practitioner loses clarity, and the mind becomes functionally ineffective and unproductive. Dullness is a form of mental depression, so to counteract it employ techniques that can help uplift the mind. Some of the more effective ways are to think about joyful objects, such as the wonderful qualities of a Buddha, or to think about the rarity of the precious human life and the opportunities it provides. You should draw inspiration from these thoughts to engage in a fruitful meditation.

In developing calm abiding, the other main obstacle to be overcome is mental excitement. This is occurs when the mind is in a state of excitement, chasing the objects of desire and recalling past experiences of joy and happiness. Grosser forms of mental excitement will cause the mind to lose the object of concentration completely: in subtler forms only a portion of the mind attends to the object. The solution to this problem is to meditate on impermanence, suffering, and so forth, which can help the mind to settle down.

> You should recognize the presence of dullness when the mind cannot see the object very clearly, when you feel as if you are blind or in a dark place or that you have dosed your eyes. If, while you are in meditation, your mind chases after qualities of external objects such as form, or turns its attention to other phenomena, or is distracted by desire for an object you have previously experienced, or if you suspect distraction is approaching, reflect that ail composite phenomena are impermanent. Think about suffering and so forth, topics that will temper the mind.

The antidote to mental dullness and excitement is introspection. The function of introspection is to observe whether or not the mind is abiding stably on the object of meditation. The function of mindfulness is to keep the mind on the object; once this is achieved, mental introspection has to watch whether the mind remains on the object or not. The stronger your mindfulness, the stronger your mental introspection will be. For example, if you constantly remember, 'It is not good to do this,' 'This is not helpful,' and so forth, you are maintaining introspection. It is important to be mindful of the negative aspects of your daily life and you should be alert to their occurrence. Therefore, one of the unique features and functions of mental introspection is to assess the condition of your mind and body, to judge whether the mind remains stably on the object or not.

> In this process, distraction should be eliminated and with the rope of mindfulness and alertness the elephant-like mind should be fastened to the tree of the object of meditation. When you find that the mind is free of dullness and excitement and that it naturally abides on the object, you should relax your effort and remain neutral as long as it continues thus.

~

TWENTY-ONE

GENERATING THE MIND OF

ENLIGHTENMENT*

To generate the mind of enlightenment we reflect on the fact that, just like ourselves, all other sentient beings equally have the natural tendency to desire happiness and the wish to avoid suffering. The only difference is that I am a single person whereas the others are limitless in number. In other words one is in the minority; the others are the majority.

Again, reflect that just as I want happiness, so too they want happiness; I do not want suffering, and they do not want suffering; and that there is a clear relation between me and them. We depend on others; without others we cannot gain any happiness: not in the past, not today, and not in the future.

If we think more about others' benefit and welfare, ultimately it is we ourselves who will reap the benefit.

Thinking on these lines we find that when comparing the two, ourselves and others, the others are more important. We come to the conclusion that the fate of ourselves is a question of only one person. If it is the case that one has to undergo suffering in order to bring about happiness for the infinite number of others, then it is really worthwhile to suffer. On the other hand, if in order to achieve happiness for one then many others have to suffer, then something is wrong in the perspective.

To approach the practice of cultivating the mind of enlightenment, the aspiration to achieve enlightenment for the sake of all sentient beings,

---

* From *Cultivating a Daily Meditation*, Library of Tibetan Works and Archives, 1991.

first we have to achieve equanimity. Equanimity in this context means to cultivate an equal state of mind towards all sentient beings, one that is not affected by desire for friends, hatred for enemies, or indifference towards neutral people. We are seeking an equal state of mind towards all sentient beings.

Generally speaking, there are four types of birth: birth from the womb, from an egg, from heat, and miraculous birth.

In birth from the womb or from an egg, we need a mother. Today, for example, I could feel, though my mother of this lifetime passed away some years ago, that at one or another time all of you have been my mother. We may logically not be certain about it, but we can develop the feeling that you have been my mother.

On the basis of that, we should reflect on kindnesses received when these beings were my mother in past lives. In the same way, we then meditate on others as having been our own fathers or close relatives or friends of past lives.

If that is the case, then we should remember that their kindness towards us must have been boundless. Since the number of our lifetimes is beginningless, we must have been conceived limitless times, on many occasions a child to each of them. That is the third stage.

The fourth is the special recollection of kindness. This really extends not only to our close relatives but to all sentient beings.

Our very survival depends entirely on others. For example, if our clothes are of cotton, cotton comes from the fields, from those labourers who worked on them not only in this generation but in previous generations. Then our houses, this room for example. Today it is rather hot, but otherwise we are very comfortable. This comfort is the result of hardships endured by many workers who gave their energy, who sweated and worked until they had sores on their hands and had bent backs.

Up to the present day our survival has depended on food. Thinking of myself, if I imagine all those loaves of bread I have consumed piled up, they would make quite a mountain. And the milk I have drunk would make a pond. If one is not vegetarian, then one consumes another mountain of meat. Vegetarians eat all sorts of fruits and vegetables. All this does not come from the sky. It does not appear from nowhere, but is produced through the hard work of many labourers.

And people's big names. Even fame comes from others. If there were only one single person, then there would be no possibility of becoming famous. Fame comes through many mouths. That also depends on others.

Food depends on others; clothing depends on others; housing depends on others. We may think, 'Oh, but I paid for all these things, I bought them for a certain amount of money. Without money I cannot get food or anything else.'

But that money did not come from your own mouth either. It came through the hands of many people. The very existence of our lives depends entirely on others. Then you may feel, 'Yes, these are facts, but the others did not deliberately help me. They did it as a by-product of their efforts to survive.'

That is true. But I cherish many things that do not return my concern. For example, if my watch fell down on the floor and broke, I would feel some kind of a loss. This does not mean that this watch has some feeling for me or is kind to me. It is useful to me, so I care.

In the same way, all those people may not have done anything for us deliberately, but as their work is useful to us we should recognize and remember their kindness. We must be aware of the fact that although others do not have the motivation to help us, we depend on their contribution and efforts for our own survival.

Thinking on these lines and reflecting on the kindness of others becomes a very extensive practice.

The practice of compassion, kindness and altruism is something very excellent. Sometimes I am fascinated by the power of the human brain. Our human heart can produce such an altruistic state of mind, one that can hold others more dear than oneself. These things are really remarkable.

We cannot practise like this without other beings. One of the most important conditions is living beings. Without others we cannot practise compassion; without others we cannot practise love, genuine kindness, altruism, the mind of enlightenment.

There is no question about it. We do respect the Buddhas, bodhisattvas and the higher beings, but in order to cultivate these good qualities, sentient beings are more important than Buddhas. On the ordinary level, our very survival depends on the kindness of other sentient beings, and even the realization of the path that one travels during spiritual purification depends on others.

For example, in order to practise genuine compassion or altruism, we need tolerance. Without tolerance, it is impossible to practise. Anger and hatred are the greatest obstacles to compassion and love. To minimize anger and hatred, tolerance is the key factor. In order to practise tolerance we need an enemy. The enemy will not want to help us deliberately, but because of our enemy's actions we get the opportunity to practise tolerance.

The golden opportunity is when we face an enemy. All sentient beings, but particularly our enemies, are very important for our mental development. Our spiritual practice depends entirely on others, and our very survival also depends on others. From that point of view, not only our close friends but all sentient beings are something very important to us.

That is the fourth step in the meditation.

The fifth step is about how to develop the thought of repaying the kindness of others.

The sixth step is equalizing oneself with others. The meaning of this is to realize that just as we ourselves do not desire suffering and wish for happiness; in the same way other sentient beings have the same natural tendencies. Thinking like this, we develop this equality of equalizing oneself with others.

We should think of others as part of our own body. In times of danger you need to protect all parts of your body.

Your attitude to other sentient beings should be that they are 'mine'. Then when something hurts another being it will hurt us. When we expand that kind of feeling to all sentient beings, then they all become like members of our own family. If anyone gets hurt, we feel it as we feel our own pain. This is the sixth stage.

The seventh stage is to reflect on the many disadvantages of the self-cherishing thought. I often tell people that a very self-centered motivation, although it comes from the selfish wish for something good for oneself, in the end brings many problems. Killing, stealing, lying: all these actions are bad, not only from the religious point of view, but also according to the law. All these negative actions arise due to selfishness.

On a human level, fighting between husband and wife, parents and children, neighbour and neighbour, nation and nation, is due to internal confusion. All these negative, unfortunate actions are ultimately due to selfishness.

On the other hand, altruism is really the key source of happiness. If we help other people, if we show other people openness and sincerity, then we will greatly benefit ourselves as well. For example, we will easily make friends.

I often feel that though we Tibetans are refugees, and are stateless people, as long as we are sincere and honest and also have a smile we will easily make friends. Even if we end up in the Soviet Union or wherever, we will find good friends. But if we are selfish and look down on other people, then we could not find friends anywhere.

Cultivating the thought of cherishing others more than ourselves produces great benefits. Our spiritual development, achievement of higher states, higher rebirth in future lives, and also the achievement of liberation and enlightenment all depend on cherishing others.

The ninth stage is the actual thought of exchanging oneself with others. This is a state of mind which was initiated in an earlier process. Here we have the natural feeling to benefit other sentient beings.

Here we engage in the meditation of 'giving and taking.' We visualize taking on ourselves the difficulties of others, which is to emphasize our practice of compassion. Then we visualize giving other sentient beings both happiness and its causes. This strengthens our practice of love.

Next follows what is known as the special attitude, the thought of universal responsibility. This is facilitated as a result of the earlier meditations.

It is this thought that eventually gives rise to the mind of enlightenment, the aspiration to achieve highest enlightenment for the sake of all sentient beings. This is the eleventh and final step of the meditation.

In this system both the tradition for cultivating the mind of enlightenment as explained by Asanga and the tradition explained by Shantideva are integrated.

On the basis of the above motivation recite the following verse.

To the Buddha, the Dharma and the Supreme Community
I turn for refuge until enlightenment is gained.
By the strength of my practices, like the six perfections,
May enlightenment be attained for the benefit of all.

Repeat these words with a strong feeling of genuine altruism, the words acting like fuel so that the actual fire burns within yourself.

Repeat the passage three times or more. This can be done in English or your own mother tongue.

TWENTY-TWO

EIGHT VERSES FOR TRAINING THE MIND*

At this point I would like to use a simple text as the basis of our discussion.

It is known as *The Eight Verses for Training the Mind*, and deals with the principles of developing the Bodhisattva spirit. It was written many centuries ago.

I received an oral transmission and teachings on *The Eight Verses for Training the Mind* from Kyabje Trijang Rinpoche, my late Junior Tutor. I have been reciting these verses every day for more than thirty-five years, and contemplating their meanings.

The composer of this text, the Kadampa master Geshe Langri Thangpa, saw the practice of the mind of enlightenment, and in particular the meditation of exchanging self with others, as most important throughout his life.

I shall explain the eight verses briefly.

With the determination to accomplish
The highest welfare of all sentient beings,
Who excel even the wish-fulfilling jewel,
May I at all times hold them dear.

Sentient beings' kindness to us is not confined to the achievement of our final goal, enlightenment. The fulfilment of our temporary aims, such as the experience of happiness, also depends on their kindness.

Therefore sentient beings are superior even to the wish-fulfilling jewel. So we make the prayer, 'May I at all times hold them dear.' We

---

★ From *Cultivating a Daily Meditation*, Library of Tibetan Works and Archives, 1991.

should regard them as being more precious than a wish-fulfilling jewel.

> Whenever I associate with others
> May I think of myself as the lowest of all
> And from the depth of my heart
> Hold the others as supreme.

When we meet others we should not think of ourselves as superior and look down on or pity them, but think of ourselves as more humble than they are. We should hold them dear and revere them because they have a capacity equal to the activities of the Buddhas to grant us happiness and enlightenment.

> In all actions may I search into my mind,
> And as soon as delusions arise
> That endanger myself and others,
> May I firmly face and avert them.

When we engage in ritual practice, we sometimes encounter obstacles. These obstacles are not external but internal; they are delusions of our own mind. The real enemy, the destroyer of our happiness, is within ourselves.

When through training and effort we are able to discipline and control our mind, then we will gain real peace and tranquillity.

Therefore Buddha said, 'You are your own master.' Everything rests on your own shoulders, depends on yourself.

Although in the practice of the mind of enlightenment we have to restrain from all negative ways, primarily we must avoid anger. Anger can never produce happiness, whereas attachment can bring about the experience of happiness in certain cases.

We have a saying in Tibet: 'If you lose your temper and get angry, bite your knuckles.' This means that if you lose your temper, do not show it to others; rather say to yourself: 'Leave it.'

> When I see beings of wicked nature,
> Oppressed by violent misdeeds and afflictions,

May I hold them dear
As if I had found a rare and precious treasure.

Some people, when they see others who are exhausted by sufferings and oppressed by delusions, tend to avoid these experiences because they are afraid of getting involved and carried away. Bodhisattvas, instead of avoiding such situations, face them bravely as an opportunity to bring happiness to other sentient beings.

When others out of envy treat me badly
With slander, abuse and the like,
May I suffer the loss and
Offer the victory to them.

When other beings, especially those who hold a grudge against you, abuse and harm you out of envy, you should not abandon them, but hold them as objects of your greatest compassion and take care of them.

Thus the practitioner should take the 'loss' on himself or herself, and offer the 'victory' to the others.

Practitioners of the mind of enlightenment take the loss on themselves and offer the victory to others, not with the motivation to become virtuous themselves but rather with the motivation to help other sentient beings.

Since it is sometimes possible, however, that taking the loss and offering the victory to others can harm them in the long run, there are cases when you should not do it.

If a practitioner of altruism finds himself in such a situation, then induced by a strong motive to help others, he should actually do the opposite.

Think in these terms. When something unpleasant happens and you get irritated, you are the loser, since irritation immediately destroys your own mental peace and in the long run brings unwanted results. Yet if someone hurts you and you do not lose your mental peace, that is a victory.

If you become impatient and lose your temper, then you lose the

179

best part of the human brain, judgement of the situation. Once you are angry, almost mad with anger, then you cannot make correct decisions.

When your mind is calm you can analyse in a clearer way. Without losing your tranquillity, analyze the circumstances, and if necessary take counteractions. This is the spiritual meaning of loss and victory.

When the one whom I have helped
And benefitted with great hope
Hurts me badly, may I behold him
As my supreme guru.

When one among those whom you have benefitted repays your kindness in the wrong way, you might feel that you do not want to help him ever again. For the very reason that it is difficult not to hold this against him—and this is a great stumbling-block for the practitioner of altruism—it is emphasized that a practitioner should care specially for such a person.

A person who harms you should be seen not only as someone who needs your special care, but also as someone who is your spiritual guide. You will find that your enemy is your supreme teacher.

In short, may I directly and indirectly offer
Benefit and happiness to all my mothers.
May I secretly take upon myself the harmful actions
And suffering of my mothers.

Since others are infinite in number, and since you yourself are only one, no matter how superior you are, others become the more valuable. If you have some power of judgment, you will find that it is worthwhile to sacrifice yourself for the sake of others, that one person must not sacrifice infinite numbers of others for the sake of oneself.

Special visualization is valuable here. See yourself as a very selfish person, and in front of you a great number of sentient beings undergoing their sufferings. Visualize them actively experiencing their sufferings while you selfishly remain neutral and unbiased. Then see which side you want to take, theirs or your own.

If selfish politicians thought like this, then they would without hesitation join the majority.

Initially it is very difficult to decrease and control your selfish attitude. But if you persevere for a long time, you will be successful.

He who from the depth of his heart practises taking onto himself all the suffering and faults of the other sentient beings should also train in sharing with them all good qualities like virtues and happiness that he has in himself.

The above seven verses deal with the practice of the conventional mind of enlightenment, which is method. The eighth verse deals with the practice of the ultimate mind of enlightenment, which is wisdom.

By engaging in the practice of the conventional mind of enlightenment, one accumulates a store of merit; and by engaging in the practice of the ultimate mind of enlightenment one accumulates a store of wisdom.

With these two forces combined, one achieves as a result the two bodies of the Buddha: the Form Body, or *Rupakaya*; and the Truth Body, or *Dharmakaya*.

May all this remain undefiled by the stains of
Keeping in view the eight worldly principles.
May I, by perceiving all phenomena as illusory,
Unattached, be delivered from the bondage of samsara.

If someone undertakes such a practice motivated by worldly concerns like wishing for a long and healthy life in which he has happiness and achieves perfection, this is basically wrong. To undertake the practice hoping that people will call one a great religious practitioner is also definitely wrong. So is viewing the objects of one's compassion as truly existent.

You should undertake this practice with the understanding that all phenomena arc like illusions.

One understands that all phenomena are like illusions through negating their supposedly true existence, leaving behind what is mere imputation, label, designation. This is the Buddhist view.

Earlier we talked about view and conduct in Buddhism. This view is called dependent arising. Although there are many different levels of meaning to dependent arising, its final meaning approaches the understanding of emptiness.

Dependent arising establishes the evidence of something as not truly existent. By gaining a complete understanding of dependent arising, one has the strong conviction of the functioning of the conventions. Therefore one engages in the practice of the mind of enlightenment and accumulates the store of merit; and by focusing on emptiness, or non-true existence, one accumulates the store of wisdom.

Supported by this strong motivation of the mind of enlightenment, one engages in the practice of the six perfections, or paramitas: generosity, discipline, patience, joyous effort, concentration and wisdom.

The six perfections can also be considered under three headings as the three higher trainings.

The first of the three higher trainings is the practice of discipline. There are three ways to effect this. The one explained in the *Pratimoksha* or *Vinaya* is called individual liberation. The second is the discipline of Bodhisattvas, and the third the discipline of tantra.

The discipline of individual liberation is of two types, that of monks and that of lay-people.

Lay-people can take two types of precepts, either for one day or for the rest of their life.

All of the vows are based on refraining from the ten negative courses of action: killing, stealing, and sexual misconduct (these three being non-virtues of the body); lying, derisive talk, harsh words, and idle gossip (these four being verbal non-virtuous actions); and covetousness, harmful intent, and wrong views (the three non-virtuous actions of the mind).

The wrong views referred to are chiefly nihilistic views, but there are also other wrong views, like acceptance of an almighty creator.

The chief way to practise the discipline of the bodhisattvas is to refrain from cherishing oneself more than others. There are many different bodhisattva precepts.

Within the discipline of tantra, there are four classes of tantra; and for the two highest tantras, certain precepts have to be taken and observed. The main precepts are to refrain from ordinary appearances and from grasping at ordinariness.

In the practice of these three disciplines, the lower one should be taken as the basis for the next higher one. Having laid the foundation for discipline, one has to engage in the practice of the two remaining higher trainings: meditation and wisdom.

Although techniques for the practice of meditation and wisdom are explained in the Mahayana sutras, the techniques explained in tantra are considered by Tibetan Buddhists to be superior.

~

TWENTY-THREE

MEDITATION ON EMPTINESS*

To realize that all deceptive phenomena are the same in their nature of emptiness, we concentrate on emptiness. When meditation on the mind of enlightenment and also training in concentration have matured, then the practice of emptiness begins.

Generally it is not necessary to withdraw the appearance of the object when we meditate on emptiness, but as we are concerned here with tantric practices, the appearance of the objects is recommended to be withdrawn.

We can start this practice in either of two ways: we can first dissolve all appearances and then meditate on emptiness; or first meditate on emptiness and then dissolve all appearances of the objects.

Now to explain briefly the actual meditation on emptiness. Here it is very important to identify what is to be negated.

The major Buddhist schools accept what are known as the four Buddhist seals. These four are as follows:

All products are impermanent;
All contaminated phenomena are in the nature of suffering;
All phenomena are selfless and empty; and
Nirvana alone is peace.
Here selflessness refers to the emptiness of a self-sufficient person.

Selflessness of phenomena is explained only by the Mahayana schools: the Mind-Only and the Middle Way.

---

* From *Cultivating a Daily Meditation*, Library of Tibetan Works and Archives, 1991.

The Mind-Only School, by relying on the *Sutra Unravelling the Thought of Buddha*, propounds the existence of two types of phenomena. One is that although form, for example, is the referent object of conceptual thought, it is not the referent object of the consciousness realizing it as from its own side. It is only a label, a referent of the term form and also the conceptual thought which gives the label. Therefore the absence of form as the referent of the term is one type of emptiness.

The other type of emptiness is the negation of existence of external objects as existing apart from mental projections. The Mind-Only School says that external things do not exist, that they are only mental projections. The presentation of emptiness of the Middle Way School is different. Although followers of the Mind-Only School refute true existence of external objects, they believe in the true existence of the subjective mind.

Looking from the point of view of the Middle Way School, we find that the followers of Mind-Only have fallen into the extremes both of eternalism or absolutism and of nihilism. Because they do not accept external objects they have fallen into the extreme of nihilism; and since they accept a truly existent subjective mind, they have fallen into the extreme of absolutism.

According to the Middle Way School, both external phenomena and the subjective mind do not exist truly, but both exist conventionally.

Within the Middle Way School, there are two divisions. One part of the school says that although external phenomena are not truly existent in the sense that they are not the objects of consciousness which analyses its true nature, there is something on the part of the object, some kind of essence within the object itself that we can find on analysis and which justifies its having such conventionalities. For example, when they search for the person or the self, they will finally come up with the statement 'consciousness is the identity of the person,' or things like that. They say that something exists from the side of the object.

Then there is the other part of the school which says that phenomena do not exist truly in the sense that they are not the object of their consciousness which sees its reality; and at the same time, even when we analytically search for the essence or the convention of something, we cannot find what it is. That is the other part of the school. The view of the latter is the more profound one for the reason that it has fewer inconsistencies.

When we examine the theories of the other schools, we will find many logical contradictions within their systems.

When the Middle Way thinkers propound the theory of emptiness, they do so by employing different kinds of reasoning. One of them is the analysis of the course of phenomena, known as 'the diamond slivers of reasoning.' This reasoning analyses from the side of the effect of the thing.

Then there are reasonings where we search for four possibilities, analysing both from the point of view of cause and from the point of view of the effect.

Reasoning is known as the king of reasonings, the reason of independent arising.

Still a different reasoning is that which observes the absence of singularity and plurality by analysing the thing itself. Within the reasoning known as absence of singularity and plurality, there exist also different styles of observation.

Now I shall explain very briefly the meditation on emptiness within the reasoning of absence of singularity and plurality.

Firstly, in order to meditate on emptiness we have to identify the emptiness on which we are meditating, the thing to be negated. Unless we identify the object of negation, we cannot have the image of its absence.

For this it is more convenient first to reflect on one's own self. When you have this natural feeling of 'I go, I eat, I stay,' just contemplate what kind of self or 'I' appears to your mind. Then try different techniques. As I mentioned earlier try to recollect unpleasant situations where, for example, you were unjustly blamed for something; or pleasant situations where you were praised. During such experiences you had a very fluctuating state of mind, and at that time it seemed you could sense that I, that self, quite clearly.

When this 'I' appeared to your mind, did it appear as something separate from your body and mind, like an independent entity? That type of 'I' or self, which appears to you so vividly that you feel you could put your finger on it, something independent from your own body and mind, that type of 'I' is the most misconceived projection, and that is the object of negation.

This is the first essential point, identifying what is to be negated.

The second essential point is to reflect whether, if such an 'I' or independent self exists, it does so as one with the body and mind; or truly separate from them; or if there is a third way in which it can exist.

You have to look at the different possibilities, and then you will find that, if it truly exists as an independent entity, it should be either one with the body and mind, the aggregates, or it should be separate, because there is no third way of existence.

That is the second essential point.

The choices are that it is either one with the aggregates or totally different from them.

Now reflect that, if it is one with the aggregates, then just as the self is one, body and mind should be one, because they are identified with the self. If the self is separate, then just as the aggregates are manifold, in the same way the self should be manifold.

Then contemplate that if this independent self or 'I' existed as something distinctly separate, truly apart from the aggregates, then it should be findable even after the aggregates ceased to exist. But this is not the case.

When you search by this mode of inquiry you will find that such an 'I' cannot be identified from the side of the aggregates.

Reasoning thus you will find that the independent 'I' or self that previously appeared to your consciousness is a misconception or projection. It does not exist.

For example, at dawn or dusk, when there is not much light, someone might get frightened and might mistake a coiled rope for a snake. Apart from the image of the snake in the mind of that person, there is no sense of true existence of snake on the part of the object, the rope.

It is the same with the aggregates. When you perceive the appearance of self in them, although such appearance seems to arise from within the aggregates, there is not the slightest particle which can be identified as the self within the aggregates. Just as in the earlier example wherein the snake is only a misconceived projection, there is no true existence of the snake.

In the same way, when we have the appearance or apprehension of person as distinct from the aggregates, from the side of the aggregates there is no true existence of the person; there is only a label imputed on the aggregates. As long as there is no essence existing on the part of the object concerned, in both cases they are the same.

As far as the status of the object from the side of the object is concerned, there is no difference at all between them. The difference has to come from the perceiving mind, from the side of the subject. When we label that coiled rope as a snake that is a mistaken convention. After awhile the sun rises, we get a clear view of the object, and can dispel the misconception of that rope as a snake by valid cognition, a different type of consciousness.

That label of snake on the coiled rope can be harmful. However, in the case of a person although there is no objective reality, if you label the aggregates as the person, it serves the purpose of the convention. There is no other type of consciousness which can dispel that.

However, if we were to say that therefore there is no person at all, then our own experiences would contradict our false conclusion.

Hence the existence of the person has to be justified only from the subjective consciousness, which gives the label. For this reason things are said to exist only nominally, there is no objective reality.

TWENTY-FOUR

TANTRA-DEITY YOGA*

The special purpose of Tantra is to provide a faster path so that qualified practitioners can be of service to others more quickly. In Tantra the power of imagination is harnessed to meditation in a practice called deity yoga. In this practice you imagine (1) replacing your mind as it ordinarily appears, full of troubling emotions, with a mind of pure wisdom motivated by compassion; (2) substituting your body as it ordinarily appears (composed of flesh, blood, and bone) with a body fashioned from compassionately motivated wisdom; (3) developing a sense of a pure self that depends on purely appearing mind and body in an ideal environment, fully engaged in helping others. As this distinctive practice of Tantra calls for visualizing yourself with a Buddha's body, activities, resources, and surroundings, it is called 'taking imagination as the spiritual path.'

Let us consider a qualm about this practice. You are considering yourself to have Buddha qualities, which you presently do not have. Is this, then, a correct type of meditative consciousness? Yes. Your mind is involved in understanding reality, out of which you are appearing as a deity. Therefore, your mind, from this viewpoint, is correct. Also, you are *purposely* imagining yourself as having a divine body even if you do not presently possess one. This is an imaginative meditation; you are not convinced from the depths that you actually have pure mind, body, and selfhood. Rather, based in clear imagination of ideal body and mind, you are cultivating the sense of being a deity, compassionately helping others.

---

* From *How to Practice—The Way to a Meaningful Life*, translated and edited by Jeffrey Hopkins, published by Rider. Reprinted by permission of the Random House Group Ltd.

To be a *special* trainee of Tantra—that is to say, the kind of trainee for whom Buddha specifically set forth the practice of Tantra—a practitioner must have sharp faculties and have already attained stable wisdom realizing emptiness, or be ready for speedy activation of this wisdom. The requirements for just practising Tantra are less rigorous; still, to engage in Tantra at any level demands a powerful intention to become enlightened for the sake of others, and a feeling that this needs to be done very quickly.

At the beginning of Tantric practice, the basic way to develop calm abiding is to meditate on your own body as if it were that of a deity. When you meditate on a divine body, first you meditate on emptiness, gaining as much awareness of the emptiness of inherent existence as you can. When you have acclimated to this state, you use that very mind itself as the basis out of which the deity appears. The mind, realizing emptiness, appears as the deity and his or her surroundings. First you meditate on emptiness; out of that the deity appears; then you concentrate on the deity.

In this way, deity yoga combines wisdom and compassionate motivation; a single consciousness realizes emptiness and also appears compassionately in the form of an altruistic deity. In the Sutra system, although there is a union of wisdom and compassionate motivation, the practice of wisdom is only *affected* by the force of the practice of motivation, and the practice of motivation is only *affected* by the force of the practice of wisdom; they are not contained within one consciousness. A distinguishing feature of Tantra is that they are. Inclusion of motivation and wisdom within one consciousness is what makes Tantra's progress so swift.

When I was a young boy, Tantra was just a matter of blind faith. At age twenty-four I lost my own country, and then after coming to India started really reading Tsong-khapa's explanations on emptiness. Then, after moving to Dharamsala, I put more effort into the study and practice of the stages of the path, emptiness, and Tantra. So it was only in my late twenties after gaining some experience of emptiness that deity yoga made sense.

One time in the main temple in Dharamsala I was performing the ritual of imagining myself as a deity of Highest Yoga Tantra, called

Guhyasamaja. My mind continuously remained on the recitation of the ritual text, and when the words 'I myself' came, I completely forgot about my usual self in relation to my combination of mind and body. Instead, I had a very clear sense of 'I' in relation to the new, pure combination of mind and body of Guhyasamaja that I was imagining. Since this is the type of self-identification that is at the heart Tantric yoga, the experience confirmed for me that with enough time I could definitely achieve the extraordinary, deep states mentioned in the scriptures.

Initiation

To practice Tantra it is especially important to gain access to the transmission of blessings from previous great beings. Blessings also exist in Sutra practice, but they are crucial in Tantra. The first means of entry to these blessings is through the door of initiation. There are four classes of Tantras—Action, Performance, Yoga, and Highest Yoga Tantra—each with it own initiations to ripen the mind for practice, and each with its own meditations.

Where do you receive initiation? In a mandala, comprised of ideal surroundings and divine residents which all are manifestations of compassion and wisdom. There are mandalas of varying complexity for all four Tantras. Some are painted. Others are constructed from coloured sands, and still others comprise a special class of concentration mandalas.

In order to receive initiation and to take vows in a mandala of Yoga Tantra or Highest Yoga Tantra, the lama conducting the ceremony must have the full complement of qualifications. All four sets of Tantras place special emphasis on the attributes of the lama, in keeping with Buddha's detailed descriptions of teachers' qualifications for the various stages of the path. Remember also Buddha's admonition to rely not just on the person but on the doctrine. You should not be overwhelmed by a teacher's reputation. Most important, the teacher must know the doctrine, the practices, well.

Pledges and Vows

In the two lower Tantra sets—Action and Performance— there is no clear indication that Tantric vows must be taken upon initiation; nevertheless, there are many pledges to be kept. In the two higher Tantra sets—Yoga and Highest Yoga—after receiving initiation with all of its facets, you must take Tantric vows in addition to pledges. Yoga Tantra and Highest Yoga Tantra have fourteen basic vows as well as lists of infractions to guard against, but as they differ in the respective paths, even the basic vows differ slightly. Since the practice of Tantra is mainly concerned with overcoming the *appearance* of yourself and your surroundings as ordinary (in order to overcome the *conception* of these as ordinary), you visualize yourself to have a Buddha's body, compassionate activities, resources, and abode. Therefore, most of the pledges are concerned with substituting ideal for ordinary appearances, and restraining your own estimation of yourself, your companions, your environment, and your activities as being ordinary.

Except for the particular vow of individual liberation that lasts for just twenty-four hours, all of the other vows of individual liberation are taken for an entire lifetime (although it is possible to rescind one's vows and give back one's ordination). By contrast, Bodhisattva and Tantric vows extend right through to the time of highest enlightenment, as long as one has not committed a root infraction.

First one assumes the morality of individual liberation, then Bodhisattva morality, and finally Tantric morality. Householders who take the Bodhisattva and Tantric vows keep a householder's version of the vows of individual liberation. The *Kalachakra Tantra,* which flourished during the eleventh century in India and became a principal Tantra of the New Translation Schools in Tibet, states that if there are three teachers of Tantra, one with householder's vows, another with the vows of a novice monastic, and a third with the vows of a full-fledged monastic, the person who has taken the vows of a full-fledged monastic should be considered higher than the others. This indicates the high estimation that even this Tantric system places on the monastic morality. The *Guhyasamaja Tantra* says that externally you should keep the discipline of the practice of individual liberation, and internally maintains an affinity for the practice of Tantra. In these ways the practice of Sutra and Tantra work together.

Using Sex in the Path

Let us begin to consider the role of sexual desire in the path in Tantra by looking at the prohibition against sexual misconduct in the morality of individual liberation, which is entirely based on the principle of refraining from harm. Specific sexual misconduct is identified in detail in Vasubandhu's Treasury of Manifest Knowledge. For a male it would be to cohabit with someone else's wife, or with someone who is under the care of her family. For a female it is the same; it is prohibited to cohabit with someone else's husband or with someone who is under the care of his family. Some have suggested, ridiculously, that since Vasubandhu's text explains the ten non-virtues from the viewpoint of a male, there is no fault if a female engages in the non-virtues—and thus there are no prohibitions for a female!

For Buddhists, sexual intercourse can be used in the spiritual path because it causes a strong focusing of consciousness if the practitioner has firm compassion and wisdom. Its purpose is to manifest and prolong the deeper levels of mind (described earlier with respect to the process of dying), in order to put their power to use in strengthening the realization of emptiness. Otherwise, mere intercourse has nothing to do with spiritual cultivation. When a person has achieved a high level of practice in motivation and wisdom, then even the joining of the two sex organs, or so-called intercourse, does not detract from the maintenance of that person's pure behaviour. Yogis who have achieved a high level of the path and are fully qualified can engage in sexual activity, and a monastic with this ability can maintain all the precepts.

One Tibetan yogi-adept, when criticized by another, said that he ate meat and drank beer as offerings to the mandala deity. Such Tantric practitioners visualize themselves as deities in a complete mandala, within realization that the ultimate deity is the ultimate bliss— the union of bliss and emptiness. He also said that his sexual practice with a consort was undertaken for the sake of developing real knowledge. And that indeed is the purpose. Such a practitioner can make spiritual use not only of delicious meat and drink, but even of human excrement and urine. A yogi's meditation transforms these into real ambrosia. For people like us, however, this is beyond our reach. As long as you cannot transform piss and shit, these other things should not be done!

Buddha set out a specific series of stages on the path precisely for this reason. The preliminary stage is training in the vows of individual liberation. If you live as a monk or nun, your conduct has a more sound basis— there is little danger of excessive distraction. Even if you cannot fully implement such vows, there is not much risk. Then simply practise, practise, practise. Once you develop inner strength, you can control the four internal elements—earth, water, fire, and wind (or five elements if inner space is included). Once you can fully control these internal elements, then you can control the outer five elements. Then you can make use of anything.

How does sexual intercourse help in the path? There are many different levels of consciousness. The potential of grosser levels is very limited, but the deeper, more subtle levels are much more powerful. We need to access these subtler levels of mind. But in order to do so, we need to weaken and temporarily stop grosser consciousness. To accomplish this it is necessary to bring about dramatic changes in the flow of inner energies.

Even though brief versions of the deeper levels of mind occur during sneezing and yawning, they obviously cannot be prolonged. Also, previous experience with manifesting the deeper levels is required to make use of their occurrence in deep sleep. This is where sex comes in. Through special techniques of concentration during sex, competent practitioners can prolong very deep, subtle, and powerful states and put them to use to realize emptiness. However, if you engage in sexual intercourse within an ordinary mental context, there is no benefit.

A Buddha has no use for sexual intercourse. Deities depicted in a mandala are often in union with a consort, but this does not suggest that Buddhas have to rely on sexual intercourse for their bliss. Buddhas have full bliss within themselves. Deities in union spontaneously appear in mandalas for the benefit of people with very sharp faculties who can make use of a consort and the bliss of sexual union in practising the quick path of Tantra. In much the same way, the Tantric Buddha

Vajradhara appears in peaceful aspects and wrathful aspects, but this does not mean that Vajradhara has these two aspects to his personality. Vajradhara is always totally compassionate. Rather, his spontaneous appearance in various ways is for the sake of trainees. Vajradhara appears in just the way that the trainee should meditate when using afflictive emotions such as lust or hatred in the process of the path. To corral such powerful emotions into the spiritual path trainees cannot be imagining that they have the peaceful body of Shakyamuni Buddha. Deity yoga is required. Since in the case of hatred, for instance, it is necessary to meditate on your own body in a fierce form, Vajradhara automatically appears in the appropriate ferocious form to show the trainee how to meditate. The same is true for sexual yoga; trainees who are capable of using the bliss arising from the desire involved in gazing, smiling, holding hands, or union must perform the appropriate deity yoga; they could not be imagining themselves as Shakyamuni, a monk.

The purpose of Vajradhara's various appearances is neither to scare the trainees nor to excite desire in them, but to show how to do imaginative meditation in those forms in order eventually to overcome afflictive emotions.

A Buddha is capable of appearing spontaneously without exertion in whatever way is appropriate. The form of these appearances is shaped by the needs of others, not for the sake of that Buddha. From a Buddha's own point of view, that Buddha has the total self-fulfillment of the Truth Body, in which he or she remains forever.

Remember that Tantric morality is built on the morality of individual liberation and on the morality of compassion. The aim of Tantra is to achieve Buddhahood on a faster path in order to be of service to others more quickly.

TWENTY-FIVE

RELYING ON A SPIRITUAL TEACHER*

The Qualities of a Teacher

Although (there is much merit to be gained from) reciting or hearing even once this manner of text (written by Atisha) that includes the essential points of all scriptural pronouncements, you are certain to amass even greater waves of beneficial collections from actually teaching and studying the sacred Dharma (contained therein). Therefore, you should consider the points (for doing this properly).

Lama Tsong Khapa's *Lines of Experience* is a key to the connections and relationships between all the various scriptural texts. Verse 8 presents how the teacher should teach and how the students should listen, so that both teaching and listening are successful and effective. It is very important that the teacher has the right motivation and attitude. If the teacher is motivated by mundane aspirations, such as wanting to be known as a great scholar, to attract money or other material offerings or to bring people under his or her influence, then that teacher's motivation is certainly polluted.

It is very important that a teacher's motivation for teaching be the pure, altruistic aspiration to be of service and benefit to others. According to traditional Tibetan teachings, not only should a teacher ensure purity of motivation but also the manner of giving the teaching should not be flawed. Teaching in a flawed way is likened to an old man eating; he chews only the soft food and puts the hard bits aside. Similarly, teachers should not just focus on the simple points and leave out the difficult

---

* From *Illuminating the Path to Enlightenment*, Thubten Dhargye Ling, 2002.

ones. It is also said that teachers should not teach Dharma like crows build nests. When crows build nests, there is no systematic order; it's totally chaotic. Similarly, Dharma teachers should not teach chaotically but should offer a correct, systematic presentation that will benefit their students.

Another quality that ideally a teacher should have is experiential knowledge of the topic being taught. If that is not possible, then the teacher should have some familiarity with the practice of that topic, in order to be able to draw on personal experience. If that is not possible either, then at least the teacher should have a thorough intellectual understanding of the topic. As Dharmakirti said, there's no way that you can reveal to others that which is hidden to yourself.

I have a friend who is a great teacher and a very learned Hindu master. One day we were talking about the issue of interreligious harmony and the need for greater communication among the different faiths. I remarked that I am completely ignorant on matters of Islam and don't have much contact with the Islamic world. He replied, 'Well, it's not that difficult. Just learn to quote a few verses from the Koran and come up with some commentary here and there. That should be enough. You don't really have to know more.'

A more serious example involves a German scholar who attended a discourse by a Tibetan teacher. During the discourse he heard things that contradicted some of the basic teachings of the Buddha, so after the lecture, he went up to the teacher in person and told him that it seemed he had made some mistakes. Instead of acknowledging these mistakes, the Tibetan teacher said, 'Oh, it doesn't matter. You can say stuff like that.' This is wrong; it's very important for teachers to be careful.

When giving teachings from a throne, teachers' physical conduct is also very important. Before sitting down, teachers should make three prostrations towards the throne. This is to remind them that teaching from a throne does not mean that they are being recognized as great or holy beings but rather reflects the respect that is being accorded to the Dharma being taught. According to the Mahayana tradition, when the Buddha gave the teachings on the perfection of wisdom, he himself made a throne to sit on in order to show respect for these sutras, which are considered to be the mother, or source, of all aryas, be they hearers, solitary realizers or fully enlightened Buddhas.

When the Buddha's sutras were compiled by the early arhats and later by other followers of the Buddha, there were times when all the members of the congregation would remove their outer yellow robes. The person supervising the compilation process would fold and stack them up to make a throne and then sit on this throne of robes and compile the sutras. All this shows the tremendous respect accorded the Dharma.

Once the lama has sat down on the throne, the Tibetan custom is for him to recite a sutra reflecting on impermanence, to keep his motivation pure and prevent pride or conceit from arising in his mind. Such practices are important in ensuring purity on the teachers part, because when you're sitting on a high throne and people start praising you, there's a real danger of pride and arrogance taking over.

Therefore, we should take to heart the instructions of the Tibetan master, Dromtonpa, who said, 'Even if the whole world venerates you by placing you on the crown of their head, always sit as low as possible and maintain humility.' In the *Precious Garland*, Nagarjuna makes aspirational prayers to be like the elements of earth, water, fire and wind, which can be enjoyed and utilized by all sentient beings. If you take such sentiments seriously, you will never think that you are better than others or to try to bring them under your control.

It is also very important to have pure motivation when you receive teachings; to ensure that you have the three qualities of the ideal student— an objective mind, intelligence and a deep interest in the teachings— and that you cultivate the appropriate attitude. In this way, you will become a suitable recipient of the teachings. You should regard the Dharma as a mirror and the actions of your body, speech and mind as what that mirror reflects. Constantly examine what you see in the mirror of Dharma and continually try to modify your behaviour.

One feature of the Buddha's teaching is that the greater the diversity of your resources and avenues of contemplation, the more effective will be your understanding and experience, and the deeper the conviction you acquire. Therefore, you must ensure that your approach to your practice is comprehensive and that your learning and understanding are vast. At the same time, you must also ensure that the things you learn do not remain merely at the intellectual level. Right from the start, your studies should be directed towards the objective of practice. If you study without the desire to relate what you are learning to your own life through practice, you run the risk of becoming hardened or apathetic.

The great Kadampa masters used to say that if the gap between the Dharma and your mind is so big that a person can walk through it, your practice has not been successful. Make sure there's not the slightest gap between the teachings and your mind. You need to integrate and unite the Dharma with your mind. A Tibetan expression says that you can soften leather by kneading it with butter, but if that leather is hard because it's been used to store butter, you can never soften it, no matter how hard you try. Since you don't store butter in skin containers in the West, perhaps that saying doesn't make sense, but you get the idea.

The Kadampa masters also used to say that the water of Dharma can moisten the earnest, fresh minds of beginners, no matter how undisciplined they are, but can never penetrate the minds of those hardened by knowledge.

Therefore, learning and knowledge must never override your enthusiasm for practice, but neither should your dedication to practice interfere with your commitment to study. Furthermore, both your knowledge and dedication to practice must be grounded in a warm, compassionate heart. These three qualities—scholarship, dedication to practice and compassion—should be combined.

If teachers and students prepare their minds as above, students can experience transformation, even while listening to teachings.

Finally, at the end of each session, both the student and teacher should dedicate their merit to the enlightenment of all sentient beings.

The Practice of Reliance

With respect to ordinary, worldly knowledge, although in the final analysis what we learn comes through our own study and maturity of understanding, still, at the beginning, we need someone to introduce us to the subject matter and guide us through it. Similarly, when it comes to spiritual transformation, although true experiences come through our own development of knowledge and practice, we again need an experienced teacher to show us the path.

Since the spiritual teacher is so crucial to our practice, Lama Tsong Khapa goes into great detail in his *Great Exposition of the Stages of the Path*, presenting the topic in three broad categories: the qualifications of the spiritual teacher, the qualities required by the student and the proper teacher-student relationship.

The Qualities of the Spiritual Teacher

The qualifications of a suitable teacher can be found in texts from the Vinaya all the way up to the Vajrayana. Since here we are discussing Mahayana teachings in general, we will consider the ten qualifications of the teacher as presented in Maitreya's *Ornament of the Mahayana Sutras*:

1. A disciplined mind (referring to the quality of having mastered the higher training in ethical discipline).
2. A calmed mind (referring to the quality of having mastered the higher training in meditation and concentration).
3. A mind that is thoroughly calmed (referring to the quality of having mastered the higher training in wisdom, particularly the wisdom of no-self (Skt: anatman; Tib: dag-med).
4. Knowledge exceeding that of the student in whatever subject is being taught.
5. Energy and enthusiasm for teaching the student.
6. Vast learning in order to have the resources from which to draw examples and citations.
7. Realization of emptiness—if possible, a genuine realization of emptiness, but at least a strong commitment to the practice of emptiness on the basis of deep admiration for the teachings on it.
8. Eloquence and skill in presenting the Dharma so that the teaching is effective.
9. Deep compassion and concern for the well-being of the student to

whom the teaching is given (perhaps the most important quality of all).

10. The resilience to maintain enthusiasm for and commitment to the student, not becoming discouraged no matter how many times the teaching has to be repeated.

The first three qualities relate to the practice and experience of the Three Higher Trainings of morality, concentration and wisdom. The other important qualities are having the realization of emptiness as the ultimate nature of reality and compassion for the student. Those who assume the role of teacher must ensure that these qualities are present within themselves.

When discussing these ten qualities in his *Great Exposition of the Stages of the Path*, Lama Tsong Khapa makes a very important point. He says that if your own mind is not disciplined, there's no way you can discipline the mind of another. Therefore, if you want to be a teacher, you must first seek to discipline your own mind. He goes on to say that the way prospective teachers should discipline their minds is through the practice of the Three Higher Trainings.

Furthermore, teachers should not be limited to teaching just one or two points of Dharma but should be able to present particular practices with complete knowledge of their place within the overall framework of the Buddha's teachings.

Lama Tsong Khapa concludes this section of his *Great Exposition* by emphasizing that practitioners seeking a spiritual teacher should familiarize themselves with these ten qualities and then look for them in those in whom they would entrust their spiritual welfare. When choosing a spiritual teacher, from the start, examine the person you have in mind to see if he or she really possesses these qualities. If you do so, you'll reduce the risk of encountering serious problems later on.

Otherwise, you may use the wrong criteria to judge a teacher's suitability. This used to happen in Tibet. Tibetans have tremendous faith in the Dharma, but their level of knowledge was not always equal to their devotion. Instead of assessing spiritual teachers by their inner qualities, people would base their judgment on external manifestations, such as the number of horses in a lama's entourage. If a lama was travelling in a large convoy, people would say, 'Oh, he must be a *very* high lama!' People like that also tended to regard what the lama was wearing—a unique hat, brocade robes and so forth—as an indicator of his spiritual greatness.

It is said that when Atisha first came to Tibet, his translator, Nagtso Lotsawa, and the Ngari king, Jangchub O, sent letters inviting all the high Tibetan lamas to come and receive this great Indian master. A large procession of lamas came to meet Atisha, and as they rode up on horseback, they could be seen from quite a distance. They were all dressed in very impressive-looking costumes with elaborate headgear shaped into fantastic designs, such as crows' heads. When Atisha saw them, he covered his head with his shawl in mock terror and exclaimed, 'Oh my! The Tibetan ghosts are coming!' When the lamas dismounted, they removed their brocades and costumes until they were wearing just their monastic robes, and walked towards Atisha, who then became very pleased.

On this subject, we can also look at the life of Milarepa, who shines as one of the crown jewels among Tibetan meditators. One day, the lama, Naro Bonchung, who had heard of Milarepa's great reputation, went to visit him. When he met Milarepa in person, however, he was taken completely by surprise, and later remarked to someone, 'This Milarepa is so famous, but when you actually see him, he looks just like a beggar.'

This reminds me of the humility of another great lama, the Kadampa master, Dromtonpa. The story goes that once, when Dromtonpa was travelling from one place to another, he met a Tibetan monk who had been walking for some time. This monk was very tired and his boots had begun to hurt his feet, so he took them off and, since Dromtonpa looked like just a humble layman, asked him to carry his boots. Dromtonpa took the heavy boots on his back without question. Later, as they approached a monastery, the monk noticed that all the monks were lined up on both sides of the road, obviously waiting to receive somebody. He thought to himself, 'They didn't know I was coming, and anyway, this reception could not possibly be for me,' so he turned to Dromtonpa and said, 'This welcome is obviously for someone important. Do you have any idea who it's for?' Dromtonpa replied, 'It could be for me.' The monk looked at him in astonishment and, realizing what he had done, ran off, leaving his boots behind.

There is also a much more recent example. Around the turn of the century, there was a great meditation master and teacher named Dza Patrul Rinpoche, who was truly a great bodhisattva and embodied the teachings of Shantideva's text, *A Guide to the Bodhisattva's Way of Life*. Dza Patrul Rinpoche had many disciples but often led the life of a wandering practitioner. Whenever he settled in one area, he would begin to attract disciples and particularly patrons. After a while, he would find it all too much and go elsewhere to seek solitude.

One of those times, Dza Patrul Rinpoche sought shelter in the home of an old lady, and started doing household chores while pursuing his spiritual practice. One day, as he was outside emptying the lady's chamber pot, some lamas stopped by the house. They told the old lady that they had heard their teacher might be residing somewhere in the region and asked if she had seen him. She asked what he looked like, and as they started to describe his general appearance, the kind of clothes he wore and so forth, she suddenly realized that the person who was outside emptying her pot was the great Dza Patrul Rinpoche. She was so embarrassed that, just like the monk in the previous story, she too ran off. I heard this story from the late Khunu Lama Tenzin Gyaltsen.

The point of all this is that a true Mahayana teacher should be someone who enjoys simplicity, yearns to be anonymous and, as Tibetans would say, hides in solitude like a wounded animal. The Tibetan tradition states that Mahayana teachers should have at least two basic qualities. First, from the depths of their heart, they should regard the future life as more important than this. Without this, nothing one does becomes Dharma. Second, teachers should regard the welfare of others as more important than their own. Without this, nothing one does becomes Mahayana.

The Qualities of the Student

In his *Great Exposition*, Lama Tsong Khapa goes on to discuss the three principal qualifications of an ideal student:

1. An objective and open mind
2. The intelligence to judge between right and wrong, appropriate and inappropriate
3. Enthusiasm for and interest in the subject

Objectivity and openness are critical, regardless of what you want to study. Bias is an obstacle to knowledge. Objectivity ensures that you are engaging in the Dharma in the right way and with the right motivation. The sutras and Nagarjuna's *Precious Garland* both emphasize this and describe four wrong ways of approaching and engaging in the Dharma:

1. Engaging in the Dharma out of attachment to a particular tradition or custom
2. Engaging in the Dharma out of hatred or hostility
3. Engaging in the Dharma to seek temporary relief from some actual or perceived threat
4. Engaging in the Dharma out of ignorance

With respect to the second point, sometimes people have so much aversion to something that they embrace whatever opposes it. For example, there are people in India who are motivated to engage in the Dharma in rebellion against their traditional caste status as untouchables. They embrace Buddhism because of negative feelings towards their traditionally inherited religion.

The second quality of the ideal student, intelligence, is also very important, since it is intelligence that allows you to discriminate between right and wrong and so forth.

When commenting on this quality and the various attitudes that practitioners must have towards their teacher, Lama Tsong Khapa writes that students should relate to their teachers as loyal and respectful children. This does not mean that you should give your leash to anybody who is willing to take it, but only to one who possesses the right qualifications. To substantiate this point, he cites a Vinaya sutra that says that if a teacher says something that contradicts the Dharma, you should not follow that teaching. Another passage states that if a teacher says something contradictory to the overall framework of the Buddha's path, the student must point this error out to the teacher.

This reminds me of a story. The Tibetan master and learned scholar, Geshe Sherab Gyatso, used to attend the discourses of one of his teachers, Muchog Rinpoche. Whenever Muchog Rinpoche made some effective point, Geshe Sherab would immediately praise it and say, 'Yes, these are powerful instructions. Deeply inspiring.' However, if Muchog Rinpoche said something contradictory to the teachings of the Buddha, Geshe Sherab would immediately rebuff what his teacher had said, saying, 'No, no, no. Nobody should say such things.'

With respect to the third quality of the student, enthusiasm for and interest in the teachings, right at the beginning of the *Great Exposition of the Stages of the Path*, when Lama Tsong Khapa states his intention for writing the text, we find a request for the attention of readers who have the quality of objectivity, are endowed with the faculty of intelligence and wish to make their human existence meaningful. In order to make your life meaningful, you need enthusiasm for and interest in practising the teachings, otherwise, whatever you learn is like the drawing of a lamp—it doesn't illuminate anything—and your knowledge remains at the level of mere information.

We find similar exhortations among the Indian masters. In the salutation verses of his commentary on Maitreya's *Ornament of Clear Realization*, Haribhadra states that his teacher, Vimuktisena, wrote a commentary on the *Perfection of Wisdom Sutras*. Vasubandhu, Vimuktisena's own teacher, had also written a commentary on these sutras, but interpreted their ultimate meaning according to Cittamatra philosophy. Recognizing that his teacher, Vasubandhu, hadn't fully understood the meaning of these sutras, Vimuktisena wrote his own commentary as a corrective. This shows that even students with great devotion and respect for their teacher should have the intelligence to point out any mistakes their teacher makes.

Another example concerns the Indian master, Dharmakirti, whose teacher was a student of the seventh century pandit, Dignaga. Dharmakirti used Dignaga's text in his study of epistemology. As he read over the text with his teacher, Dharmakirti realized that even his own teacher hadn't fully understood Dignaga's meaning. When

Dharmakirti mentioned this to his teacher, he invited him to write a commentary that would take his own interpretation as an object of critique.

All these examples show clearly that the great masters truly took to heart the Buddha's own advice that his followers should not accept his words simply out of reverence but should scrutinize them in the way a goldsmith examines gold by rubbing, cutting and scorching and accept the validity of his teachings only on the basis of their own analysis.

The Mahayana has a long tradition of subjecting the Buddha's words to detailed analysis and examination, following that with an interpretative approach to discriminate between teachings that can be taken at face value and those that require further interpretation. This is necessary because there are certain scriptural teachings that, if taken literally, actually contradict reasoning and experience. These interpretations have been made by Mahayana practitioners and masters who have unwavering, single-pointed faith in the Buddha, some of whom have actually been willing to give up their lives in the service of the Dharma. Even such devoted masters subject the word of the Buddha to critical analysis.

Establishing Proper Reliance

In his *Great Treatise*, Lama Tsong Khapa goes on to describe the actual manner in which proper reliance on a spiritual teacher should be developed and established. 'Reliance on a spiritual teacher,' he writes, 'is the foundation of the path, because the spiritual teacher is the source of all temporary and (particularly) ultimate gain.' The point here is that if we encounter a genuine spiritual teacher, this person may be able to help us open our eye of awareness and lead us on the path.

The actual practice of relying on a spiritual teacher is performed through both thought and action, but relying through thought is the key. This entails the cultivation of two principal qualities, faith and respect. In the *lam-rim*, we often find citations from Vajrayana texts stating that we should perceive our teacher as a truly enlightened being. It is important to understand the significance of this practice.

By encouraging you to cultivate a perception of your teacher as an enlightened being, the *lam-rim* texts do not mean that such reliance on a spiritual teacher is indispensable. If you look at the structure of the *lam-rim* teachings, although all the practices are organized within the framework of the three scopes, those of the initial and middling scopes are regarded as common practices, the term 'common' implying that they are not full or complete practices in and of themselves.

The *initial scope* teachings discuss the need to cultivate the yearning for a better rebirth and contain practices related to that aspiration. The *middling scope* teachings deal with the practices of the Three Higher Trainings of morality, meditation and wisdom, but even here they are not presented in full because they are still in the context of the Mahayana path. The point is that *lam-rim* texts are written assuming that the ultimate aim of the practitioner is to enter the Vajrayana path in order to reach enlightenment (*the great scope*). Therefore, even though the *lam-rim* teachings present the idea of perceiving your teacher as a truly enlightened being, it does not mean that every single spiritual practice depends upon that kind of reliance. Cultivating the perception of your teacher as a fully enlightened being is relevant only in the context of Vajrayana but not in the common practices.

The actual reliance on a spiritual teacher is done through the cultivation of certain thoughts, particularly faith, admiration and respect, based on the recognition of your teacher's great kindness. It does not end there, however. In fact, the very purpose of cultivating such attitudes is to arouse enthusiasm for and dedication to your practice. By cultivating such thoughts as admiration and respect, you develop a deeper appreciation of what your spiritual teacher embodies, and your commitment and dedication to practice naturally increase. The best way of making an offering to your teacher is to practise what you have been taught. As Milarepa wrote, 'I do not have any material things to offer my teacher, but still I have the best offering—my practice and experiences.'

Questions

Q: If I did not misunderstand what you said before, part of the practice of guru devotion is to point out where you think your teacher has gone wrong. First, what do you do when it is nearly impossible to express a dissenting opinion to your teacher because those around him or her tend to block the expression of criticism? Second, how do you reconcile holding fundamentally different views on certain issues from those expressed by your guru?

His Holiness: If a lama or spiritual teacher has done something wrong that needs to be pointed out, there could be two kinds of motivation for those immediately around the teacher—such as attendants or close disciples—trying to hide it or prevent people from disclosing it or pointing it out to the teacher. On the one hand, their motivation could be quite innocent; they might just be trying to protect and help their teacher. Such motivation is more the result of ignorance rather than wilful manipulation of the situation. However, even if that's the case, there is still the danger of causing harm to the teacher. In fact, a Tibetan expression says that extremely devout students can turn a true teacher into a false one.

On the other hand, the motivation of the attendants and close disciples could be more mundane they may not want to make their teacher's wrongdoing public for fear of harming his or her reputation. This is completely wrong, and you must find a way of expressing your concerns to your teacher. However, it is also very important to ensure that your own motivation is pure. You should not act out of hostility towards your teacher or out of the desire simply to express your displeasure. As the Mahayana teachings state, we must ensure that everything our teacher teaches accords with the principal teachings of the Buddha. We must also practice the motto of relying on the teaching and not the person.

In response to your second question, it's unlikely that you will have disagreements with your teacher on every single issue. That's almost impossible. Basically, you should embrace and practise the teachings that accord with the fundamental teachings of the Buddha and disregard those that do not.

Q: Do we need a guru to get enlightened or is it sufficient just to study Dharma, live a moral life, attend teachings and practise meditation?

His Holiness: Of course it is possible to practise, study and lead a moral life without actually seeking a guru. However, you must understand that when you talk about enlightenment, you are not talking about something that can be attained within the next few years but about a spiritual aspiration that may, in some cases, take many lifetimes and eons. If you do not find a qualified teacher to whom you can entrust you spiritual well-being then, of course, it is more effective to entrust yourself to the actual Dharma teachings and practise on that basis.

I can tell you a story related to this. Dromtönpa was a great spiritual master who truly embodied the altruistic teachings of exchanging self and others. In fact in the latter part of his life, he dedicated himself to serving people who suffered from leprosy. He lived with them and eventually lost his own life to this disease, which damaged his chin in particular.

As Dromtönpa lay dying, his head rested on the lap of one of his chief disciples, Potowa, and he noticed that Potowa was crying. Then Potowa said, 'After you pass away, in whom can we entrust our spiritual well-being? Who can we take as our teacher?' Dromtönpa replied, 'Don't worry. You'll still have a teacher after I'm gone—the Tripitaka, the threefold collection of the teachings of the Buddha. Entrust yourself to the Tripitaka; take the Tripitaka as your teacher.'

However, as we progress along the spiritual path, at some point we will definitely meet an appropriate and suitable teacher.

Q: Many texts describe the practitioner's goal as that of Buddhahood itself, yet among seasoned Western Dharma teachers there seems to be a trend towards accepting partial results, as if Buddhahood is unattainable. The new attitude is that of accepting samsaric mind punctuated by spiritual phases and seems to be based on those dilligent teachers' inability to achieve complete liberation themselves. Is seeking Buddhahood in this very lifetime still a viable goal in what the Buddha declared would be a dark age for Buddhism?

His Holiness: If you understand the process of attaining Buddhahood from the general Mahayana perspective, the attainment of Buddhahood within the period of three countless aeons is actually said to be the quick version. Some texts speak about forty countless aeons! However, according to the general Vajrayana teachings, practitioners with high levels of realization can prolong their lifespan and attain Buddhahood within a single lifetime. The Highest Yoga Tantra teachings recognize that even within this short human lifetime, the possibility of full enlightenment exists.

There is also the idea of someone being able to attain full enlightenment after a three-year retreat, which is not too dissimilar from Chinese communist propaganda. I make this comment partly as a joke, but partly in all seriousness—the shorter the time period of your expectation, the greater the danger of losing courage and enthusiasm. Leaving aside the question of whether it takes three or forty countless aeons to reach enlightenment, when you cultivate deeply such powerful sentiments as those articulated in Shantideva's prayer,

> For as long as space exists,
> For as long as sentient beings remain,
> Until then, may I too remain
> And dispel the miseries of the world,

time is totally irrelevant; you are thinking in terms of infinity. Also, when you read in the Mahayana scriptures passages pertaining to the bodhisattva's practice of what is called armour-like patience, again time has no significance. These are tremendously inspiring sentiments.

IV

A WORLD IN HARMONY

~

TWENTY-SIX

ETHICS AND SOCIETY*

Education and the Media

Living a truly ethical life in which we put the needs of others first, and provide for their happiness, has tremendous implications for our society. If we change internally—disarm ourselves by dealing constructively with our negative thoughts and emotions—we can literally change the whole world. We have so many powerful tools for creating our ethical and peaceful society already in place. Yet some of these tools are not being used to their full potential. At this point, I would like to share some of my views on how and in which arenas we can begin to bring about a spiritual revolution of kindness, compassion, patience, tolerance, forgiveness and humility.

When we are committed to the ideal of concern for all others, it follows that this should inform our social and political policies. I say this not because I suppose that thereby we will be able to solve all society's problems overnight. Rather, it is my conviction that unless this wider sense of compassion which I have been urging on the reader inspires our politics, our policies are likely to harm instead of serve humanity as a whole. We must, I believe, take practical steps to acknowledge our responsibility to all others both now and in the future. This is true even where there may be little practical difference between those policies that are motivated by this compassion and those that are motivated by, for example, national interest.

Now although it is certainly the case that if all my suggestions

---

* From *Ethics for the New Millennium*, Riverhead Books, Penguin Putnam Inc., 1999.

concerning compassion, inner discipline, wise discernment, and the cultivation of virtue were to be implemented widely, the world would automatically become a kinder, more peaceful place, I believe that reality compels us to tackle our problems at the level of society at the same time as that of the individual. The world will change when each individual makes the attempt to counter their negative thoughts and emotions and when we practise compassion for its inhabitants irrespective of whether or not we have direct relationships with them.

In view of this, there are, I believe, a number of areas to which we need to give special consideration in the light of universal responsibility. These include education, the media, our natural environment, politics and economics, peace and disarmament, and inter-religious harmony. Each has a vital role to play in shaping the world we live in, and I propose to examine them briefly in turn.

Before doing so, I must stress that the views I express are personal. They are also the views of someone 'who claims no expertise' with respect to the technicalities of these matters. But if what I say seems objectionable, my hope is that it will at least give the reader pause for thought. For although it would not be surprising to see a divergence of opinion concerning how they are to be translated into actual policies, the need for compassion, for basic spiritual values, for inner discipline and the importance of ethical conduct generally are in my view incontrovertible.

The human mind *(lo)* is both the source and, properly directed, the solution to all our problems. Those who attain great learning but lack a good heart are in danger of falling prey to the anxieties and restlessness which result from desires incapable of fulfillment. Conversely, a genuine understanding of spiritual values has the opposite effect. When we bring up our children to have knowledge without compassion, their attitude toward others is likely to be a mixture of envy of those in positions above them, aggressive competitiveness toward their peers, and scorn for those less fortunate. This leads to a propensity toward greed, presumption, excess, and, very quickly, to loss of happiness. Knowledge is important. But much more so is the use toward which it is put. This depends on the heart and mind of the one who uses it.

Education is much more than a matter of imparting the knowledge and skills by which narrow goals are achieved. It is also about opening the child's eyes to the needs and rights of others. We must show children that their actions have a universal dimension. And we must somehow find a way to build on their natural feelings of empathy so that they come to have a sense of responsibility toward others. For it is this which stirs us into action. Indeed, if we had to choose between learning and virtue, the latter is definitely more valuable. The good heart which is the fruit of virtue is by itself a great benefit to humanity. Mere knowledge is not.

How, though, are we to teach morality to our children? I have a sense that, in general, modern educational systems neglect discussion of ethical matters. This is probably not intentional so much as a by-product of historical reality. Secular educational systems were developed at a time when religious institutions were still highly influential throughout society. Because ethical and human values were and still are generally held to fall within the scope of religion, it was assumed that this aspect of a child's education would be looked after through his or her religious upbringing. This worked well enough until the influence of religion began to decline. Although the need is still there, it is not being met. Therefore, we must find some other way of showing children that basic human values are important. And we must also help them to develop these values.

Ultimately, of course, the importance of concern for others is learned not from words but from actions: the example we set. This is why the family environment itself is such a vital component in a child's upbringing. When a caring and compassionate atmosphere is absent from the home, when children are neglected by their parents, it is easy to recognize their damaging effects. The children tend to feel helpless and insecure, and their minds are often agitated. Conversely, when children receive constant affection and protection, they tend to be much happier and more confident in their abilities. Their physical health tends to be better too. And we find that they are concerned not just for themselves but for others as well. The home environment is also important because children learn negative behaviour from their parents. If, for example, the father is always getting into fights with his associates, or if the father and mother are always arguing destructively, although at first the child may find this objectionable, eventually they will come to understand it as quite normal. This learning is then taken out of the home and into the world.

It also goes without saying that what children learn about ethical conduct at school has to be practised first. In this, teachers have a special responsibility. By their own behaviour, they can make children remember them for their whole lives. If this behaviour is principled, disciplined, and compassionate, their values will be readily impressed on the child's mind. This is because the lessons taught by a teacher with a positive motivation *(kun long)* penetrate deepest into their students' minds. I know this from my own experience. As a boy, I was very lazy. But when I was aware of the affection and concern of my tutors, their lessons would generally sink in much more successfully than if one of them was harsh or unfeeling that day.

So far as the specifics of education are concerned, that is for the experts. I will, therefore, confine myself to a few suggestions. The first is that in order to awaken young people's consciousness to the importance of basic human values, it is better not to present society's problems purely as an ethical matter or as a religious matter. It is important to emphasize that what is at stake is our continued survival. This way, they will come to see that the future lies in their hands. Secondly, I do believe that dialogue can and should be taught in class. Presenting students with a controversial issue and having them debate it is a wonderful way to introduce them to the concept of resolving conflict non-violently. Indeed, one would hope that if schools were to make this a priority, it could have a beneficial effect on family life itself. On seeing his or her parents wrangling, a child that had understood the value of dialogue would instinctively say, 'Oh, no. That's not the way. You have to talk, to discuss things properly.'

Finally, it is essential that we eliminate from our schools' curricula any tendency toward presenting others in a negative light. There are undoubtedly some parts of the world where the teaching of history, for example, fosters bigotry and racism toward other communities. Of course this is wrong. It contributes nothing to the happiness of humanity. Now more than ever we need to show our children that distinctions between 'my country' and 'your country,' 'my religion' and 'your religion' are secondary considerations. Rather, we must insist on the observation that my right to happiness carries no more weight than others' right. This is not to say that I believe we should educate children to abandon or ignore the culture and historical tradition they were born into. On the contrary, it is very important they be grounded in these. It is good for children to learn to love their country, their religion, their culture, and so on. But the danger comes when this develops into narrow-minded nationalism, ethnocentricity, and religious bigotry. The example of Mahatma Gandhi is pertinent here. Even though he had a very high level of Western education, he never forgot or became estranged from the rich heritage of his Indian culture.

If education constitutes one of our most powerful weapons in our quest to bring about a better, more peaceful world, the mass media is another. As every political figure knows, they are no longer the only ones with authority in society. In addition to that of newspapers and books, radio, film, and television together have an influence over individuals unimagined a hundred years ago. This power confers great a responsibility on all who work in the media. But it also confers great responsibility on each of us who, as individuals, listen and read and watch. We, too, have a role to play. We are not powerless before the media. The control switch is in our own hand, after all.

This does not mean that I advocate bland reporting or entertainment without excitement. On the contrary, so far as investigative journalism is concerned, I respect and appreciate the media's interference. Not all public servants are honest in discharging their duties. It is appropriate, therefore, to have journalists, their noses as long as an elephant's trunk, snooping around and exposing wrongdoing where they find it. We need to know when this or that renowned individual hides a very different aspect behind a pleasant exterior. There should be no discrepancy between external appearances and the individual's inner life. It is the same person, after all. Such discrepancies suggest them to be untrustworthy. At the same time, it is vital that the investigator does not act out of improper motives. Without impartiality and without due respect for the other's rights, the investigation itself becomes tainted.

With regard to the question of the media's emphasis on sex and violence, there are many factors to consider. In the first instance, it is clear that much of the viewing public enjoys the sensations provoked by this sort of material. Secondly, I very much doubt that those producing material containing a lot of explicit sex and violence·intend harm by it. Their motives are surely just commercial. As to whether this is positive or negative in itself is to my mind less important than the question of whether it can have an ethically wholesome effect. If the result of seeing a film in which there is a lot of violence is that the viewer's compassion is aroused, then perhaps that depiction of violence would be justified. But if the accumulation of violent images leads to indifference, then I think it is not. Indeed, such a hardening of heart is potentially dangerous. It leads all too easily to lack of empathy.

When the media focuses too closely on the negative aspects of human nature, there is a danger that we become persuaded that violence and aggression are its principal characteristics. This is a mistake, I believe. The fact that violence is newsworthy suggests the very opposite. Good news is not remarked on precisely because there is so much of it. Consider that at any given moment there must be hundreds of millions of acts of kindness taking place around the world. Although there will undoubtedly be many acts of violence in progress at the same time, their number is surely very much less. If therefore, the media is to be ethically responsible, it needs to reflect this simple fact.

Clearly it is necessary to regulate the media. The fact that we prevent our children from watching certain things indicates that we already discriminate between what is and is not appropriate according to different circumstances. But whether legislation is the right way to go about this is hard to judge. As in all matters of ethics, discipline is only really effective when it comes from within. Perhaps the best way to ensure that the output various media provides is healthy lies in the way we educate our children. If we bring them up to be aware of their responsibilities, they will be more disciplined when they become involved in the media.

Although it is perhaps too much to hope that the media will actually promote the ideals and principles of compassion, at least we should be able to expect that those involved will take care when there is the potential for negative impact. At least there should be no room for the incitement of negative acts such as racist violence. But beyond this, I don't know. Perhaps we might be able to find a way to connect more directly those who create stories for news and entertainment with the viewer, the reader, and the listener?

The Natural World

If there is one area in which both education and the media have a special responsibility, it is, I believe, our natural environment. Again, this responsibility has less to do with questions of right or wrong than with the question of survival. The natural world is our home. It is not necessarily sacred or holy, it is simply where we live. It is therefore in our interest to look after it. This is common sense. But only recently have the size of our population and the power of science and technology grown to the point that they can have a direct impact on nature. To put it another way, until now, Mother Earth has been able to tolerate our sloppy house habits. The stage has been reached where she can no longer accept our behaviour in silence. The problems caused by environmental degradation can be seen as her response to our irresponsible behaviour. She is warning us that there are limits even to her tolerance.

Nowhere are the consequences of our failure to exercise discipline in the way we relate to our environment more apparent than in the case of present-day Tibet. It is no exaggeration to say that the Tibet I grew up in was a wildlife paradise. Every traveller who visited Tibet before the middle of the twentieth century remarked on this. Animals were rarely hunted, except in the remotest areas where crops could not be grown. Indeed, it was customary for government officials annually to issue a proclamation protecting wildlife: 'Nobody,' it read, 'however humble or noble, shall harm or do violence to the creatures of the waters or the wild.' The only exceptions to this were rats and wolves.

As a young man, I recall seeing great numbers of different species whenever I travelled outside Lhasa. My chief memory of the three-month journey across Tibet from my birthplace at Takster in the east to Lhasa, where I was formally proclaimed Dalai Lama as a four-year-old boy, is of the wildlife we encountered along the way. Immense herds of *kiang* (wild asses) and *drong* (wild yak) freely roamed the great plains. Occasionally we would catch sight of shimmering herds of *gowa*, the shy Tibetan gazelle, of *wa*, the white-lipped deer, or of *tso*, our majestic antelope. I remember, too, my fascination for the little *chibi*, or pika, which would congregate on grassy areas. They were so friendly. I loved to watch the birds, the dignified *gho* (the bearded eagle) soaring high above monasteries perched up in the mountains, the flocks of geese (*nangbar*), and occasionally, at night, to hear the call of the *wookpa* (the long-eared owl).

Even in Lhasa, one did not feel in any way cut off from the natural world. In my rooms at the top of the Potala, the winter palace of the Dalai Lamas, I spent countless hours as a child studying the behaviour of the red-beaked *khyungkar* which nested in the crevices of its walls. And behind the Norbu-lingka, the summer palace, I often saw pairs of *trung trung* (Japanese black-necked crane), birds which for me are the epitome of elegance and grace that lived in the marshlands there. And all this is not to mention the crowning glory of Tibetan fauna: the bears and mountain foxes, the *chanku* (wolves), and *sazik* (the beautiful snow leopard), and the *sik* (lynx) which struck terror into the hearts of the nomad farmer or the gentle-faced giant panda, which is native to the border area between Tibet and China.

Sadly, this profusion of wildlife is no longer to be found. Partly due to hunting but primarily due to loss of habitat, what remains half a century after Tibet was occupied is only a fraction of what there was. Without exception, every Tibetan I have spoken with who has been back to visit Tibet after thirty to forty years has reported on a striking absence of wildlife. Whereas before wild animals would often come close to the house, today they are hardly anywhere to be seen.

Equally troubling is the devastation of Tibet's forests. In the past, the hills were all thickly wooded; today, those who have been back report that they are clean-shaven like a monk's head. The government in Beijing has admitted that the tragic flooding of western China, and farther afield, is in part due to this. And yet I hear continuous reports of round-the-clock convoys of trucks carrying logs east out of Tibet. This is especially tragic given the country's mountainous terrain and harsh climate. It means that replanting requires sustained care and attention. Unfortunately, there is little evidence of this.

None of this is to say that, historically, we Tibetans were deliberately 'conservationist.' We were not. The idea of something called 'pollution' simply never occurred to us. There is no denying we were rather spoiled in this respect. A small population inhabited a very large area with clean, dry air and an abundance of pure mountain water. This innocent attitude toward cleanliness meant that when we Tibetans went into exile, we were astonished to discover, for example, the existence of streams whose water is not drinkable. Like an only child, no matter what we did, Mother Earth tolerated our behaviour. The result was that we had no proper understanding of cleanliness and hygiene. People would spit or blow their nose in the street without giving it a second thought. Indeed, saying this, I recall one elderly Khampa, a former bodyguard who used to come each day to circumambulate my residence in Dharamsala (a popular devotion). Unfortunately, he suffered greatly from bronchitis. This was exacerbated by the incense he carried. At each corner, therefore, he would pause to cough and expectorate so ferociously that I sometimes wondered whether he had come to pray or just to spit!

Over the years since our first arriving in exile, I have taken a close interest in environmental issues. The Tibetan government in exile has paid particular attention to introducing our children to their responsibilities as residents of this fragile planet. And I never hesitate to speak out on the subject whenever I am given the opportunity. In particular, I always stress the need to consider how our actions, in affecting the environment, are likely to affect others. I admit that this is very often difficult to judge. We cannot say for sure what the ultimate effects of, for example, deforestation might be on the soil and the local rainfall, let alone what the implications are for the planet's weather systems. The only clear thing is that we humans are the only species with the power to destroy the earth as we know it. The birds have no such power, nor do the insects, nor does any mammal. Yet if we have the capacity to destroy the earth, so, too, do we have the capacity to protect it.

What is essential is that we find methods of manufacture that do not destroy nature. We need to find ways of cutting down on our use of wood and other limited natural resources. I am no expert in this field, and I cannot suggest how this might be done. I know only that it is possible, given the necessary determination. For example, I recall hearing on a visit to Stockholm some years ago that, for the first time in many years, fish were returning to the river that runs through the city. Until recently, there were none due to industrial pollution. Yet this improvement was by no means the result of all the local factories closing down. Likewise, on a visit to Germany, I was shown an industrial development designed to produce no pollution. So, clearly, solutions do exist to limit damage to the natural world without bringing industry to a halt.

So far as the individual is concerned, the problems resulting from our neglect of our natural environment are a powerful reminder that we all have a contribution to make. And while one person's actions may not have a significant impact, the combined effect of millions of individuals' actions certainly does. This means that it is time for all those living in the industrially developed nations to give serious thought to changing their lifestyle. Again, this is not so much a question of ethics. The fact that the population of the rest of the world has an equal right to improve their standard of living is in some ways more important than the affluent being able to continue their lifestyle. If this is to be fulfilled without causing irredeemable violence to the natural world— with all the negative consequences for happiness that this would entail— the richer countries must set an example. The cost to the planet, and thus the cost to humanity, of ever-increasing standards of living is simply too great.

Politics and Economics

We all dream of a kinder, happier world. But if we wish to make it a reality, we have to ensure that compassion inspires all our actions. This is especially true with regard to our political and economic policies. Given that probably half the world's population lacks the basic necessities of adequate food, shelter, medical care, and education, I believe we need to question whether we are really pursuing the wisest course in this regard. I think not. If it seemed likely that after another fifty years of carrying on as we are, we could definitely eradicate poverty, perhaps our present inequity of wealth distribution could be justified. Yet, on the contrary, if present trends continue, it is certain that the poor will get poorer. Our basic sense of fairness and justice alone suggests that we should not be content to let this happen.

Of course, I don't know much about economics. But I find it hard to avoid the conclusion that the wealth of the rich is maintained through neglect of the poor, especially by means of international debt. Saying this, I do not mean to suggest that the undeveloped countries have no share of responsibility for their problems. Nor can we put all social and economic ills down to politicians and public officials. I do not deny that even in the world's most established democracies it is quite usual to hear politicians making unrealistic promises and boasting about what they are going to do when elected. But these people do not drop out of the sky. So if it is true that a given country's politicians are corrupt, we tend to find that the society is itself lacking in morality and that the individuals who make up the population do not lead ethical lives. In such cases, it is not entirely fair for the electorate to criticize its politicians. On the other hand, when people possess healthy values, and where they practice ethical discipline in their own lives out of concern for others, the public officials produced by that society will quite naturally respect those same values. Each of us, therefore, has a role to play in creating a society in which respect and care for others, based on empathy, are given top priority.

So far as the application of economic policy is concerned, the same considerations apply here as to every human activity. A sense of universal responsibility is crucial. I must admit, however, that I find it a bit difficult to make practical suggestions about the application of spiritual values in the field of commerce. This is because competition has such an important role to play. For this reason, the relationship between empathy and profit is necessarily a fragile one. Still, I do not see why it should not be possible to have constructive competition. The key factor is the motivation of those engaged in it. When the intention is to exploit or destroy others, then clearly the outcome will not be positive. But when competition is conducted with a spirit of generosity and good intention, the outcome, although it must entail a degree of suffering for those

223

who lose, will at least not be too harmful.

Our problems of economic disparity pose a very serious challenge to the whole human family. Nevertheless, as we enter the new millennium, I believe there are a good number of reasons for optimism. During the early and middle years of the twentieth century, there was a general perception that political and economic power was of more consequence than truth. But I believe that this is changing. Even the wealthiest and most powerful nations understand that there is no point in neglecting basic human values. The notion that there is room for ethics in international relations is also gaining ground. Irrespective of whether it is translated into meaningful action, at least words like 'reconciliation,' 'non-violence,' and 'compassion' are becoming stock phrases among politicians. This is a useful development. Then, according to my own experience, I note that when I travel abroad I am often asked to speak about peace and compassion to quite large audiences—often in excess of a thousand. I doubt very much whether these topics would have attracted such numbers forty or fifty years ago. Developments such as these indicate that collectively we humans are giving more weight to fundamental values such as justice and truth.

I also take comfort in the fact that as the world economy evolves, the more explicitly interdependent it becomes. As a result, every nation is to a greater or lesser extent dependent on every other nation. The modern economy, like the environment, knows no boundaries. Even those countries openly hostile to one another must cooperate in their use of the world's resources. Often, for example, they will be dependent on the same rivers. And the more interdependent our economic relationships, the more interdependent must our political relationships become. Thus we have witnessed, for example, the growth of the European Union from a small caucus of trading partners into something approaching a confederation of states with a membership now well into the double figures. We see similar, though presently less-well-developed, groupings throughout the world: the Association of South East Asian Nations, the Organization for African Unity, the Organization of Petroleum Exporting Countries, to name but three. Each of these testifies to the human impulse to join together for the common good and reflects the continuing evolution of human society. What began with relatively small tribal units has progressed through the foundation of city-states to nationhood and now to alliances comprising hundreds of millions of people, which increasingly transcend geographical, cultural, and ethnic divisions. This is a trend which I believe will and must continue.

TWENTY-SEVEN

SCIENCE AND SPIRITUALITY*

I feel that the topic of the relation between matter and consciousness is a place where Eastern philosophy—particularly Buddhist philosophy—and western science could meet. I think this should be a happy marriage, with no divorce! If we work along the lines of a joint effort by Buddhist scholars—not mere scholars, but those who also have some experience—and pure unbiased physicists, to investigate, study and engage in deeper research in the field of the relation between matter and consciousness, by the next century we may find beautiful things that may be helpful. This does not have to be considered the practice of religion, but can be engaged in simply for the extension of human knowledge.

Also, the scientists who are working in the field of the neurology of the human brain could benefit from Buddhist explanations about consciousness—how it functions, how it changes in terms of levels, and so on.

Because of Buddhism's emphasis on self-creation, there is no creator deity, and thus, from this viewpoint, some people consider it, strictly speaking, not a religion. A western Buddhist scholar told me, 'Buddhism is not a religion; it is a kind of science of mind.' In this sense, Buddhism does not belong to the category of religion. I consider this to be unfortunate, but in any case it means that Buddhism gets closer to science. Furthermore, from the pure scientist's viewpoint, Buddhism is naturally considered a type of spiritual path. Again, it is unfortunate that it does not belong to the category of science.

The fundamental view or philosophy of Buddhism is that of

---

* From *The Heart of Compassion*, published by Full Circle Publishing and Foundation for Universal Responsibility of HH The Dalai Lama, 1997.

dependent arising. When one talks about the view of dependent arising, one means that things exist in dependence, or that they are imputed depending on something or the other. In the case of a physical phenomenon, one would specify that it exists in dependence on its parts, whereas non-physical composite phenomena would be described as existing in dependence either on their continuity or an aspect of their continuity. Consequently, whether it is external or internal phenomena, there is nothing that exists, except in dependence upon its parts or aspects.

If one were to investigate to find a basis for the imputation in any given phenomenon—since one would not find anything at all which is actually the phenomenon, no solid lump of anything that one could point one's finger at, which represents the phenomenon—then one says that phenomena exist through the imputation of the mind.

As phenomena do not exist independently of the imputing mind, one speaks of emptiness, which means the lack of any intrinsic existence that does not depend upon the imputing mind. Since things do not exist just of their own accord, but in dependence on conditions, they change whenever they encounter different conditions. Thus, they come into existence in dependence on conditions and they cease in dependence on conditions. That very lack of any intrinsic existence, independent of cause and conditions, is the basis for all the changes that are possible in a phenomenon, such as birth, cessation and so on.

It may be interesting to compare the scientific interpretation of the role of the observer or participator with the Buddhist view that observed phenomena do not exist merely as a mental image, a projection or vision of the mind, but rather as separate entities from the mind. Mind and matter are two separate things. Matter is separate from the mind which cognizes it and denominates it. This means that, with regard to all phenomena without exception—though they are not simply a creation or manifestation of the mind with no entity of their own—their ultimate mode of existence is dependent on the mind that imputes them, the imputer. Their mode of existence is therefore quite separate from the imputer, but their existence itself is dependent on the imputer. This point of view perhaps corresponds to the scientific explanation of the role of the observer. Though different terms are employed to explain them, their meanings are somewhat related.

On the surface, dependent arising and emptiness may seem quite contrary. Yet, if one analyses them at a much deeper level, one can come to understand that phenomena, on account of their being empty, are dependently arising or dependently existing; and, because of that dependent existence, are empty by nature. Thus, one can establish both emptiness and dependent arising on one single basis; and two faces, which, at a general level, seem to be contradictory, when understood at a very profound level, will be seen to fit together in a very complementary fashion.

The mode of existence of phenomena is differentiated from their mode of appearance. Phenomena appear to the mind differently from their actual mode of existence.

When the mind apprehends their way of appearing, accepts that appearance as true, and follows that particular idea or concept, then one makes mistakes. Since that concept is completely distorted in its apprehension of the object, it contradicts the actual mode of existence, or reality itself. So this disparity or contradiction between what is and what appears is due to the fact that, although phenomena are in reality empty of any intrinsic nature, yet they do appear to the ordinary mind as if they exist inherently, though they lack any such quality. Similarly, although, in reality, things which depend on causes are impermanent and transient, undergoing constant change, they do appear as though they were permanent and unchanging. Again, something that in its true nature is suffering appears as happiness. And something which is in reality false appears as true. There are many levels of subtlety regarding this contradiction between the mode of existence of phenomena and their mode of appearance. As a result of the contradiction between what is and what appears, all manner of mistakes are made. This explanation may have much in common with scientists' views of the difference in the modes of appearance and existence of certain phenomena.

We might ask, 'How do the different levels of the consciousness or mind that apprehends an object actually come to exist themselves?' Different levels of consciousness are established in relation to the different levels of subtlety of the inner energy that activates and moves the consciousness towards a given object. So, the level of their subtlety and strength in moving the consciousness towards the object determines and establishes the different levels of consciousness. It is very important to reflect upon the relationship between the inner consciousness and outer material substances. Many eastern philosophies and Buddhism in particular, speak of four elements: earth, water, fire and air; or five elements, with the addition of space. The first four elements—earth, water, fire and air—are supported by the elements of space, which enables them to exist and function. Space or ether serves, then, as the basis for the functioning of all the other elements.

These five elements can be divided into two types: the outer five elements and the inner five elements. There is a definite relationship between the outer and inner elements. As regards the element space or ether, according to certain Buddhists texts, such as the Kalachakra Tantra, space is not just a total voidness, devoid of anything at all, but it is referred to in terms of empty particles. These empty particles therefore serve as the basis for the evolution and dissolution of the other four elements. They are generated from it and finally absorbed back into it.

The process of dissolution evolves in this order: earth, water, fire and air; and the process of generation in this order: air, fire, water and earth. These four are better understood in terms of solidity (earth), liquidity (water), heat (fire), and energy (air). The four elements are generated from the subtle level to the gross, out of this basis of empty particles, and dissolve from the gross level to the subtle into the empty particles. Space, or the empty particle, is the basis for the whole process. The Big-Bang model of the beginning of the universe perhaps has something in common with this empty particle. Such parallels do present something that I feel it would be worthwhile to reflect upon.

From the spiritual point of view of Buddhism, the state of our mind, whether it is disciplined or undisciplined, produces what is known as karma. This is accepted in many eastern philosophies. Karma, meaning action, has a particular influence upon the inner elements, which in turn affect the outer elements. This, too, is a point for further investigation.

Another area in Tibetan Buddhism, which may be of interest to scientists, is the relationship between the physical elements and the nerves,

229

and consciousness; in particular, the relationship between the elements in the brain and consciousness. Involved here are the changes in consciousness, happy or unhappy states of mind and so on, the kind of effect they have on the elements within the brain; and the consequent effect on the body. Certain physical illnesses improve or worsen according to the state of mind. Regarding this kind of relationship between body and mind, Buddhism can definitely make a contribution to modern science.

Buddhism also explains, with great precision, the different levels of subtlety within consciousness itself. These are very clearly described in the Tantras. Consciousness is classified, from the point of view of its levels of subtlety, into three levels: the waking state or the gross level of consciousness; the consciousness of the dream state, which is more subtle; and consciousness during deep, dreamless sleep, which is subtler still.

Similarly, the three stages of birth, death and the intermediate state are also established in terms of the subtlety of their levels of consciousness. During the process of dying, a person experiences the innermost, subtle consciousness; the consciousness becomes grosser after death in the intermediate state, and progressively more gross during the process of birth. Upon the basis of the continuity of the stream of consciousness is established the existence of rebirth and re-incarnation. There are currently a number of well-documented cases of individuals who clearly remember their past lives, and it would seem very worthwhile to investigate these phenomena, with a view to expanding human knowledge.

~

TWENTY-EIGHT

BUDDHIST CONCEPT OF NATURE*

Nagarjuna said that for a system where emptiness is possible, it is also possible to have functionality, and since functionality is possible, emptiness is also possible. So when we talk about nature, the ultimate nature is emptiness. What is meant by emptiness, or *shunyata*? It is not the emptiness of existence but the emptiness of true or independent existence, which means that things exist by dependence upon other factors.

So whether it be the environment that is inhabited, or the inhabitants, both of them are composed of five or four basic elements. These elements are earth, wind, fire, water and vacuum, that is space. About space, in Kalachakra Tantra, there is a mention of what is known as the atom of space, particles of space. So that forms the central force of the entire phenomena. When the entire system of the universe first evolved, it evolved from this central force which is the particle of space, and also a system of universe would dissolve eventually into this particle of the space. So it is on the basis of these five basic elements that there is a very close inter-relatedness or interrelation between the habitat that is the natural environment and the inhabitants, the sentient beings living within it.

Also, when we talk of the elements there are internal elements which are existent inherently within sentient beings; they are also of different levels—some are subtle and some are gross.

So ultimately, according to Buddhist teaching, the innermost subtle consciousness is the sole creator itself, consisting of five elements, very subtle forms of elements. These subtle elements serve as conditions for

---

* From *The Spirit of Tibet: Universal Heritage*, Allied Publishers, 1995.

producing the internal elements which form sentient beings, and that in turn causes the existence or evolution of the external elements. So there is a very close interdependence or interrelationship between the environment and the inhabitants. Within the meaning of interdependency, there are many different levels, that things are dependent upon their causal factors, or upon their own parts or the conceptual mind which actually gives the label, the designation.

Then, another very significant thing again, as I am always saying, is the importance of compassionate thought. As I mentioned earlier, even from one's own selfish viewpoint, one needs other people. So, by showing concern for other people's welfare, sharing other people's suffering, and by helping other people, ultimately one will benefit. If one thinks only of oneself and forgets about others, ultimately one will be lost. This also is something like nature's law. I think it is quite simple. If you do not give a smile to other people, and give some kind of bad look or something like that, the other side will also give a similar response. Isn't that right? If you show other people a very sincere and open attitude there will also be similar response. So it is quite simple logic.

Now in this respect, another thing which I feel is very important is, what is consciousness, what is mind? Up to now, I think specially in the Western world, during the last one or two centuries science and technology have been very much emphasized and that mainly deals with matter.

Now, today, some of the nuclear physicists and neurologists have started investigating and analyzing particles in great detail and depth. While doing so they found some kind of involvement on the part of the observer, which they sometimes call 'the knower'. Who is 'the knower'? Simply speaking, it is the human being, like the scientist. Through which ways do scientists know? I think through the brain. Now, about the brain. Western scientists have not yet fully identified billions of cells of the brain. I think out of a hundred billions only a few hundred have been identified so far. So now the mind, whether you call it mind or a special energy of the brain or consciousness, you will see that there is a relationship between the brain and the mind and the mind and matter. This I think is something important. I feel there should be some sort of dialogue between Eastern philosophy and Western science on the basis of the relationship between mind and matter.

TWENTY-NINE

A WISH FOR HARMONY*

(AMONG RELIGIONS)

Religious traditions are as relevant as ever. Yet, as in the past, conflicts and crises arise in the name of different religious traditions. This is very, very unfortunate. We must make every effort to overcome this situation. In my own experience, I have found that the most effective method to overcome these conflicts is close contact and an exchange among those of various beliefs, not only on an intellectual level, but in deeper spiritual experiences. This is a powerful method to develop mutual understanding and respect. Through this interchange, a strong foundation of genuine harmony can be established!

Since it is my belief that harmony among different religious traditions is extremely important, extremely necessary, I would like to suggest a few ideas on ways it can be promoted. First, I suggest we encourage meetings among scholars from different religious backgrounds to discuss differences and similarities in their traditions, in order to promote empathy and to improve our knowledge about one another. Some of you may have already heard me mention that on a visit to the great monastery at Montserrat in Spain, I met a Benedictine monk there. He came especially to see me—and his English was much poorer than mine, so I felt more courage to speak to him. After lunch, we spent some time alone, face to face, and I was informed that this monk had spent a few years in the mountains just behind the monastery. I asked

---

* From *The Good Heart: A Buddhist Perspective on the Teachings of Jesus* by the Dalai Lama, translated by Geshe Thupten Jinpa, published by Rider and reprinted by permission of the Random House Group Ltd.

him what kind of contemplation he had practised during those years of solitude. His answer was simple: 'Love, love, love.' How wonderful! I suppose that sometimes he also slept. But during all those years he meditated simply on love. And he was not meditating on just the word. When I looked into his eyes, I saw evidence of profound spirituality and love—as I had during my meetings with Thomas Merton.

These two encounters have helped me develop a genuine reverence for the Christian tradition and its capacity to create people of such goodness. I believe the purpose of all the major religious traditions is not to construct big temples on the outside, but to create temples of goodness and compassion inside, in our hearts. Every major religion has the potential to create this. The greater our awareness is regarding the value and effectiveness of other religious traditions, then the deeper will be our respect and reverence toward other religions. This is the proper way for us to promote genuine compassion and a spirit of harmony among the religions of the world.

In addition to encounters among scholars and experienced practitioners, it is also important, particularly in the eyes of the public, that leaders of the various religious traditions occasionally come together to meet and pray, as in the important meeting at Assisi in 1986. This is a third simple yet effective way to promote tolerance and understanding.

A fourth means of working toward harmony among the world's religions is for people of different religious traditions to go on pilgrimages together to visit one another's holy places. A few years ago, I started doing this practice myself in India. Since then, I have had the opportunity to travel as a pilgrim to Lourdes, the holy place in France, and to Jerusalem. In these places, I prayed with the followers of the various religions, sometimes in silent meditation. And in this prayer and meditation, I felt a genuine spiritual experience. I hope this will set an example, serve as a sort of precedent, so that in the future it will be regarded as quite normal for people to join together in pilgrimages to holy sites and share the experience of their different religious backgrounds.

Finally, I would like to come back to the subject of meditation and to my Christian brothers and sisters who practise meditation in their daily lives. I believe this practice is extremely important. Traditionally

THE ESSENTIAL DALAI LAMA

in India, there is samadhi meditation, 'stilling the mind,' which is common to all the Indian religions, including Hinduism, Buddhism, and Jainism. And in many of these traditions, certain types of *vipas'yand*, 'analytical meditation,' are common as well. We might ask why samadhi, 'stilling the mind,' is so important. Because samadhi, or focusing meditation, is the means to mobilize your mind, to channel your mental energy. Samadhi is considered to be an essential part of spiritual practice in all the major religious traditions of India because it provides the possibility to channel all one's mental energy and the ability to direct the mind to a particular object in a single-pointed way.

It is my belief that if prayer, meditation, and contemplation—which is more discursive and analytic—are combined in daily practice, the effect on the practitioner's mind and heart will be all the greater. One of the major aims and purposes of religious practice for the individual is an inner transformation from an undisciplined, untamed, unfocussed state of mind toward one that is disciplined, tamed, and balanced. A person who has perfected the faculty of single-pointedness will definitely have a greater ability to attain this objective. When meditation becomes an important part of your spiritual life, you are able to bring about this inner transformation in a more effective way.

Once this transformation has been achieved, then in following your own spiritual tradition, you will discover that a kind of natural humility will arise in you, allowing you to communicate better with people from other religious traditions and cultural backgrounds. You are in a better position to appreciate the value and preciousness of other traditions because you have seen this value from within your own tradition. People often experience feelings of exclusivity in their religious beliefs—a feeling that one's own path is the only true path—which can create a sense of apprehension about connecting with others of different faiths. I believe the best way to counter that force is to experience the value of one's own path through a meditative life, which will enable one to see the value and preciousness of other traditions.

In order to develop a genuine spirit of harmony from a sound foundation of knowledge, I believe it is very important to know the fundamental differences between religious traditions. And it is possible to understand the fundamental differences, but at the same time recognize the value and potential of each religious tradition. In this way, a person may develop a balanced and harmonious perception. Some people believe that the most reasonable way to attain harmony and solve problems relating to religious intolerance is to establish one universal religion for everyone. However, I have always felt that we should have different religious traditions because human beings possess so many different mental dispositions: one religion simply cannot satisfy the needs of such a variety of people. If we try to unify the faiths of the world into one religion, we will also lose many of the qualities and richnesses of each particular tradition. Therefore, I feel it is better, in spite of the many quarrels in the name of religion, to maintain a variety of religious traditions. Unfortunately, while a diversity of religious traditions is more suited to serve the needs of the diverse mental dispositions among humanity, this diversity naturally possesses the potential for conflict and disagreement as well. Consequently, people of every religious tradition must make an extra effort to try to transcend intolerance and misunderstanding and seek harmony.

These are a few points that I thought would be useful at the beginning of the Seminar. Now I am looking forward to the challenge of exploring texts and ideas that are not familiar to me. You've given me a heavy responsibility, and I will try my best to fulfill your wishes. I really feel it a great honour and privilege to be asked to comment on selected passages of the Holy Scripture—a scripture I must admit I am not very familiar with. I must also admit that this is the first time I have tried to do such a thing. Whether it will be a success or failure, I don't know! But in any case, I will try my best.

THIRTY

BUDDHIST PERSPECTIVES ON THE
TEACHINGS OF JESUS*

Since this dialogue has been organized by the World Community for
Christian Meditation and the main audience attending here is practising
Christians who have a serious commitment to their own practice and
faith, my presentation will be aimed primarily toward that audience.
Consequently, I shall try to explain those Buddhist techniques or methods
that can be adopted by a Christian practitioner without attaching the
deeper Buddhist philosophy. Some of these deeper, metaphysical
differences between the two traditions may come up in the panel
discussion.

My main concern is this: how can I help or serve the Christian
practitioner? The last thing I wish to do is to plant seeds of doubt and
scuepticism in their minds. As mentioned earlier, it is my full conviction
that the variety of religious traditions today is valuable and relevant.
According to my own experience, all of the world's major religious
traditions provide a common language and message upon which we
can build a genuine understanding.

In general, I am in favour of people continuing to follow the religion
of their own culture and inheritance. Of course, individuals have every
right to change if they find that a new religion is more effective or
suitable for their spiritual needs. But, generally speaking, it is better to
experience the value of one's own religious tradition. Here is an example

---

*   From *The Good Heart: A Buddhist Perspective on the Teachings of Jesus* by the
    Dalai Lama, translated by Geshe Thupten Jinpa, published by Rider
    and reprinted by permission of the Random House Group Ltd.

of the sort of difficulties that may arise in changing one's religion. In one Tibetan family in the 1960s, the father of the family passed away, and the mother later came to see me. She told me that as far as this life is concerned she was Christian, but for the next life there was no alternative for her but Buddhism. How complicated! If you are Christian, it is better to develop spiritually within your religion and be a genuine, good Christian. If you are a Buddhist, be a genuine Buddhist. Not something half-and-half! This may cause only confusion in your mind.

Before commenting on the text, I would like to discuss meditation. The Tibetan term for meditation is *gom*, which connotes the development of a constant familiarity with a particular practice or object. The process of 'familiarization' is key because the enhancement or development of mind follows with the growth of familiarity with the chosen object. Consequently, it is only through constant application of the meditative techniques and training of the mind that one can expect to attain inner transformation or discipline within the mind. In the Tibetan tradition there are, generally speaking, two principal types of meditation. One employs a certain degree of analysis and reasoning, and is known as contemplative or analytical meditation. The other is more absorptive and focusing, and is called single-pointed or placement meditation.

Let us take the example of meditating on love and compassion in the Christian context. In an analytical aspect of that meditation, we would be thinking along specific lines, such as the following: To truly love God one must demonstrate that love through the action of loving fellow human beings in a genuine way, loving one's neighbour. One might also reflect upon the life and example of Jesus Christ himself, how he conducted his life, how he worked for the benefit of other sentient beings, and how his actions illustrated a compassionate way of life. This type of thought process is the analytical aspect of meditation on compassion. One might meditate in a similar manner on patience and tolerance.

These reflections will enable you to develop a deep conviction in the importance and value of compassion and tolerance. Once you arrive at that certain point where you feel totally convinced of the preciousness of and need for compassion and tolerance, you will experience a sense of being touched, a sense of being transformed from within. At this point, you should place your mind single-pointedly in that conviction, without applying any further analysis. Your mind should rather remain single pointedly in equipoise; this is the absorptive or placement aspect of meditation on compassion. Thus, both types of meditation are applied in one meditation session.

Why are we able, through the application of such meditative techniques, not only to develop but to enhance compassion? This is because compassion is a type of emotion that possesses the potential for development. Generally speaking, we can point to two types of emotion. One is more instinctual and is not based on reason. The other type of emotion—such as compassion or tolerance—is not so instinctual but instead has a sound base or grounding in reason and experience. When you clearly see the various logical grounds for their development and you develop conviction in these benefits, then these emotions will be enhanced. What we see here is a joining of intellect and heart. Compassion represents the emotion, or heart, and the application of analytic meditation applies the intellect. So, when you have arrived at that meditative state where compassion is enhanced, you see a special merging of intellect and heart.

If you examine the nature of these meditative states, you will also see that there are different elements within these states. For example, you might be engaged in the analytic process of thinking that we are all creations of the same Creator, and therefore, that we are all truly brothers and sisters. In this case, you are focusing your mind on a particular object. That is, your analytic subjectivity is focusing on the idea or concept that you are analyzing. However, once you have arrived at a state of single-pointedness—when you experience that inner transformation, that compassion within you—there is no longer a meditating mind and a meditated object. Instead, your mind is generated in the form of compassion.

These are a few preliminary comments on meditation. Now I will read from the Gospel.

You have head that they were told, 'an eye for an eye, a tooth for a tooth.' But what I tell you is this: do not resist those who wrong you. If anyone slaps you on the right cheek, turn and offer him the other also. If anyone wants to sue you and takes your shirt, let him have cloak as well. If someone in authority presses you into service for one mile, go with him two. Give to anyone who asks, and do not turn your back on anyone who wants to borrow (Matthew: 5:38-42)

The practice of tolerance and patience which is being advocated in these passages is extremely similar to the practice of tolerance and patience which is advocated in Buddhism in general. And this is particularly true in Mahayana Buddhism in the context of the bodhisattva ideals in which the individual who faces certain harms is encouraged to respond in a nonviolent and compassionate way. In fact, one could almost say that these passages could be introduced into a Buddhist text, and they would not even be recognized as traditional Christian scriptures.

You have heard that they were told, 'Love your neighbour and hate your enemy.' But what I tell you is this: Love your enemies and pray for your persecutors; only so can you be children of your heavenly Father, who causes the sun to rise on good and bad alike, and sends rain on the innocent and wicked. If you love only those who love you, what reward can you expect? Even the tax collectors do as much as that. If you greet only your brothers, what is there extraordinary about that? Ever the heathens do as much. There must be no limit to your goodness, as your heavenly Father's goodness knows no bounds. (Mathew 5:43-48)

This reminds me of a passage in a Mahayana Buddhist text known as the *Compendium of Practices* in which Shantideva asks, 'If you do not practice compassion toward your enemy then toward whom can you practice it?' The implication is that even animals show love, compassion, and a feeling of empathy toward their own loved ones. As we claim to be practitioners of spirituality and a spiritual path, we should be able to do better than the animals.

These Gospel passages also remind me of reflections in another Mahayana text called *A Guide to the Bodhisattva's Way of Life*, in which

Shantideva states that it is very important to develop the right attitude toward your enemy. If you can cultivate the right attitude, your enemies are your best spiritual teachers because their presence provides you with the opportunity to enhance and develop tolerance, patience, and understanding. By developing greater tolerance and patience, it will be easier for you to develop your capacity for compassion and, through that, altruism. So even for the practice of your own spiritual path, the presence of an enemy is crucial. The analogy drawn in the Gospel as to how 'the sun makes no discrimination where it shines' is very significant. The sun shines for all and makes no discrimination. This is a wonderful metaphor for compassion. It gives you the sense of its impartiality and all-embracing nature.

As I read these passages, I feel that the Gospel especially emphasizes the practice of tolerance and feelings of impartiality toward all creatures. In my opinion, in order to develop one's capacity for tolerance toward all beings, and particularly toward an enemy, it is important as a precondition to have a feeling of equanimity toward all. If someone tells you that you should not be hostile toward your enemy or that you should love your enemy, that statement alone is not going to move you to change. It is quite natural for all of us to feel hostility toward those who harm us, and to feel attachment toward our loved ones. It is a natural human feeling, so we must have effective techniques to help us make that transition from these inherently biased feelings toward a state of greater equanimity.

There are specific techniques for developing this sense of equanimity toward all sentient creatures. For instance, in the Buddhist context, one can refer to the concept of rebirth to assist in the practice of generating equanimity. As we are discussing the cultivation of equanimity in the context of Christian practice, however, perhaps it is possible to invoke the idea of Creation and that all creatures are equal in that they are all creations of the same God. On the basis of this belief, one can develop a sense of equanimity. Just before our morning's session, I had a brief discussion with Father Laurence. He made the point that in Christian theology there is the belief that all human beings are created in the image of God— we all share a common divine nature. I find this quite similar to the idea of Buddha-nature in Buddhism. On the basis of this belief that all human beings share the same divine nature, we have a very strong ground, a very powerful reason, to believe that it is possible for each of us to develop a genuine sense of equanimity toward all beings.

However, we should not see equanimity as an end in itself. Nor should we feel that we are striving for a total state of apathy in which we have no feelings or fluctuating emotions toward either our enemies or our loved ones and friends. That is not what we are seeking to achieve. What we aspire to achieve is, first of all, to set the foundation, to have a kind of clear field where we can then plant other thoughts. Equanimity is this even ground that we are first laying out. On the basis of this, we should then reflect on the merits of tolerance, patience, love, and compassion toward all. We should also contemplate the disadvantages and the negativities of self-centered thinking, fluctuating emotions toward friends and enemies, and the negativities of having biased feelings toward other beings.

The crucial point is how you utilize this basic equanimity. It is important to concentrate on the negativities of anger and hatred, which are the principal obstacles to enhancing one's capacity for compassion and tolerance. You should also reflect upon the merits and virtues of enhancing tolerance and patience. This can be done in the Christian context without having to resort to any belief in rebirth. For example, when reflecting upon the merits and virtues of tolerance and patience, you can think along the following lines: God created you as an individual and gave you the freedom to act in a way that is compatible and in accordance with the Creator's wishes—to act in an ethical way, in a moral way, and to live a life of an ethically disciplined, responsible individual. By feeling and practising tolerance and patience toward fellow creatures, you are fulfilling that wish: you are pleasing your Creator. That is, in a way, the best gift, the best offering that you can make to the divine Creator.

There is an idea in Buddhism of something called offering of practice (*drupai chopa*): of all the offerings you can make to someone that you revere—such as material offerings, singing songs of praise, or other gifts—the best offering you can make is to live a life according to the principles of that being. In the Christian context, by living life in an ethically disciplined way, based on tolerance and patience, you are, in a way, making a wonderful gift to your Creator. This is in some sense much more effective than having only prayer as your main practice. If you pray but then do not live according to that prayer, it is not of much benefit.

One of the great yogis of Tibetan Buddhism, Milarepa, states in one of his songs of spiritual experience, 'As far as offerings of material gifts are concerned, I am destitute; I have nothing to offer. What I have to offer in abundance is the gift of my spiritual practice.' We can see that, generally, the person who has a tremendous reserve of patience and tolerance has a certain degree of tranquility and calmness in his or her life. Such a person is not only happy and more emotionally grounded, but also seems to be physically healthier and to experience less illness. The person possesses a strong will, has a good appetite, and can sleep with a clear conscience. These are all benefits of tolerance and patience that we can see in our own daily lives.

One of my fundamental convictions is that basic human nature is more disposed toward compassion and affection. Basic human nature is gentle, not aggressive or violent. This goes hand in hand with Father Laurence's statement that all human beings share the same divine nature. I would also argue that when we examine the relationship between mind, or consciousness, and body, we see that wholesome attitudes, emotions, and states of mind, like compassion, tolerance, and forgiveness, are strongly connected with physical health and well-being. They enhance physical well-being, whereas negative or unwholesome attitudes and emotions—anger, hatred, disturbed states of mind—undermine physical health. I would argue that this correspondence shows that our basic human nature is closer to the wholesome attitudes and emotions.

After you have reflected upon the virtues of tolerance and patience and feel convinced of the need to develop and enhance them within you, you should then look at different types and levels of patience and tolerance. For example, in the Buddhist texts three types of tolerance and patience are described. The first is the state of resolute indifference—one is able to bear pain or suffering and not be overwhelmed by them. That is the first level. In the second state, one is not only able to bear such sufferings, but is also, if necessary, prepared and even willing to take upon oneself the hardships, pain, and suffering that are involved in the spiritual path. This involves a voluntary acceptance of hardships for a higher purpose. The third is a type of patience and tolerance arising from a sound conviction about the nature of reality. In the context of Christian practice this kind of patience would be based on a firm faith and belief in the mysteries of the Creation. Although the distinctions between these three levels of tolerance are found in Buddhist texts, they are also applicable in the Christian context. This is especially true of the second type of tolerance and patience—deliberately taking upon yourself the hardships and pains that are involved in your spiritual path.

~

THIRTY-ONE

THE SHELTERING TREE OF

INTERDEPENDENCE

Lord Tathagata born of the Iksvakus tree
Peerless One
Who, seeing the all-pervasive nature
Of interdependence
Between the environment and sentient beings
Samsara and Nirvana
Moving and unmoving
Teaches the world out of compassion
Bestow thy benevolence on us

The Saviour
The One called Avalokitesvara
Personifying the body of compassion
Of all Buddhas
We beseech thee to make our spirits ripen
And fructify to observe reality
Bereft of illusion

Our obdurate egocentricity
Ingrained in our minds
Since beginningless time
Contaminates, defiles and pollutes
The environment
Created by the common karma
Of all sentient beings

Lakes and ponds have lost
Their clarity, their coolness
The atmosphere is poisoned
Nature's celestial canopy in the fiery firmament
Has burst asunder
And sentient beings suffer diseases
Unknown before

Perennial snow mountains resplendent in their glory
Bow down and melt into water
The majestic oceans lose their ageless equilibrium
And inundate islands

The dangers of fire, water and wind are limitless
Sweltering heat dries up our lush forests
Lashing our world with unprecedented storms
And the oceans surrender their salt to the elements

Though people lack not wealth
They cannot afford to breathe clean air
Rain and streams cleanse not
But remain inert and powerless liquids

Human beings
And countless beings
That inhabit water and land
Reel under the yoke of physical pain
Caused by malevolent diseases
Their minds are dulled
With sloth, stupor and ignorance
The joys of body and spirit
Are far, far away

We needlessly pollute
The fair bosom of our mother earth
Rip out her trees to feed our short-sighted greed

Turning our fertile earth into a sterile desert

The interdependent nature
Of the external environment
And people's inward nature
Described in Tantras
Works on medicine, and astronomy
Has verily been vindicated
By our present experience.

The earth is home to living beings;
Equal and impartial to the moving and unmoving
Thus spoke the Buddha in truthful voice
With the great earth for witness

As a noble being recognizes the kindness
Of a sentient mother
And makes recompense for it
So the earth, the universal mother
Which nurtures all equally
Should be regarded with affection and Care

Forsake wastage
Pollute not the clean, clear nature
Of the four elements
And destroy the well being of people
But absorb yourself in actions
That are beneficial to all

Under a tree was the great Sage
Buddha born
Under a tree, he overcame passion
And attained enlightenment
Under two trees did he pass in Nirvana
Verily, the Buddha held the tree in great esteem

Here, where Manjusri's emanation
Lama Tson Khapa's body bloomed forth
Is marked by a sandal tree
Bearing a hundred thousand images of the Buddha

Is it not well known
That some transcendental deities
Eminent local deities and spirits
Make their abode in trees?

Flourishing trees clean the wind
Help us breathe the sustaining air of life
They please the eye and soothe the mind
Their shade makes a welcome resting place

In Vinaya, the Buddha taught monks
To care for tender trees
From this, we learn the virtue
Of planting, of nurturing trees

In times of yore
Our forbears ate the fruits of trees
Wore their leaves
Discovered fire by the attrition of wood
Took refuge amidst the foliage of trees
When they encountered danger

Even in this age of science of technology
Trees provide us shelter
The chairs we sit in
The beds we lie on
When the heart is ablaze
With the fire of anger
Fuelled by wrangling
Trees bring refreshing, welcome coolness

In the trees lie the roots
Of all life on earth
When it vanishes
The land exemplified by the name
Of the Jambu tree
Will remain no more
Than a dreary, desolate desert

Nothing is dearer to the living than life
Recognizing this, in the Vinaya rules
The Buddha lays down prohibitions
Like the use of water with living creatures

In the remoteness of the Himalayas
In the days of yore, the land of Tibet
Observed a ban on hunting, on fishing
And, during designated periods, even construction.
These traditions are noble
For they preserve and cherish
The lives of humble, helpless,
defenceless creatures

Playing with the lives of other beings
Without sensitivity or hesitation
As in the act of hunting or fishing for sport
Is an act of heedless, needless violence
A violation of the solemn rights
Of all living beings

Being attentive to the nature
Of interdependence of all creatures
Both animate and inanimate
One should never slacken in one's efforts
To preserve and conserve nature's energy

On a certain day, month and year
One should observe the ceremony
Of tree planting
Thus, one fulfils one's responsibilities
Serves one's fellow beings
Which not only brings one happiness
But benefits all

May the force of observing that which is right
And abstinence from wrong practices and evil deeds
Nourish and augment the prosperity of the world
May it invigorate living beings and help them blossom
May sylvan joy and pristine happiness
Ever increase, ever spread and encompass all that is.

COPYRIGHT ACKNOWLEDGEMENTS

and edited by Jeffrey Hopkins, published by Snow Lion Publications, 1984.

HarperCollins*Publishers* for 'Compassion', 'Karma', and 'Interdependence' from *The Heart of the Buddha's Path* © The Dalai Lama, 1999.

Ralph Vicinanza Agency for 'Refuge: The Three Jewels' and 'Meditation: A Beginning' from *An Open Heart* by HH the Dalai Lama, published by Little, Brown and Company.

Thubten Dhargye Ling for 'Universal Responsibility' 'Introduction' and 'Relying on a Spiritual Teacher' from *Illuminating the Path to Enlightenment* © Tenzin Gyatso, the fourteenth Dalai Lama, 2002. Permission given with the approval of the Office of His Holiness the Dalai Lama.

Foundation for Universal Responsibility for HH the Dalai Lama for:

    'Buddhist Concept of Nature' and the 'Nobel Oration' from *Spirit of Tibet: Universal Heritage*; 'The Buddha' from *The Joy of Living and Dying in Peace* (Library of Tibet);

    'Four Noble Truths' and 'The Bodhisattva Ideal' from *The Way To Freedom* (Library of Tibet); 'Creating the Perspective for Practice' from *Awakening the Mind, Lightening the Heart*; 'Environment/Symbols/Posture/Breathing', 'Generating the Mind of Enlightenment', 'Meditation on Emptiness' and 'Eight Verses for Training the Mind' from *Cultivating a Daily Meditation*; 'Science and Spirituality' from *The Heart of Compassion*; 'the Nature of the Mind' extracted from *Opening the Mind and Generating a Good Heart and Universal Responsibility and the Good Heart Part 2*; 'Words of Truth' and 'Sheltering Tree of Interdependence' (previously unpublished poems by HH the Dalai Lama). Permission given in consultation and with the approval of the Office of HH the Dalai Lama.

~

THE FOUNDATION FOR UNIVERSAL

RESPONSIBILITY OF HIS HOLINESS THE

DALAI LAMA

To meet the challenges of our times, I believe that humanity must develop a greater sense of Universal Responsibility. Each of us must learn to work not just for our own individual self, family or nation, but for the benefit of all mankind.

—His Holiness the Dalai Lama

The Foundation for Universal Responsibility of His Holiness The Dalai Lama is a not-for-profit, non-sectarian, non-denominational organization established with the Nobel Peace Prize awarded to His Holiness in 1989. In the spirit of the Charter of the United Nations, the Foundation brings together men and women of different faiths, professions and nationalities, through a range of initiatives and mutually sustaining collaborations.

It works to promote Universal Responsibility in a manner that respects difference and encourages a diversity of beliefs and practices; to enrich educational paradigms that tap the transformative potential of the human mind; to build a global ethic of non-violence, coexistence, gender equity and peace by facilitating processes of personal and social change.

PROJECTS

Interfaith Confluence

Exploring Meditation is an interfaith-guided meditation programme that seeks to celebrate the diversity in different faiths through firsthand exploration of a range of spiritual mind-training techniques.

Interfaith Dialogue brings together groups of young people to stay in monasteries ashrams and other spiritual centres. Participants spend time studying and exploring the basic tenets of Christianity, Buddhism, Sikhism, Hinduism, Islam, Judaism, Zoroastrianism, Jainism and other lesser-known faiths.

Peace-building and Coexistence

Peacemakers is a lecture series designed to invigorate the discourse on peace-building and non-violence in South Asia and the world. Speakers have included: Shri I.K. Gujral (former Prime Minister of India), Justice J.S. Verma (former Chief Justice of India) and Ela Gandhi

WISCOMP (Women in Security, Conflict Management and Peace) is a South Asian research and training initiative, which facilitates the leadership of women in the areas of peace, security, and international affairs. It provides a unique interface between academia and the NGO sector, and positions its work at the confluence of Security Studies, Conflict Transformation, and Peace-building. The intersection of these with gender concerns provides the focus of its programs.

- The *Conflict Transformation* project offers an annual Summer School for women and men from the South Asian region in the theory and practice of conflict transformation.
- *Engendering Security* facilitates research and discourse on ways in which gender and emerging formulations of security intersect in South Asia. Themes of research include: Gender, Identity and Armed Conflict, Gender and the Politics of Water Security and Gender and Terrorism.
- *Building Constituencies of Peace* empowers women from regions

of protracted conflict such as Jammu and Kashmir and Sri Lanka with the skills and expertise to engage in processes of conflict transformation in their local communities and regions as well as in official peace negotiations. The Initiative in Jammu and Kashmir called Athwaas (a handshake), comprises a group of Muslim, Hindu and Sikh women who work to build peace through a range of activities including active listening, trauma counselling and articulation of the concerns of women to policymakers and government interlocutors.

Ethics and Education

Student Interface comprises a range of educational interactions and materials, such as debates, films, and workshops, for school students that encourage discussion and reflection on contemporary issues and alternative ways of life.

Gurukul facilitates inspirational contact with masters of different spiritual traditions, particularly Tibetan Buddhism. The participants, mainly university students, live in Tibetan monasteries and nunneries where they learn about Tibetan culture, art and philosophy.

Tibetan Heritage is an ongoing series of workshops and visits intended to introduce people to important elements of the unique heritage and culture of Tibet.

Mind Science is an ongoing series of round tables and seminars intended to strengthen linkages between science and spirituality. By sharing knowledge and experience, eminent spiritualists and scientists generate new understandings of the mind in these creative interactions.

Fellowships and Scholarships

The Tibetan Scholarship Program provides an opportunity to motivated Tibetan youth to pursue professional degrees in reputed institutions of higher education in India. Special scholarships are also available for young Tibetans to attend prestigious primary and secondary schools.

The Scholar of Peace Fellowship Program encourages innovative, multidisciplinary, theoretical engagement and research on issues of gender, security and conflict transformation.

Lectures and Seminars

The Foundation organizes periodic lecture series and seminars on topics such as *Creeds of Our Times* and *Sadhana-The Experiential Journey of Artistic Expression*.

Publications

The Foundation produces print and audiovisual material on themes and issues related to its mission. It houses a library of books, journals and films on subjects such as universal responsibility, non-violence, peace-building, gender studies and Tibetan Buddhism.

Trustees
(July 2005)

Contact:

The Foundation for Universal Responsibility
of His Holiness the Dalai Lama

257

Core 4 A, UGF
India Habitat Centre
Lodhi Road
New Delhi – 110003
India
Tel: 91-11-24648450
Fax: 91-11-24648451
Email: furhhdl@vsnl.com
Website: http://www.furhhdl.org